Rethinking Macroeconomics

Macroeconomics has always played host to contesting schools of thought, but recent events have exacerbated those differences. To fully understand the subject, students need to be aware of these controversies. *Rethinking Macroeconomics: A History of Economic Thought Perspective* introduces students to the key schools of thought, equipping them with the knowledge needed for a true understanding of today's economy.

The text guides the reader through multiple approaches to macroeconomic analysis before presenting the data for several critical economic episodes, all in order to explore which analytical method provides the best explanation for each event. It covers key background information on topics such as the basics of supply and demand, macroeconomic data, international trade and the balance of payments, the creation of the money supply, and the global financial crisis. This anticipated second edition contains new chapters on Modern Monetary Theory, the Japanese economy, the European Union, and the COVID-19 crisis, bringing the story up to date and broadening the international coverage.

Offering the context that is missing from existing introductory textbooks, this work encourages students to think critically about received economic wisdom. This is the ideal complement to any introductory macroeconomics textbook and is ideally suited for undergraduate students who have completed a principles of economics course.

The book is fully supported with additional online resources, which include lecture slides and an instructor manual.

John F. McDonald is Adjunct Professor of Economics at Temple University, Emeritus Professor of Economics at the University of Illinois at Chicago, and Gerald W. Fogelson Distinguished Chair in Real Estate Emeritus at Roosevelt University.

Rethinking Macroeconomics

A History of Economic Thought Perspective

Second Edition

John F. McDonald

Routledge
Taylor & Francis Group

LONDON AND NEW YORK

Second edition published 2022
by Routledge
2 Park Square, Milton Park, Abingdon, Oxon, OX14 4RN

and by Routledge
605 Third Avenue, New York, NY 10158

Routledge is an imprint of the Taylor & Francis Group, an informa business

© 2022 John F. McDonald

First edition published by Routledge 2016

British Library Cataloguing-in-Publication Data
A catalogue record for this book is available from the British Library

Library of Congress Cataloging-in-Publication Data
Names: McDonald, John F., 1943- author.
Title: Rethinking macroeconomics : a history of economic thought perspective / John F. McDonald.
Description: Second Edition. | New York : Routledge, 2022. | Revised edition of the author's Rethinking macroeconomics, 2016. | Includes bibliographical references and index.
Subjects: LCSH: Macroeconomics.
Classification: LCC HB172.5 .M37435 2022 (print) | LCC HB172.5 (ebook) | DDC 339—dc23
LC record available at https://lccn.loc.gov/2021011660
LC ebook record available at https://lccn.loc.gov/2021011661

ISBN: 978-0-367-76358-9 (hbk)
ISBN: 978-0-367-76292-6 (pbk)
ISBN: 978-1-003-16662-7 (ebk)

Typeset in Bembo
by Apex CoVantage, LLC

Access the Support Material: www.routledge.com/9780367762926

For Glena, Elizabeth, Charles, Elliot, and Madeleine

Contents

Figures

Tables

About the author

John F. McDonald is Adjunct Professor of Economics at Temple University, Emeritus Professor of Economics at the University of Illinois at Chicago (UIC), and Gerald W. Fogelson Distinguished Chair in Real Estate Emeritus at Roosevelt University. He earned his PhD in economics from Yale University in 1971 and joined the UIC faculty that year. At UIC he served as Professor of Economics and Finance, Department Head, Senior Associate Dean for Academic Affairs and Research, and Interim Dean in the College of Business Administration. He joined the Roosevelt faculty in 2009 as Fogelson Chair and retired in 2013. He is the author of 10 books, including *Economic Analysis of an Urban Housing Market* (1979), *Urban Economics and Real Estate* with D. McMillen (2011), *Postwar Urban America* (2015), and *Chicago: An Economic History* (2016). He served as editor of Urban Studies from 2000 to 2005 and edited *Journal of Real Estate Literature* from 2005 to 2010. He was elected a fellow of the Regional Science Association International in 2008 and was awarded the David Ricardo Medal by the American Real Estate Society in 2013. He was named a Penn Institute for Urban Research Scholar in 2015.

Preface

This book is a revised and expanded version of *Rethinking Macroeconomics: An Introduction*, which was published in 2016. New features are:

- Addition of an international perspective by including the United Kingdom, Japan, and some nations in the Euro zone.
- Chapter 1 is now much expanded to provide an introduction to economics so that the book can be used as a textbook for Principles of Macroeconomics.
- A new chapter presents Modern Monetary Theory as an additional approach to macroeconomics.
- A chapter examines Japan's recovery from World War II and its subsequent "lost decade."
- Another chapter discusses the European Union and the experience with a common currency, the Euro. Data on Germany, France, Spain, and Greece are included.
- The chapter on the financial crisis and recession of 2008–2009 is expanded to include the United Kingdom, Germany, and Japan.
- Another new chapter examines the macroeconomic experience of the United States, the United Kingdom, Japan, and Germany during the pandemic year of 2020.

This book is still a text in macroeconomics that follows a teaching strategy different from all of the texts of which I am aware. Macroeconomics is a contentious field. Several different theories exist, their adherents have strongly held views, and some of the people in the field really do not like each other. My view is that the student should not be kept from this state of affairs. Rather, an educated person deserves to know about the differences that exist. Beyond knowing about the different theories, the educated person needs to be able to look at the evidence and make judgments about the various explanations that these theories offer. Students who study this book will know about the different theories and be able to figure out how the theories comport with evidence.

My work is influenced by three fundamental ideas. First, John Maynard Keynes famously said that we are all dead in the long run. What matters is what he said next. We are alive in the short run, and economics should be used to solve short-run problems. Economics is useless if all it can do is tell us what will happen in the long run. The American artist Georgia O'Keefe said that we can get to the real essence of experience by eliminating unneeded details and concentrating on what really matters. And the economist and statesman George Shultz said that the accumulation of facts does not help us much if there is no theory to provide understanding. On the other side of the coin, spinning theories with no factual basis is worse. Theories with facts or facts with theories, these are the coins of the realm.

The book still has a simple format. The first chapter is introductory and includes background information that is needed to read the book. This chapter will be review for some students, but others will need to study the material carefully. The topics are the production possibility curve, the basics of supply and demand, macroeconomic data, international trade and the balance of payments, the creation of the money supply, and fiscal policy. The different theories are presented in the following six chapters. These chapters are followed by chapters containing empirical examinations of macroeconomic episodes in the United States, the United Kingdom, the Euro zone, and Japan. Basic macroeconomic data are presented, and a narrative is laid out for each episode. Then a comparison is made between the narrative and the implications of each of the theories. Each of these empirical chapters ends with a judgment as to which theory seems to work best. The judgment is based on a "preponderance of the evidence," not on the basis of "beyond a reasonable doubt."

Teaching is required at every step. Each of the theories must be taught and learned. Students must gain familiarity with the data sources. Then they must be taught how to look at the data with a discerning eye and how to compose a narrative of what they see. I have supplied a narrative for each episode, but these narratives are in print – not carved in stone. And students must learn how to compare the facts from the narrative with the implications of the theories. Furthermore, the instructor is free to present some other episode from another country (and maybe omit one from the book). Once the students get with the program, the instructor has this flexibility. Indeed, the instructor could assign the students the task of assembling data, composing the narrative, and judging the theories for episodes not in the book. The Instructor's Manual includes more suggestions for exercises and some exam questions.

I imagine that this book is suitable for a course of one academic term, with about two weeks for Chapter 1 and one week for each theory and each episode. The book is best suited for undergraduate students who have had an introductory course in economics or for graduate students in fields other than economics (e.g., MBA students). The book is relatively short, so it could be supplemental reading for a semester course in macroeconomics at the intermediate level.

I wish to thank those who have made this book possible. Natalie Tomlinson, my editor at Routledge, is at the head of this list. She suggested that the book should include material about other advanced nations besides the United States. And the title of the book is her idea. Chloe James and Emma Morley took the manuscript through the publication process. Next, I thank the reviewers of the book proposal for their encouragement, especially the one who used the term "engaging writing." I admit that, for better or worse, some of the writing is based on how I talk in class. Then there are thanks to my family "pod." The book was written during the fall of 2020, a time of pandemic. I divided my time between teaching online, writing the book, and helping with the grandchildren. My wife, Glena, served as quartermaster, and food was delivered. Our daughter Elizabeth taught our grandson Elliot kindergarten at home, while Glena and I occupied our granddaughter Madeleine, age 3. And our son-in-law Charles worked from home in the basement. We all observed the recommended quarantine procedures so it all could work safely.

John F. McDonald
Philadelphia
February 2021

1

Rethinking macroeconomics
Introduction to economics

Introduction

How can economics be defined? The standard definition begins with the notion that a society has limited resources that can be used for different purposes. Economics studies the choices for the use of those resources made by individuals, firms, governments, and society as a whole. Furthermore, economics focuses on the incentives that influence and reconcile those choices.

The part of economics that studies the choices made by individual people and businesses is called microeconomics. Those choices are added up to be the study of markets. The choices made by governments in the use of resources and in the regulation of markets are also the purview of microeconomics. Furthermore, economists contend that those choices are rational. Choices are made in response to incentives – monetary and otherwise. Microeconomics looks at the economy from the "bottom up."

Macroeconomics is the study of the behavior of the economy as a whole. The idea is to understand the determinants of aggregate economic activity – the total output of goods and services and its main components, unemployment, inflation, and other indicators of aggregate economic activity. Macroeconomics is concerned with identifying policies that will improve the performance of the aggregate economy, such as reducing the volatility of the economy and keeping unemployment and inflation low. The subject is of obvious importance. Macroeconomics looks at the economy from the "top down."

At this time (2021), the field of macroeconomics continues to undergo quite a lot of rethinking. Several schools of thought are, or least their adherents think they are, in contention to provide the best model for future thinking and policy action. In fact, contending schools of thought have been in the pot for decades, but the financial crisis and deep recession that started in 2007 and 2008 have brought the pot to a boil. What is an educated person to think, and do? The editorial pages and the semi-popular books on economics present the views of various economists and other experts, and the voracious reader can come away very confused. The person who reads only the authors who represent one particular school of thought does not come away confused but, I would submit, does not come away educated.

The purposes of this book are to introduce you to the field of economics in general, and then to explore these contending schools of thought in the context of those facts that Secretary Schulz mentioned. At the same time, we shall be mindful that details are confusing, and that emphasis is needed to get at the real meaning of things. The schools of thought – Keynesian, Monetarist, and others – are described first. Then macroeconomic data for several time periods for the United States and a few other nations are presented. The last step is to assess the ability of each of the schools of thought to provide a reasonable explanation for what happened in each of those time periods. It may be that one school of thought is not "best" for all of the selected time periods. Indeed, real-world experience produced a rethinking of macroeconomics in the 1920s, the 1930s, the 1970s, the 1980s, and in the past few years. The various schools of thought were born out of the seeming failure of the prevailing macroeconomic theory. The educated person deserves to know what's what and who's who of all of this.

The most important example of this rethinking was conducted by J. M. Keynes in the *General Theory of Employment, Interest, and Money* (1936). The *General Theory* was written during the depths of the Great Depression of the early 1930s, and it can be regarded as the founding document for the field of macroeconomics. It is a product of its time, to be sure. Indeed, Keynes believed that useful economics is a product of its time. His purpose was to develop a theory that explained the obvious facts that the capitalist economies of the day were not generating anything close to full employment, and that this state of affairs had existed for several years. The economic theory of the time, which Keynes called the postulates of classical economics and dismissed in a few pages, was not capable of providing an explanation of these overwhelming facts.

Progress in economic analysis and policy making (and in other scientific fields as well) proceeds by

- being confronted with facts that cannot be explained by the existing theories,
- devising new theoretical explanations (or modifying the existing theories) so as to account for the new facts,
- working out the implications of the new theory,
- conducting tests of the new theory, and
- using the new theory to make economic policy in those situations with the conditions contemplated in the new theory.

The highest accolades in economics often are conferred on those who devise the new theory that turns out to be successful. Keynes provided the new theory but devoted very little space in the *General Theory* to empirical testing or policy recommendations. Indeed, the lack of details pertaining to economic policy is striking and perhaps is surprising, given that much macroeconomic policy now has been based on Keynesian principles for decades. But Keynes's purpose in his book was to develop a new theory that could explain, to the satisfaction of his fellow economists, the overwhelming facts of the depression in the private economy. Here is a famous quote attributed to Keynes: "When the facts change, I change my mind.

What do you do sir?" Unfortunately, there is no evidence that he ever said this, but it sounds like something he would have said.

As I neared the completion of the first version of this book, a new book by the economist Dani Rodrik (2015) arrived. The title of the book, *Economics Rules*, means that economics as a discipline operates with certain rules. The rules include (2015, p. 213):

- Economics is a collection of models; cherish their diversity.
- It's a model, not *the* model.
- Make your model simple enough to isolate specific causes and how they work, but not so simple that it leaves out key interactions among causes.
- Unrealistic assumptions are OK; unrealistic *critical* assumptions are not OK.
- To map a model to the real world, you need explicit empirical diagnostics, which is more craft than science.

A summary of Rodrik's view is that economics expands horizontally by adding more models that can be used to understand particular situations. There is no one model that explains all situations. Models that fail in certain situations are not discarded but rather saved and still used to understand other situations to which they do apply. This book is written in this spirit. Macroeconomics consists of a collection of models that keeps expanding because the world and the questions we ask keep changing.

This chapter introduces you to the background information and tools that you need to read the rest of the book.

The big questions

The big questions that must be answered in any economy are:

- what goods and services to produce,
- how to produce those goods and services, and
- for whom shall the goods and services be produced?

Any economy is somehow organized to allocate its scarce resources to produce goods and services for people.

How can we judge how well the society has accomplished these basic tasks? One method is to determine the efficiency with which the resources have been used. Could more have been produced with the given resources? Could more of one good have been produced without a reduction in the production of anything else? Or would an increase in the output of one good have required a reduction in the output of another good? If the answer to the first two questions is "yes," then the society has not been as efficient as possible.

A second method for judging the outcome of an economy is the fairness with which the goods and services are distributed to the people (the "for whom" question). If the society has, in principle, enough resources to provide for the basic needs of all, does it? Beyond that, does the society generate a highly unequal distribution of goods and services even if the basic needs of all are met? Does such an unequal outcome meet with the approval of most people? The issue of distribution has been argued by economists, philosophers, and everyone else since the beginning of civilization. The economist falls back on a simple rule that mirrors the rule for production efficiency. If the well-being of one person can be improved without reducing the well-being of any other person, then make the change indicated, especially if that one person is poor compared to the majority of society.

In a nutshell, the economic way of thinking, always in an economist's head, is the understanding that a choice is a tradeoff – something must be given up to get something else. An efficient economy, as defined earlier, is one in which this rule applies. In order to have more of one good, you must give up the opportunity to have the same amount of some other good. What must be given up is called the *opportunity cost*. More of one good requires giving up the opportunity to have some of the other good. Note that opportunity cost occurs at the "margin" – one more of this means less of that. So how are those choices made? As noted, economists believe that choices are made in response to incentives. Rational choice involves reckoning the opportunity cost of an action in comparison to its benefits. For example, a person goes shopping for food. The price of steak is $9.00 a pound. The decision to buy the pound of steak means that, ultimately, the person has $9.00 less to spend on other items. That is what a price means, after all. Is a pound of steak worth the price to the shopper? Only that person can answer the question, of course.

How does production occur? How are the "what" and "how" questions answered? An economy uses what are called the basic "factors of production" to produce goods and services. Those factors are:

- land
- labor (both quantity and quality)
- capital (plants, office buildings, machinery, etc.)
- technology
- entrepreneurship (the capacity to recognize what goods and services to produce and the ability to organize the inputs to get the job done)

The quality of labor is otherwise known as "human" capital – knowledge, experience, and expertise. College students are considered by economists to be investing in human capital (at least some of the time). But experience on the job also counts as valuable human capital.

Basic concepts I: production possibilities

A simple diagram captures the "what" and "how" questions. Consider Figure 1.1. On the vertical axis we measure units of an all-purpose consumption good, and the horizontal axis is used to chart units of investment goods. Investment goods are things such as plants, equipment, and houses that are used to produce consumption goods in the future. The diagram depicts consumption and investment, because these are basic concepts in macroeconomics. In essence, Figure 1.1 is showing the options available for the production of goods and services for use *now* versus the

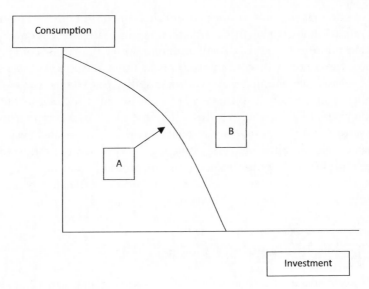

FIGURE 1.1 Production Possibilities

capacity to produce goods and services *later* – the now-versus-later choice. The curve is called the *production possibilities curve.*

The diagram is drawn for given supplies of the basic factors of production – land, labor, capital, technology, and entrepreneurship. Any point on the curve shows the maximum amount of consumption goods that can be produced given the indicated amount of investment goods – hence, production *possibilities.* The curve is drawn with a negative slope because more of one good means that less of the other good can be produced given the resources available. Each and every point on the curve is based on an allocation of the basic factors of production. Suppose one more unit of investment goods is contemplated as shown in Figure 1.1. The curve shows how much consumption goods must be given up – the opportunity cost of investment goods. As the slope is the "rise over the run" of the curve (in this case, the "rise" is negative), the opportunity cost of investment is the slope of the production possibility curve. Furthermore, that increase in investment at the expense of consumption will require some shifting of the basic factors of production from one use to another – a different allocation of resources. For example, some farmers will become construction workers.

The points on the production possibilities curve represent efficient allocations of resources, because more of one good can come only with a reduction in the other good. On the other hand, a point inside the curve (such as point A) is a point of inefficient use of resources, because more output of one or both goods can be achieved by moving to the curve (as shown by the arrow). And a point outside the curve (such as point B) cannot be reached with the available resources. Point B can be reached only if there is some increase in the resources available to the society. How can an increase happen? Increases can occur by an increase in the labor force, by an increase in capital through use of resources to produce investment goods, or by an improvement in the technology of production. But none of that can happen immediately.

There is one more feature of the production possibilities curve to point out. The curve has been drawn bowed out – not a straight line. As shown in Figure 1.1, the curve says that the opportunity cost of investment goods gets larger as the amount of investment is greater. At the smaller amount of investment goods, the amount of consumption given up is a small amount. But at the larger amount of investment goods, the amount of consumption given up at the margin is larger. Why? The basic idea is that resources vary in their ability to produce the two goods. At the smaller amount of investment, an increase in investment output would be accomplished by moving resources that are adept at producing investment goods away from consumption goods. That would be an efficient way to get it done. However, if the amount of investment already is large, getting more investment goods production requires moving resources out of consumption goods production that are less adept at the new task. But one does the best that is possible to be efficient.

Basic concepts II: supply and demand

This book makes use of a basic economic theory apparatus, supply and demand. Economic analysis usually is done with diagrams (or equations), and this book is no exception. So here is an explanation of the fundamental tool that is used. A few simple equations also are used and explained along the way.

Start with the supply and demand diagram that depicts the market for an individual consumer good (see Figure 1.2). The horizontal axis measures the quantity of the good demanded or supplied, and the vertical axis measures the price of the item. The demand curve slopes downward because households buy more when the price is lower. The supply curve slopes upward because suppliers provide more quantity at a higher price. The market is assumed to be competitive, i.e., there are many suppliers and demanders who take the market price as given, suppliers are producing the same product, and the features of the product are well known to all in the market. The market price is set by the impersonal forces of

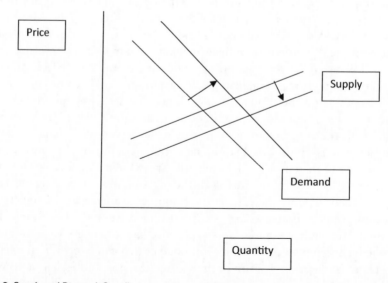

FIGURE 1.2 Supply and Demand: Suppliers supply more, and demanders demand less, if the price goes up

competition. Figure 1.2 depicts two supply and two demand curves. These curves are explained next.

The basic model of supply and demand is based on rather extreme assumptions; actors in the market take the market price as given, all suppliers produce the same product, and all actors in the market have complete knowledge of the product and the market. Some actual markets satisfy, or come very close to satisfying, these assumptions. For example, the markets for basic agricultural products (corn, wheat, etc.) are considered to be competitive. However, the usefulness of the model has been found to extend to other markets. For example, while the various brands of automobiles are different in some respects, a simple supply-and-demand model of total auto sales can be used to study overall trends. The market is no longer dominated by a very small number of firms, so the market can for some purposes be treated as competitive. The course in microeconomics includes extensive examination of different types of markets that range from competitive to monopoly (single seller).

The market price in a competitive market is determined by the intersection of the supply and demand curves. At this price, the quantity supplied is just equal to the quantity demanded. If the price somehow gets set at a level higher than at that intersection, some suppliers are unable to sell their output and therefore will reduce the price at which they are willing to sell. This process forces other sellers to lower the price and, fortunately, more is demanded as the price comes down. The process stops – you know where. What happens if the price starts out below the intersection of supply and demand? You say it….

Now comes the hard part, the part that confounds many students upon their first encounter with economics. Standing behind the supply and demand curves are several factors that determine the position of the curves. The demand curve represents the amount demanders plan to purchase at alternative prices, *holding all factors other than price constant*. In particular, the demand curve is drawn for a given number of households with given incomes and tastes and preferences for goods that they may purchase. In addition, the prices of other goods are assumed to be constant. What if the number of households increases? More of the good will be purchased at each possible price – the entire demand curve shifts up. We say that demand has increased. The result of the shift in demand is that the quantity purchased goes up and the price increases along the given supply curve. Figure 1.2 depicts a shift in the demand curve. The same idea applies if they change their preferences in favor of the good, and usually applies if households have an increase in their incomes. A more complex point is that, if the price of a good that is a substitute for the good in question increases, the demand curve in Figure 1.2 shifts up. And if the price of the substitute good declines, the demand curve in Figure 1.2 shifts down. If the price of hot dogs increases, the demand for hamburgers increases.

On the supply side, the supply curve is drawn for a given level of production technology, given costs of the relevant inputs (labor, materials, etc.), and a given number of (the numerous) suppliers. In addition, the "state of nature" is given; for example, bad weather interrupts production. Producers plan to offer the amounts shown by the curve at alternative prices because they can make a "normal" profit, given that these other factors are held constant. If production costs decline because technology improves or input costs decline, more will be supplied at each possible price. The entire supply curve shifts to the right. We say that supply has increased.

Figure 1.2 also depicts a shift in the supply curve. Note that an increase in supply (shift to the right) brings about a lower price and a larger quantity of the good bought and sold along a given demand curve.

The basic supply and demand apparatus facilitates what I like to call the one-thing-at-a-time rule. Economic analysis is designed to enable us to figure out what happens if one thing changes and everything else remains the same. Now the fact is that, in the real world, lots of things are changing at the same time. Figuring out what is going on in the real world is difficult. Economics says, "Let's break all of that down into its different pieces." That way we at least have a chance to understand what is going on. Suppose we observe that the price went up and the quantity did not change. What might have happened? We would look behind the curves. Did production costs rise? That would shift the supply curve to the left and make prices rise. If the demand curve does not move, then the supply curve shift tells the story. But what if household incomes increased as well? Then a greater quantity would be purchased at each possible price. So the combination of cost increases and household income increases can explain why the price went up and quantity was constant. It all depends on how the factors standing behind supply and demand change. Can you think of a set of reasons why price can decrease while quantity remains constant? Have fun.

The basic supply–demand diagram can be used to make one of the fundamental points of this book. Movements in the demand and/or supply curves cause changes in the quantity of output and the price. If demand increases, both output and price increase. If demand decreases, output falls and the price declines. Or, if supply increases, output rises and the price declines; and if supply decreases, output falls and the price increases. In short, changes in the position of the demand curve make output and price move in the same direction, while changes in the position of the supply curve result in output and price movements in opposite directions. This basic insight can (and will) be used to distinguish among the contending macroeconomic theories.

Basic concepts III: macroeconomic data

The purpose of the book is to confront the different macroeconomic theories with data. So what data would that be? A conventional set of macroeconomic variables exists, and it will be used here. The annual *Economic Report of the President* has a very useful appendix that contains the data for the United States in recent decades. The Bank of England provides macroeconomic data for the United Kingdom, and the Organisation for Economic Co-operation and Development (OECD) has data for other advanced economies.

The first variable is the measure of the total output of the economy, now called gross domestic product (GDP). This is the dollar value of the *final* output for a year. For example, one might think that the output of an auto company is simply the dollar value of the final output, the cars and trucks sold. But the auto company has purchased many parts from its suppliers. The final output of the auto company is the value that is added to the parts purchased from other companies and is produced by the labor and services of its plant and equipment employed in the process of turning parts into a car. Furthermore, the parts suppliers purchased materials from firms that produce materials (steel, rubber, aluminum, etc.). The final output of a parts supplier is the value added to the purchased materials by the firm's labor and capital services. In short, the GDP is the total of *value added* by the producers in the economy. Alternatively, the GDP is the total amount paid for the services of labor, existing capital equipment (including buildings), and land. In other words, the total final output must equal the income paid to these basic inputs. One bit of terminology – GDP measures the dollar value of total final output produced within the confines of the borders of the nation. Previously the term used was gross national product (GNP), but a change in terminology and measurement was made to eliminate output produced in other countries by U.S. firms.

The measure of GDP we shall use is spending on final goods and services, and spending is broken down into four basic parts; these are consumption, gross investment, government purchases of goods and services, and net exports of goods and services (exports minus imports). Consumption consists of purchases of goods and services by households for current use. It does include some items that will last for some years (clothing, shoes, stoves, home computers, and so on) as well as food, haircuts, and electricity. Consumption can be broken down into nondurable and durable goods. Housing consumption is reckoned as rent paid for the services of housing units – which means that the GDP includes the implicit rent that a homeowner is paying to himself or herself. Households use their disposable personal income (income after taxes) to purchase consumption goods and services. They also save out of disposable personal income.

Gross investment is the amount spent by private producers for new plants (including office buildings, stores, factories, etc.), equipment (computers, assembly lines, and so on), and inventories of goods to be sold later. Gross investment also includes amounts spent to build new housing units. Some gross investment simply replaces plants, equipment, and houses that have worn out, and investment that adds to the stocks of capital is called net investment. The difference between gross and net investment is the amount spent to cover the depreciation of existing capital. Inventories of goods are also an important component of gross investment. Changes in inventories can be signals for economic upturn or downturn. An increase in inventories often means that business is slowing down – goods are not being sold but are instead stacking up in the warehouse. Or an increase in inventories can mean that an increase in business is expected. A reduction in inventories can mean that business is picking up, to be followed by an increase in production and employment, or it can mean that firms are cutting back on production because business is expected to decline. (Some variables are just not clear indicators.) Firms use profits (after taxes), increases in ownership shares (e.g., issuing more stock in the case of corporations), and borrowing to pay for investment. Profits earned by corporations are also used to pay dividends to the shareholders (the owners of the firm). Profits earned by businesses that are not corporations (i.e., partnerships and sole proprietorships) are used for investment or income for the owners of the firm as well.

Government purchases of goods and services count as part of the GDP. Government purchases many things from private producers – from paper clips to B-1B bombers and office buildings. Some government purchases are actually forms of capital (B-1B bombers and office buildings), but government purchases are not normally broken down into current and capital spending. And, very importantly, much of government spending consists of wages paid to government employees. It is assumed that the wages paid are equal to the value of the services provided by those employees. Government collects taxes to spend on its purchases, but also borrows money to finance its spending.

The fourth major category of GDP is net exports. Exports of goods and services to foreign countries obviously are part of domestic production. But why do we subtract imports? The answer is that the other three categories of GDP include spending on imports. Household consumption spending includes clothing made abroad, investment spending includes computers made abroad, and government spending includes subway cars made abroad. The subtraction of total imports adjusts for all of these types of imports.

So far, GDP and its components are measured in dollar terms, but if prices are rising (or falling), then changes in GDP from one year to the next give a misleading picture of the change in output in a "real" sense. Indeed, if all prices rise by 5% but actual outputs do not change, and the economy has not produced any more goods and services, the total dollars say otherwise. This issue is addressed by the construction of a price index. Actually, there are several price indexes, and the most popular one is called the Consumer Price Index (CPI). This variable measures the dollar cost of a given basket of consumer goods, and then over time turns the measures into an index. The price index used for GDP is called the GDP price deflator. The GDP price deflator in the early 2010s was based on the cost of the relevant basket of goods in 2009, so the value of the index for 2009 is 100. The values for this price index for some recent years are:

	GDP Price Deflator
2009	100.00
2010	101.22
2011	103.31
2012	106.17
2013	106.73

These figures mean that overall prices were higher in 2010 compared to 2009 by 1.22 percent. Prices were higher in 2013 compared to 2009 by 6.73 percent. And, for example, prices increased by 2.06 percent between 2010 and 2011. This is figured as (103.31 − 101.22) divided by 101.22. The modern price indexes change the basket of goods included in the index as spending patterns change. Another piece of notation that we will use is:

GDP = PY

where P is the price index (divided by 100) and Y is GDP corrected for the price level, i.e., Y = GDP/P. For example, using 2009 as the base year, the real output of the economy for 2009 was $14,418 billion. GDP for 2013 was $16,768 billion, but Y = $16,768/1.0673 = $15,711 billion in real terms.

The basic equation that you should now commit to memory is:

$$Y = C + I + G + X$$

where X stands for net exports, the other terms are obvious, and the components of GDP are stated in real terms (i.e., corrected for the price level).

In our notation, GDP is output stated in nominal terms, i.e., not corrected for inflation. And Y is output stated in real terms, i.e., corrected for inflation. Real output will also be called real GDP. The distinction between nominal and real amounts will be used repeatedly.

Various measures are used to assess the extent to which the economy is falling short of its full output potential. The most popular measure is the unemployment rate. This variable is measured monthly and is based on a survey of households in which people are asked:

Are you employed?

Are you not working?

If you are not working, do you want to work?

Are you actively looking for work?

(Various methods of looking for work are indicated.)

The total labor force is defined as those currently working plus those actively looking for work. The unemployment rate is the number of people actively looking for work divided by the total labor force. The unemployment rate so defined is a very useful indicator of the state of the macro economy, but at times it is deficient. What about people who want to work, but gave up looking because they were having no success at landing a job (or even getting an interview)? For this reason, these days we also look at the labor-force participation rate, which measures the percentage of the population aged 16 years and older that is included in the total labor force. A decline in the labor-force participation rate may mean that some people have simply given up looking for work, although it can also mean that people are retiring because they no longer need to work. Also, the unemployment rate does not measure the employed workers who are working on a part-time basis but would prefer to be working full time. The survey tracks part-time and full-time workers. Wage rates are another measure of the labor market that is included in our macroeconomic "dashboard." We will make the distinction between nominal wages and real wages (corrected for inflation).

Financial measures are also included in the standard set of macroeconomic variables. We keep track of interest rates, the payment at which lenders lend and borrowers borrow. Basic interest rates, such as the home mortgage rate and the rate on overnight loans between banks (called the federal funds rate), are reported in the press. But financial instruments produce yields for investors, and those yields are figured differently for different types of instruments. The yield of a certificate of deposit at a bank is simply the interest paid each month. Bonds pay a coupon every six months. Suppose you bought a new bond one year ago for $10,000 with a coupon rate of 3 percent. You receive $150 every six months. However, if the market value of the bond falls to $9,500, then you have a net yield of minus $200 for the year (2 percent of your investment). However, if you sell your bond for $9,500 to someone else (and if the value of the bond does not change again), then that person gets a yield of $300 divided by $9,500 for the next year, which is 3.16 percent. The same idea applies for home mortgages. The home buyer borrows $100,000 at 4 percent and pays interest accordingly. The owner of the mortgage gets the interest but also may see the market value of the mortgage change. Banks and other mortgage lenders used to hold the mortgages they issued, but they found that they were subject to a great deal of risk because the market value of the mortgages is subject to change. The secondary market for mortgages is very active and enables lenders to pass the risk on to other investors. The yield on stocks is figured as the dividend paid plus the change in the value of the stock. If you bought Google stock at $300 per share and they paid $15 in dividends over the year, and the stock increased in value to $320, then your yield is 11.67 percent ($35/$300). The basic point: The issuer of the bond or the stock is paying the coupon or dividend, but the investor's yield also depends upon the change in the value of the asset.

The last measure we shall consider here is the stock of money. As we know, "Money makes the world go round." Money is a medium of exchange, a unit of account, and a store of value. In other words, we use money to make transactions, keep records, and hold wealth. We cannot do without it. The basic measure of the stock of money is the amount of currency in circulation (excluding currency stashed in bank vaults) and money sitting in checking accounts. The latter is much larger than the former. This amount, currency in circulation plus checkable deposits, is called M1. A more comprehensive measure includes amounts held in time deposits (certificates of deposit), savings accounts, and money market mutual funds and is called M2. A fundamental relationship that economists have noted for over 200 years is that a greater stock of money usually means that prices are higher. Much more about this will follow.

Here is our list of variables:

Gross domestic product (GDP)

P = Price index

Y = Real GDP = GDP/P and its components in real terms

    C = Consumption

     I = Gross investment

        Fixed investment

           Nonresidential

           Residential

        Inventory investment

    G = Government purchases of goods and services

    X = Net exports (exports minus imports)

Unemployment rate

Wage rates

Interest rates

M = Money supply (generic money, type unspecified)

M1 = Money supply, consisting of currency and demand deposits

M2 = M1 plus money market mutual funds, time deposits, and savings accounts

These are the basic variables, but some additional variables will be introduced as needed to provide a clearer picture of what happened during particular episodes. This notation will be used throughout the book, so keep this list handy. Maybe mark this page with a paper clip.

Basic concepts IV: balance of payments, foreign exchange markets, and international trade

The purpose of this section is to introduce the international sector. Basic theoretical topics are covered: balance of payments, foreign exchange markets, and comparative advantage. The first subsection contains a method to integrate the balance of payments and the foreign exchange market into one diagram. The second subsection presents two methods for teaching comparative advantage. David Ricardo's original numerical example from 1819 is included, and a combined production possibility frontier for two countries is derived and discussed. The final subsection is a brief discussion of international trade policy.

Balance of payments and foreign exchange markets

The purpose of this subsection is to integrate the balance of payments and the market for foreign exchange. A brief survey of principles of economics textbooks reveals that this integration is not presented. Some texts cover the two topics in two separate chapters. Those that cover both topics in the same chapter do not show how the balance of payments can be depicted on a foreign exchange market diagram. The method presented here has been taught – and learned – by several classes of principles students.

The balance of payments of a nation consists of the current account and the financial account, and the sum of these accounts is zero. The basic rule is money coming in equals money going out. Because sellers in each nation are paid in their own currency, buyers must purchase that currency with their own currency. The main elements of the balance of payments are:

	Money Flow
Current Account	
Exports of Goods and Services	+
Imports of Goods and Services	−
Financial/Capital Account	
Foreign Investment in the Home Country	+
Home Country Investment in Foreign Countries	−

Suppose that the home country is the United States and the only foreign country is the European Union (E.U.) (the usual simplifying assumption of a two–country world). The demand for U.S. dollars on the foreign exchange market is expressed by the people of the E.U. and consists of two parts – the demand for U.S. exports of goods and services and the demand to purchase U.S. assets. The price of U.S. dollars is expressed as euros per dollar. The demand curve slopes negatively because a lower price of dollars means that each euro is worth more in these international transactions. The demand for U.S. exports of goods and services shifts when there are changes in E.U. incomes, E.U. population, prices of other goods, preferences, and price expectations. These are the usual suspects for changes in demand. In addition, the demand for U.S. assets shifts when there are changes in interest rates, i.e., rates of return, to assets in the U.S. and the E.U.

The supply of dollars in foreign exchange is expressed by people in the United States and is driven by the demand for E.U. exports of goods and services and for E.U. assets. The supply curve slopes positively because an increase in the price of dollars means that each dollar can buy more euros and thus more E.U. goods and services or assets. Yes, the supply curve of dollars is actually a demand curve, an idea that is counterintuitive and must be explained to students carefully. The shifters of this supply curve are the usual shifters of the demand for goods and services plus the interest rates that determine the demand for E.U. assets. Note that a change in the rate of return to U.S. assets will shift both the supply and demand for dollars in foreign exchange because, say, an increase in the returns to U.S. assets will increase the demand for those assets by investors in both the U.S. and the E.U. The demand for dollars by E.U. investors increases and the supply of dollars by U.S. investors to invest in the E.U. assets declines. Assume that the market for dollars is perfectly competitive. The exchange rate "floats," as it actually does according to U.S. and E.U. policy. Figure 1.3 is the basic diagram.

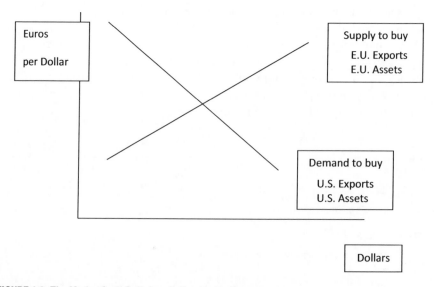

FIGURE 1.3 The Market for U.S. Dollars in Foreign Exchange

Market equilibrium is, of course, the point at which the demand for and supply of dollars are equal. An equilibrium exchange rate (euros per dollar) is established. In equilibrium:

> Dollars spent on U.S. exports and U.S. assets equal dollars spent for E.U. exports and E.U. assets.

To "prove" that the balance of payments must balance, move the terms on the right-hand side of the equation to the left-hand side to obtain:

> [Dollars spent on U.S. exports minus E.U. exports]
>
> plus
>
> [Dollars spent on U.S. assets minus E.U. assets] = 0

Consider some shifts in the demand and supply curves. Suppose that the initial equilibrium is point E, and the demand for U.S. dollars increases because incomes in the E.U. have increased, as shown in Figure 1.4. The price of the dollar in terms of euros rises and the quantity of dollars exchanged increases. As usual, the price and quantity move in the same direction when the demand shifts. U.S. exports increase, and because the value of the dollar in foreign exchange has increased, E.U. exports and/or purchases of E.U. assets increase as well. At the same time, purchases of U.S. assets will decline because no change in interest rates is posited (although interest rates may change as a result of income changes in both countries).

Now consider a shift in the supply of dollars. The demand for E.U. exports declines because preferences change as a result of a "buy American" campaign. The supply of dollars on the foreign exchange market declines and the supply curve shifts to the *left* as shown. Recall that the supply of dollars is actually a demand curve for E.U. exports and E.U. assets. The decline in the supply of dollars results in

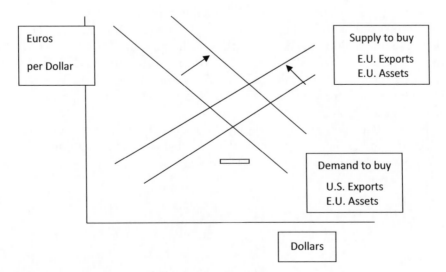

FIGURE 1.4 Effects of an Increase in the Demand for Dollars

an increase in the price of a dollar in terms of the euro and a decline in the number of dollars bought and sold. As usual, a shift in supply means that price and quantity move in opposite directions. E.U. exports of goods and services decline, but the increase in the value of the dollar will tend to offset some of that decline.

The exchange rate that matters for the real economy is the real exchange rate. The real exchange rate can be written as the nominal exchange rate that appears in the newspapers times the price level in the home country divided by the price level in the other country. In equation form:

$$\text{Real exchange rate} = E(P_h/P_f)$$

Here, E is the nominal exchange rate, P_h is the price level in the home country, and P_f is the price level in the other country. A home country with a high price level will have a difficult time selling its export products. The equation tells us that there are two methods for devaluing the home country currency in real terms: reduce the nominal exchange rate or lower its price level. Changing the nominal exchange rate is the more convenient method.

Comparative advantage

Comparative advantage is the basis for trade, is fundamental to economic analysis, and is a topic covered by all principles textbooks. This subsection includes two methods that have been used with some success. There is nothing really new in this section, but I find the methods satisfying. My mantra is (with apology to Shakespeare): "Opportunity cost, opportunity cost, all is opportunity cost."

Evidently, David Ricardo's demonstration of comparative advantage as the basis for trade is a stroke of genius. The first seven chapters of his famous book (1821, p. 82) present his model of an economy in which agricultural land is supplied in discrete amounts – a given amount of the best land, a given amount of next-best land, and so on. As the population grows, land of lower quality must be used, which generates land rent for the land of higher quality. The economy is hampered by the nature of land supply and by the tendency for land rent to increase as the population grows. What to do? Ricardo hit upon the idea that England could specialize in the production of cloth, export cloth, and import agricultural products – instead of imposing tariffs (Corn Laws) on the importation of agricultural products. As a Member of Parliament and public intellectual, he argued his case, and the Corn Laws eventually were eliminated after his death in 1823.

Here is Ricardo's example, slightly modified. England and Portugal produce wine and cloth. The number of workers needed to produce a "shipload" of wine and cloth in the two countries are as follows:

	Wine	Cloth
Portugal	80	90
England	120	100

Note that Ricardo built in the assumption that Portugal has the absolute advantage in both products because fewer workers are needed in Portugal than in England to produce either product (even though by 1819, England was the world's premier manufacturer of cloth). Because the opportunity cost of wine for cloth (and cloth for wine) is different in the two countries, there is "room for a deal." Here's the deal.

Suppose Portugal shifts 80 workers from cloth production to wine production, thus gaining one shipload of wine at the opportunity cost of 8/9 shipload of cloth. The opportunity cost of cloth is 9/8 shiploads of wine.

At the same time, suppose that England shifts 100 workers from wine production to cloth production, thus gaining one shipload of cloth at the opportunity cost of 5/6 shipload of wine. The opportunity cost of cloth is 6/5 shiploads of cloth.

Assume that the (barter) exchange rate is one shipload of wine for one shipload of cloth. Portugal ships the shipload of wine and England ships the shipload of cloth. I imagine one ship going back and forth. Portugal now has the original amounts of cloth and wine, and England now has the original amounts of cloth and wine as well. But look again. Portugal has gained the output of 10 workers. And England has gained the output of 20 workers. Both countries have gained output with no change in the number of workers because each country has specialized in the product with the lower opportunity cost.

The whole business relies on finding an exchange rate at which both countries gain. An exchange rate of one shipload of wine for one shipload of cloth was assumed. But given that the opportunity costs differ in the two countries, such an exchange rate (really a range of exchange rates) exists and there is a strong incentive for the two countries to find an exchange rate at which to strike a deal.

Ricardo's example is convincing, but another method makes explicit use of production possibility frontiers. Refer to Figure 1.5. England's production possibility frontier is labeled E, and Portugal's is P. The outer line is their combined production possibility curve. The diagram is drawn so that neither country has an absolute advantage, but the opportunity costs in the two countries are different. England has the comparative advantage in cloth, while Portugal has the comparative advantage in wine.

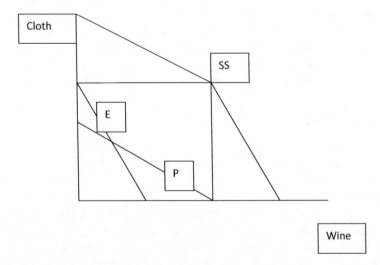

FIGURE 1.5 Production Possibility Curves: England, Portugal, and Both

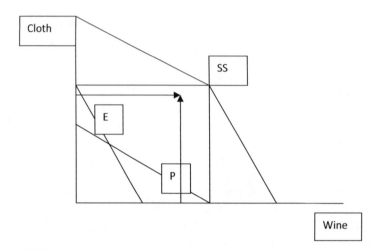

FIGURE 1.6 Why Specialization Pays Off

The combined production possibility curve is derived as follows. Suppose each country produces only the product in which it has the comparative advantage. England produces only cloth, and Portugal produces only wine. The resulting output combination is labeled SS, which is one point on the combined production possibility frontier (CPPF). The upper portion of the combined CPPF is derived by moving Portugal's production possibility curve up to the cloth level at SS. Along this portion of the CPPF, Portugal produces some cloth and less than its maximum wine, while England continues to produce only cloth.

The right-hand portion of the CPPF is derived by moving England's production possibility frontier to the right until it reaches the amount of wine at SS. Along this portion of the CPPF, Portugal continues to produce only wine, while England produces some wine and less than its maximum cloth.

What does Figure 1.5 prove? Here is the classroom demonstration. Select any point on the production possibility frontiers of each country – other than the maximum amount for the good with the lower opportunity cost. Compute the total amounts of the two goods and enter the corresponding point on the diagram. The point is inside the CPPF. See Figure 1.6, where the midpoint of each country's production possibility frontier is selected. You already know that points inside the production possibility frontier are inefficient. Together the two countries can have more of both goods, which is exactly what Ricardo was telling us.

International trade policy

There are two basic parts to international trade policy – exchange rate policy, and policies that directly impact exports and imports. Consider these in turn.

Exchange rate policy has three basic types. The first one is a floating exchange rate in which the rate is determined by demand and supply in the market for a currency, as shown in Figure 1.4. However, the central bank of the nation can change interest rates and thereby influence the exchange rate by altering the demand and supply of interest-earning assets. The third policy is to maintain a fixed exchange rate with the rest of the world. In this case, the central bank must buy or sell currency to maintain the same exchange rate. In other words, the central bank steps into the market and shifts the supply or demand for its own currency. If the central bank wishes to lower the exchange rate (the price of its own currency in terms of other currencies), it sells its own currency on the international market. To raise the exchange rate, the central bank buys its own currency.

What objective might be pursued using exchange rate policy? If the nation wishes to expand its exports, the central bank can keep the exchange rate lower than it otherwise would be. For example, China did in fact pursue such a policy from about 1997 to 2006. However, as export industries expand, prices of output may eventually go up. Since 2006, the price of the yuan has gone from about 8 yuan per dollar to 6 yuan per dollar, pushing up the price of Chinese goods.

What about trade policy that involves direct intervention into export and import markets? Intervention into import markets usually comes in the form of tariffs, which are taxes on the imported goods. The prices of the goods increase to those who purchase them, and the government collects tax revenue from the firms that sell these goods. In effect, the taxes are paid by the consumers. The firms in the exporting nation see a reduction in the quantity of exports and likely no change in the price at which they sell the product. If the tariff is targeted at the exports of one particular exporting nation, purchasers of those products can switch to imports from other nations. Domestic firms that produce the same product in the nation imposing the tariff may see their outputs rise as well.

Other trade policies pertaining to imports include import quotas and health and safety regulations. These policies also reduce imports, but the government receives no tax revenue. Domestic firms will see outputs rise.

Trade policies can also target exports. Export subsidies are used to promote exports. Such subsidies may permit the exporting firms to sell in export markets at below the actual cost of production. International organizations, such as the World Trade Organization (WTO), attempt to limit selling below cost, but proving "dumping" often is difficult.

What are the arguments for and against trade protection policies? The arguments in favor include:

- Infant industries; protect an emerging industry from foreign competition until that industry gets going and can compete against foreign imports. However, when should the protection be removed? When does the child industry go out on its own?

- Save jobs; keep domestic industries going, but the cost is not being able to buy at lower prices on international markets.

- Compete with cheap foreign labor; but what matters is labor productivity. If domestic workers are more productive and get paid well, low wages for less productive foreign workers will not matter. So maybe focus on making domestic workers more productive.

- Lax environmental standards; the idea is to reduce imports so that domestic firms are not disadvantaged by the fact that they face stricter environmental regulations than do firms in other countries. One can hope that those other countries will tighten their environmental regulations because it is the right thing to do for their own well-being.

■ Avoid exploiting people abroad; child labor and slave labor are odious practices that exist in some other nations. Send the message that if you want to export to us, you need to end exploiting your own people. Sometimes this message is sent to companies controlled by domestic owners that produce "offshore."

None of these arguments is crazy. They all make some sense, but the attempt to take these factors into consideration makes international trade policy extremely complex and controversial. Is there a simpler and better way?

The simpler and, most economists argue, better solution is to avoid trade wars. Instead, provide education and training for the nation's own workers so as to better pursue comparative advantages. In addition, if trade patterns change so that some workers are losing their jobs, then provide adequate compensation for those workers and help them make the transition to other lines of work. Helping people make the transition to other jobs is not easy, and the United States does not do a good job at providing compensation either. All of this has been a tough pill to swallow for nations that have seen their manufacturing jobs migrate to foreign countries. The argument about what to do in such circumstances will go on.

In the end, what other reasons exist for trade restrictions? Some nations need the tariff revenue. For example, tariff revenue was the main source of funding for the national government of the United States in the first half of the 19th century. And some domestic producers are doing what is called "rent seeking" – in other words, they have policies that increase their profits by doing nothing besides lobbying for trade restrictions. Some of this lobbying occurs because losers in the game of international trade are not compensated well by the government.

Basic concepts V: how monetary policy works

You need to know how the supply of money is created. The United States has had a central bank, the Federal Reserve System (the Fed), since 1913. And the United Kingdom has had the Bank of England since the 17th century. Countries with advanced economies have central banks. A central bank is not a regular bank but a government agency charged with two missions – to prevent financial panics and to stabilize the economy. A central bank prevents (or at least lessens) a financial panic by being the "lender of last resort" for financial institutions that are running short of cash because creditors are demanding their money. As former Fed chairman Ben Bernanke (2013, 2015) explained, the Federal Reserve undertook a great deal of this sort of effort during the financial crisis that began in 2008, and these actions will be discussed in Chapter 14.

Central banks attempt to stabilize the economy through the use of monetary policy. Here is a simplified balance sheet of a typical bank – call it Bank A.

Assets	Liabilities
Loans to Customers	Deposits
Government Bonds	
Reserves	
	Net Worth

The basic balance sheet equation is assets equal liabilities plus net worth (A = L + NW). Banks take in deposits, both checking accounts and time deposits (certificates of deposit), and make loans to customers, such as home mortgages and loans to businesses. Banks also invest in government bonds and hold reserves. Consider how it works in the United States. Banks are required to hold a certain amount of reserves, and the Fed is responsible for seeing that this requirement is met. Reserves consist of cash on hand (called vault cash) and the bank's reserve account at the Fed. Assets minus liabilities equal net worth, the value of the bank. As a simple example, suppose that the bank is required to hold reserves in the amount of 10 percent of its deposits. Remember that the supply of money (M1) is the total of the public's bank accounts and currency in circulation, where bank accounts are the greater part of the money supply. Currency in circulation includes only currency held by the public.

Here is how the Fed exercises control over the money supply. The Fed (through its government bond desk in New York) purchases a $10,000 government bond from a bond dealer using a check written on itself, and the dealer deposits the check in his/her bank. The bank presents the check to the Fed and the Fed adds that amount to the bank's reserve account at the Fed. This transaction has increased the bank's deposits (liabilities) and reserves (assets) by $10,000. The bank now has the ability to make more loans to customers. In fact, the bank can make a loan of $9,000 to a customer, leaving $1,000 (10 percent) in its reserve account. The bank places the $9,000 into the customer's checking account, and the customer spends the money by writing a check. All of the bank's accounts are in balance. Loans are up by $9,000, deposits are up by the original $10,000, and reserves are up by $1,000 (10 percent of the increase in deposits). The money supply has increased by $9,000 because the check for $9,000 is deposited in another bank. Here are the *changes* in the balance sheet for Bank A.

Assets		Liabilities	
Loans to Customers	+$9,000	Deposits	+$10,000
Government Bonds	0		+$9,000
Reserves	+$1,000		−$9,000
		Net Worth	0

The loan is spent by purchasing something from Firm #1. Firm #1 deposits the money in its bank account with another bank – call it Bank B. Bank B has seen an increase in deposits of $9,000 and an increase in reserves of $9,000 because the Fed credits that amount to Bank B's reserve account. Bank B now has the ability to make a loan to another customer in the amount of $8,100 (with $900, 10% of the deposit, held in reserve). Suppose Bank B's customer walks out the door with $8,100 in cash, which is an increase in the money supply because the vault cash is now in circulation. You can guess what happens next. The money is spent and winds up as a deposit in Bank C, which can now make a loan, and so on. Where does it end? If every customer spends the money and every bank lends up to the limit, then the money supply will increase by $100,000, i.e., $10,000 times 10, because the banking system has had an increase of $10,000 in reserves and the reserve requirement is 10 percent.

That is how the money supply can increase. However, the money supply increases only if banks are willing to make more loans after their reserves are increased. The first bank can stop the process by simply refusing to make a new loan, or borrowers can stop the process if nobody has a reason to borrow more money from the bank. Monetary policy often is likened to "pushing on a string." The whole process can work in reverse. The Fed can sell a $10,000 government bond to a bond dealer, which reduces the dealer's checking account. The reduction in deposits at the dealer's bank must be matched by reductions in assets, which means reducing loans by $9,000 and reserves by $1,000 (10% of the reduction in deposits).

By the way, a bank can go bankrupt in at least a couple of different scenarios. Suppose there is a run on the bank, i.e., depositors demand their money as in the movie *It's a Wonderful Life*. Vault cash is used at first to pay them, but the bank runs out of this money pretty quickly if the run is not stopped. Next the bank might borrow cash from another bank or attempt to liquidate some bonds and loans (sell them to someone). This might work, but if there is a general financial crisis, the other banks are losing cash too, and those bonds and loans may not be worth very much. If the market value of the outstanding loans (plus other assets) is less than the value of the deposits, the bank has a negative net worth and is therefore bankrupt. A loan from the Fed (say in the form of a truckload of Federal Reserve notes) can be used to increase reserves so that the bank does not have to sell its assets, thereby preventing bankruptcy.

Or consider this scenario. The bank makes money by taking in deposits (i.e., borrowing money) and paying a low rate of interest on those deposits and making loans at a higher rate of interest. Banks "borrow short" and "lend long," a recipe for potential disaster. The difference in interest rates is the return to the bank's owners for providing its services, called financial intermediation. But suppose that the loans made by the bank were made at a particular interest rate that remains fixed over the relatively long lives of loans such as home mortgages. And suppose that the interest rate in the overall economy increases sharply. Now depositors expect to be paid a higher rate of interest or they will withdraw their deposits. If the rate of interest that must be paid to depositors is greater than that earned by the bank on its loan portfolio, the bank is losing money and will be bankrupt when it runs out of vault cash and sells its assets, and net worth falls to zero. To put it another way, the increase in the interest rate in the overall economy means that the value of the loans made by the bank has declined. This is called interest rate risk. It could happen, and it did happen big-time in the early 1980s. The Fed can mitigate the crisis by providing a loan to the bank to tide it over.

Basic concepts VI: how fiscal policy works

Fiscal policy involves making changes in government spending and taxation. Both the amounts of government spending and taxation change with overall economic activity. In a recession, tax revenues decline because households and firms have less taxable income. And expenditures increase because government programs for unemployment insurance and welfare payments rise. When the economy is booming, the reverse happens; tax revenues go up and these types of expenditures decline.

There is basic algebra for tax revenue that you need to understand. Tax revenue (Rev) equals the tax rate (T) times the tax base (B), or

$$Rev = T \times B$$

So in a recession, the tax base declines and revenue falls unless the tax rate is increased. And if the tax rate is increased, revenue will rise as long as the increase in the tax rate does not cause the tax base to decline "too much." Now comes the big idea. A reduction in the tax rate might cause the tax base to increase enough so that revenue will go up. Does this happen? With a lower tax rate, will workers and firms work more and increase their taxable incomes? After all, their efforts now pay off more. But will those increased efforts increase the tax base enough to make revenue increase? Or will workers and firms actually work less because they can make the same after-tax income with less effort? Or will there be no change in work effort? Under these last two scenarios, tax revenue definitely will fall. These questions will pop up later in the book, especially when we encounter what is called supply-side economics.

So let us get back to fiscal policy. There two basic types of fiscal policy: automatic stabilizers and discretionary policy. Automatic stabilizers are those policies built into the fiscal system that will increase expenditures during a macroeconomic downturn and decline during an upturn. Unemployment compensation and welfare programs are examples. On the taxation side, a progressive tax means that a taxpayer with a higher tax base pays a higher tax rate at the margin (the tax on an additional dollar or pound of income). For example, a household might face the following tax schedule:

Income range	Tax rate	On amount over
$0 to $19,400	10%	$0
$19,400 to $78,950	12%	$19,400
$78,950 to $168,400	22%	$78,950
$168,400 to $321,450	24%	$168,400
etc.		

During an economic downturn, the household might experience a decline in taxable income from $90,000 to $60,000 that puts it in a lower "tax bracket." The household sees a decline in its marginal tax rate from 22% to 12% – quite a decline. In fact, the tax payment falls from $18,486 to $6,812, a decline of 64% with a decline in income of 33%. (I invite you to figure the taxes under both scenarios. Remember that the tax on the first $19,400 is $1,940.) With a progressive tax system, the household is somewhat cushioned in a downturn by a disproportional drop in its tax payment.

Discretionary fiscal policy means that action must be taken to change either taxation or spending policy. Ordinarily, major discretionary fiscal policy actions take the approval of the legislative branch of the government. The legislature passes laws regarding tax rates and the spending budgets for the various departments of the government. Such actions are taken in response to perceived needs. A new government program may be needed to deal with an important issue. The blizzard of new programs begun in the New Deal of the 1930s in the United States is discussed in detail in Chapter 8. More recently, for example, advanced nations realized that actions should be taken to control air pollution, water pollution, and other environmental problems. Governments had not paid much attention to such matters prior to the 1960s or 1970s. Policies were formed, and agencies were budgeted. Another big example is military policy. External threats of various types appear, and funds are needed to prepare to meet those threats. During the Cold War with the Soviet Union, both the United States and the Soviet Union competed to have the better military hardware. Enormous amounts of money were spent to develop the next generation of airplanes, naval ships, and weapons. See the book *Skunk Works* by Ben Rich and Leo Janos (1994) for the story of how Lockheed developed generations of advanced military airplanes for the United States. By the way, U.S. policy is that it does not supply the best version of its weapons to other nations, whoever they are. Ah well, the beat goes on.

Now consider discretionary policy to respond to macroeconomic issues. The economy takes a nosedive. What to do? Is the downturn serious enough that something discretionary should be done? The use of discretionary fiscal policy proceeds through a series of steps:

- recognition, which takes some time to figure out what is happening and what can be done;
- legislative lag, which means that time is needed to draft legislation and martial support for the program in the legislature; and
- implementation lag, which pertains to the time schedule for spending money and changing tax systems.

All of this can mean that discretionary fiscal policy is not timely. We want to use money quickly on "shovel-ready" projects, but there are few of those already in the pipeline. Rather, it will take time to design more worthy projects. All that said, sometimes discretionary fiscal policy has responded quickly and effectively. In particular, tax cuts can be implemented quickly so that households have more money to spend. But will they spend the money, or will the money be saved for a rainy day? That is another question. Some empirical evidence suggests that temporary tax cuts are not very effective at boosting economic activity. We will meet episodes in which discretionary policy was employed in the second half of the book.

Conclusion

So we have completed the preliminary topics. I am sure that some of this chapter has been review for many of you. I trust reading over the material did not do you any harm. It is good to review sometimes. Now let us go on to macroeconomic theories.

Appendix: How to compute percentage change

The appendix can be skipped upon the first reading of the book but will need to be studied when you begin to read chapters about the macroeconomic episodes that involve looking closely at data.

Very often, we shall examine percentage changes in many of the macroeconomics variables such as GDP, investment, prices, and money supply. You must get used to computing percentage changes, so here is a quick tutorial. You should have a calculator handy that includes the option of providing the natural logarithm of a number. We'll use the GDP deflator index numbers seen earlier, which are

2009	100.00
2010	101.22
2011	103.31
2012	106.17
2013	106.73

The basic computation for percentage change from one year to the next, in this case from 2010 to 2011, is

$(103.31 - 101.22)/101.22 = .0206$, or 2.06 percent.

Here is the quick way to do this one – one calculation instead of two:

$103.31/101.22 = 1.0206$, so the percentage change is 2.06.

If the change is negative, you still compute percentage change by subtracting the earlier number from the later number and dividing by the earlier number. For example, if investment falls from \$70 billion to \$60 billion, compute $(60 - 70)/70 = -.143$, or −14.3 percent.

It is obvious that the percentage change from 2009 to 2013 is 6.73 percent because the index for 2009 is 100.00. In general, one would compute

$106.73/100.00 = 1.0673$.

What is the average percentage change over the four years from 2009 to 2013? One method is simply to divide 6.73 by 4, or 1.68 percent. This method can be inaccurate if the elapse of time is long or if the changes are large. Here is the technically correct way to do it. Write

$(1 + i)(1 + i)(1 + i)(1 + i) = (1 + i)^4 = 1.0673$.

Here, i is the annual percentage change that produces an increase of 6.73 percent over four years. This is the equation for compound interest from investing \$1 for four years at interest rate i. The trick is to solve for i. Clearly $(1 + i)$ is equal to the fourth root of 1.0673, but the higher roots are difficult to compute. Instead, take the natural logarithm of both sides of the equation, where ln stands for natural logarithm:

$$4 \ln(1 + i) = \ln(1.0673).$$

The natural logarithm of a number is the exponent to which the base is raised to obtain the number in question. The base of natural logarithms is called e and is approximately equal to 2.71. So $1.0673 = e^{\ln(1.0673)}$.
    The next steps are as follows:

$4 \ln(1 + i) = 0.0651$ (using a calculator that provides natural logs)
$\ln(1 + i) = 0.0163$
    $(1 + i) = e^{0.0163}$ (computation of the anti–log)
    $(1 + i) = 1.0164$, so $i = 0.0164$, or 1.64 percent.

The calculator will compute what is called the anti–logarithm. We see that computing the simple average introduces a small error (1.68 vs. 1.64). The correct method takes account of the compound interest. This more complex method will be used to compute rates of change for variables in a long time horizon.
    As an exercise, compute $1.0 \times 1.0164 \times 1.0164 \times 1.0164 \times 1.0164$. In other words, compound 1.0 at 1.64 percent forward for four years. You will get the correct answer, 1.0673, or very, very close to it. Now do the same for 1.0168. You will get what? An answer that is a little larger than 1.0673.
    The same method is followed if the total change over the years is negative, except in this case, for example, $(1 + i)^4$ is something less than 1.0. Now the solution for i will turn out to be negative, the annual rate of decline. Suppose that a variable is 90 percent of its starting value after four years, i.e., $(1 + i)^4 = 0.90$. The annual rate of change is −2.60 percent (not −2.50 percent). See if you can replicate this answer.

2

Keynesian theory and policy

Introduction: schools of thought in macroeconomics

The field of macroeconomics can be broken down into several schools of thought, and this book provides an introduction to each of them. No doubt the scholars who have spent their lives developing and refining a particular school of thought will find that I have simplified things too much. I submit that simplification cannot be avoided in an introductory treatment. That is what textbooks do. The purpose of the book is to provide a sensible introduction to each theory, and to see how each theory stacks up against the data for various episodes. Most textbooks cover only one theory, and do not systematically assess how well that theory accounts for what actually happened. One textbook by Snowdon and Vane (2005) covers all of the schools of thought up to 2005 and includes interviews with important scholars associated with each one. Some discussion of actual events is included here and there. But the book is over 700 pages in length and is more appropriate for graduate students.

The schools of thought presented in this book are as follows:

- Keynesian theory, with discussion of financial instability and other additions to basic Keynesian theory made over the years. Keynesians emphasize the role of aggregate demand and its components as the source of fluctuations in the economy. The shift in the demand curve in Figure 1.1 gives the basic idea. They advocate the use of active monetary policy and fiscal policy (government spending and taxation) to influence aggregate demand and stabilize the economy.

- Monetarism associated with Milton Friedman and others, with extension to include rational expectations (the idea that people form realistic expectations that influence their current behavior). Monetarists see changes in the supply of money as a principal cause of the ups and downs of the economy. Changes in the supply of money are thought mainly to influence the demand side of the economy. They argue that activist monetary policy is dangerous and should be avoided. They think that the supply of money should be governed by a simple rule.

- New classical theory called real business cycle analysis as formulated by Robert Lucas and associates, with extension to supply-side economics. This group sees shocks to the supply side of the economy as the primary source of fluctuations. The shifting supply curve in Figure 1.1 illustrates the basic point. They believe that supply and demand will reach equilibrium quickly without "help" from the government. Supply-side economics emphasizes tax cuts to stimulate the private economy.

- Austrian capital and business cycle theory warns against any activist macroeconomic policy. A free-market economy will recover quickly from a downturn, provided that the government does not attempt to help by lowering interest rates and causing a misallocation of resources. Demand and supply will reach equilibrium without interference from the government.

- Modern Monetary Theory (MMT) is the most recent entry in the macroeconomic sweepstakes. This theory is based on the idea that a sovereign nation issues money that is used to pay the taxes the nation imposes on the public. In short, taxes are used to convince people to accept government-issued fiat money, money that is not backed by anything other than its general acceptance as legal tender. Governments do not impose taxes to raise money to spend. Rather, under MMT governments can create and spend as much money as needed to pursue the macroeconomic objective of full employment, and need not worry about the size of the government deficit. The idea is called functional finance; the function of spending money is to generate prosperity. MMT advocates recognize that spending "too much" money leads to inflation. So do not spend too much. Are you shocked? We will consider MMT in detail in Chapter 7.

Different schools of thought have very different policy conclusions. As noted, the Keynesians think that the national government should use monetary policy and the federal budget (taxes and spending) in such a manner to stabilize the economy. If the economy is operating below full employment, increase the supply of money, cut taxes, and increase spending in some combination to put unemployed resources to work. Advocates for Modern Monetary Theory go even further. They turn the idea of taxation on its head and say that government deficits do not matter unless the government is spending too much money as to generate inflation. They put discretionary fiscal policy first on their list of policy actions, but they also propose a guaranteed employment program as an automatic stabilizer. The other schools of thought, while based on different sorts of economic models, all imply that the national government should not attempt to stabilize the economy. The Keynesians and MMT people are the "liberals," in the sense they think that the government is capable of carrying out economic policy that is of benefit to the nation. The members of the other schools of thought are "conservatives" who think that either the government does not know enough to conduct good economic policy and is likely to make mistakes (the Monetarists), or that no government policy will do any good, i.e., any government attempt to stabilize the economy is a mistake (the real business cycle economists and the Austrians).

It is fair to say that members of one school of thought have been known to disagree sharply with the work of members of another school of thought. Indeed, some of the remarks are insulting and impugn a person's motives. Here are some examples.

Keynes began *The General Theory of Employment, Interest, and Money* (p. 3) with a comment on the classical school as it was taught to him:

> I shall argue that the postulates of the classical theory are applicable to a special case only and not to the general case, the situation which it assumes being a limiting point of the possible positions of equilibrium. Moreover, the characteristics of the special case assumed by the classical theory happen not to be those of the economic society in which we actually live, with the result that its teaching is misleading and disastrous if we attempt to apply it to the facts of experience.

He went on to name names – Alfred Marshall, F. Edgeworth, and especially A. C. Pigou. Pigou was his contemporary and colleague at Cambridge.

Van Overtveldt (2007, pp. 85–87) assembled some of the immediate reactions by economists at the University of Chicago to Keynes's *General Theory*.

Jacob Viner:	"I believe in the virtues of professional division of labor, however, I am troubled, therefore, when economists adopt the role and the tactics of the prophet or the politician, especially when there is any ground for suspicion that what is involved is false prophecy."
Frank Knight:	"I regard Mr. Keynes's views with respect to money and monetary theory in particular . . . as figuratively speaking, passing the keys to the citadel out of the window to the Philistines hammering at the gates."
Henry Simons:	". . . Keynes may succeed in becoming the academic idol of our worst cranks and charlatans – not to mention the possibilities of the book as the economic bible of a fascist movement."
Milton Friedman:	". . . has contributed greatly to the proliferation of overgrown governments increasingly concerned with every phase of their citizens' lives."

James Tobin, a leading Keynesian and a fellow Nobel Prize recipient, was Milton Friedman's gentlemanly nemesis. He did comment on popular writings in which Friedman advocated very conservative policies, but mostly restricted his comments to Friedman's research. Tobin wrote a 22-page review for the *American Economic Review* (1965) of *A Monetary History of the United States, 1867–1960* by Friedman and Schwartz (1963). This is their landmark master work of Monetarism. Tobin (1965, p. 481) famously wrote:

> Consider the following three propositions: Money does not matter. It does too matter. Money is all that matters. It is all too easy to slip from the second proposition to the third, to use reasoning and evidence which support the second claim to claim the third. In this book F&S have ably and convincingly marshaled evidence for the proposition that money matters. They have put to

rout the neo-Keynesian, if he exists, who regards monetary events as mere epiphenomena, postscripts added as afterthoughts to the nonmonetary factors that completely determine income, employment, and even prices. But in their zeal and exuberance Friedman and his followers often seem to go – though perhaps less in this book than elsewhere – beyond their own logic and statistics to the other extreme, where the stock of money becomes the necessary and sufficient determinant of money income. Much as I admire their work, I cannot follow them there.

What a gentlemanly way to say that Milton Friedman is a zealot.

Later in the same review, Tobin (1965, p. 482) wrote:

Many controversies on monetary theory and policy pit Friedman and his followers against the rest of the profession. But consensus among Friedman's opponents generally extends no further than the proposition that Friedman is wrong.

Robert Solow, a prominent Keynesian and another winner of the Nobel Prize, commenting on the real business cycle work of Robert Lucas, said, as quoted in Klamer (1983, p. 146), that

Now Bob Lucas and Tom Sargent like nothing better than to get drawn into technical discussions, because then you have tacitly gone along with their fundamental assumptions; your attention is attracted away from the basic weakness of the whole story. Since I find that fundamental framework ludicrous, I respond by treating is as ludicrous – that is by laughing at it.

Milton Friedman's comment on Austrian business cycle theory was (1993, p. 172):

For one thing, it (the empirical evidence) would cast grave doubt on those theories that see as the source of deep depressions the excesses of the prior expansion (the Mises cycle theory is a clear example).

We have a pretty good idea that a theory about which there is grave doubt belongs in the cemetery. Friedman had common cause with the Austrians in that both opposed economic policies to stabilize the economy, but he thought that their theory was refuted by the evidence. But macroeconomics is remarkable in that old theories never die, and they have adherents who prevent those theories from fading away.

Recent comments by economists about each other are just as harsh. John Quiggin (2010) published a book with Princeton University Press, a distinguished academic publisher, titled *Zombie Economics: How Dead Ideas Still Walk Among Us*. Paul Krugman, a Nobel Prize winner and columnist for *The New York Times*, wrote an article for *The New York Times Magazine* (2009b) titled "How did economists get it so wrong?" Both the Quiggin book and the Krugman article are heavily critical of modern macroeconomics in general, and especially of economists associated with the real business cycle school in particular, for being too enamored of mathematical models that do not capture our current reality. Krugman's writing style was rather flippant, and he named a few names, including John Cochrane of the University of Chicago. Cochrane (2009) wrote an angry response titled "How did Paul Krugman get it so wrong?" This piece includes the following:

> Paul Krugman has no interesting ideas whatsoever about what caused our current financial and economic problems, what policies might have prevented it, or what might help us in the future, and has no contact with people who do.

Modern Monetary Theory has been met with a hail of criticism, which is the normal procedure in the field of macroeconomics. The Austrian economist Robert Murphy (2019) concludes that

> The MMT worldview is intriguing, if only because it is so different from even the way conventional Keynesians think about fiscal and monetary policy. Unfortunately, it seems to me dead wrong. The MMTers concentrate on accounting tautologies that do not mean what they think.

Paul Krugman (2020b, p. 152) has taken MMT on:

> Well, it looks as if policy debates over the next couple of years will be at least somewhat affected by the doctrine of Modern Monetary Theory, which some progressives appear to believe means that they don't need to worry about how to pay for their initiatives. That's actually wrong even if you set aside concerns about MMT analysis. But first it seems to me that I need to set out what's right and what's wrong about MMT.
>
> Unfortunately, that's a very hard argument to have – modern MMTers are messianic in their claims to have proved even conventional Keynesianism wrong, tend to be unclear about what exactly their differences with conventional views are, and also have a strong habit of dismissing out of hand any attempt to make sense of what they are saying.

Krugman goes on to discuss fiscal policy as formulated by Abba Lerner in the 1940s. All of this is examined in Chapter 7.

Some additional critical remarks about the various theories are sprinkled throughout the book. You, the reader, can decide which of these remarks are justified or really go too far. The fact that macroeconomists disagree so strongly leaves the normal person in a quandary. The purpose of this book is to provide the student with an ability to understand the issues and to reach his or her own informed conclusions.

How are we going to decide which theory is the best at explaining a particular macroeconomic episode? The basic data will be presented in tabular form, and a narrative will tell the story. I have enough familiarity with each episode to be able to write what I hope is a pretty good narrative. Then we will match implications of each theory with the main events in the narrative. Which theory has the right implications? A judgment will be made about which theory does the best job of matching the narrative. This judgment is not based on formal statistical tests – because introductory students are not expected to know about formal statistical tests. Further study, such as majoring in or even getting a graduate degree in economics, will be needed to apply statistical tests to the issues. Instead, we shall follow the legal procedure of awarding judgment based on a preponderance of the evidence (the standard in civil lawsuits between private parties). We shall not seek evidence beyond a reasonable doubt, the standard used in criminal cases in which society (the people) judges an alleged criminal. Preponderance of the evidence is, admittedly, a vague standard. But in the end, you as a member of the jury will be able to think about the issues and form judgments for yourself. You are a budding economist if, after reading this book, you conclude that more study is needed.

Keynesian theory

John Maynard Keynes (1883–1946) is generally regarded as the most important economist of the 20th century. Prior to the publication in 1936 of his most important book, *The General Theory of Employment, Interest, and Money*, the field of economics was known just as economics (or as political economy). After Keynes, economics was divided into microeconomics and macroeconomics. The purposes of this chapter are to present Keynesian theory as Keynes himself did, to explain why it was (and is) important. Then, Chapter 3 shows how Keynesians interpreted and extended the theory – somewhat at variance from Keynes in the *General Theory*. I believe that you, the student of macroeconomics, should know what Keynes said and why he said it. John Maynard Keynes is the subject of a three-volume biography by Robert Skidelsky (1983, 1992, 2000) that is the best biography of any economist.

  Keynes was the son of the English economist John Neville Keynes and a brilliant student of philosophy, mathematics, and economics at Cambridge University. He pursued an academic career at Cambridge and achieved international fame with the publication in 1919 of *The Economic Consequences of Peace*, a strong critique of the Versailles Treaty at the end of World War I that imposed harsh conditions on Germany that would inhibit the recovery of the entire European economy. He was a prominent member of the Bloomsbury Group, the remarkable literary group that flourished in London in the 1920s and 1930s. Keynes made a living from his writing, his investments, and lecturing at Cambridge. He also served as bursar of Kings College, Cambridge, which meant that he managed the investments of the college. He held a position at the Treasury during World War I and was recalled to an unpaid position at the Treasury in 1940 by the government of Prime Minister Winston Churchill. He suffered a heart attack on May 16, 1937 at age 53 after a series of illnesses and symptoms during the winter of 1936–1937. He spent the years of World War II working very hard on behalf of his country. While the *General Theory* is devoted to the analysis of a single nation, Keynes was also an internationalist who worked to improve the system of international trade for his entire career. He was England's chief representative at the Bretton Woods conference in 1944 that set up the postwar international financial system that includes the International Monetary Fund and the World Bank. Given the fragile nature of his health after 1937, Keynes's biographer Robert Skidelsky (2000, p. xvii) began the third volume of his biography with:

> This is a story, above all else, about Keynes's patriotism. When he died, Lionel Robbins wrote to his widow: 'Maynard had given his life for his country, as surely as if he had fallen on the field of battle.'

Keynes suffered a fatal heart attack on April 21, 1946, a victim of heart disease at age 62. Thus, within the span of a year did heart disease claim at a relatively young age the century's most important economist as well as the century's most important political leader, Franklin Delano Roosevelt. FDR died on April 12, 1945 at age 63. Heart disease was little understood and was essentially untreatable in those days. Thankfully, much progress has been made on heart disease since the days of FDR and Keynes.

If Keynes had lived to the age of 86, he very likely (surely?) would have received the first Nobel Prize in economics that was awarded in 1969. That first Nobel Prize was awarded jointly to Ragnar Frisch and Jan Tinbergen for their statistical and modeling work in macroeconomics that had served to further Keynesian economics. Frisch had begun his work prior to the publication of the *General Theory*, but Tinbergen's first book was published in 1939 and clearly is a statistical implementation of Keynesian theory.

We begin with a brief introduction to the state of macroeconomic thinking prior to the *General Theory*.

Macroeconomics before Keynes: classical macroeconomics

The boom–and–bust cycles of a market economy had been an important topic for economists long before Keynes. Indeed, it was a topic of vital concern for Keynes before he became the Keynes of the *General Theory*. There was no unified classical (i.e., pre-Keynesian) macroeconomic theory, but now there is some agreement on the major features of monetary theory prior to Keynes's *General Theory*. This presentation follows the Snowdon and Vane (2005) history of macroeconomics. In essence, the classical economists separated the real and the monetary economies. Output and employment are determined in a perfectly competitive economy in which all markets clear and all participants in the economy have stable expectations, and the supply of money determines the overall price level.

The demand for labor depends upon the real wage rate. In the short run, capital is fixed and the demand for labor is equal to labor's marginal product. The output produced by the last worker hired is presumed to decline as more workers are hired because the capital stock is fixed. Workers are hired as long as the marginal product of the last worker exceeds the real wage rate (by as little as one cent). The supply of labor increases with the real wage. The competitive labor market establishes a real wage equal to the marginal product of labor, so the total supply of output (in the short run) is set by the fixed capital stock, the schedule of the marginal product of labor, and the supply of labor. See Figure 2.1. This level of output is the full-employment output because there is no unemployment – other than the normal, temporary movement of workers from one job to another.

How is the demand for output determined in the classical system? As you already know, and ignoring government and foreign trade for now, output of final goods and services is demanded for current consumption and for real investment goods. Workers earn wages and spend on consumption or save. Saving is presumed to be a function of the return to saving – the interest rate. Firms earn the return to capital, which is passed on to the owners, who also either spend on consumption or save. Total expenditure in real terms must equal total income, which equals the sum of

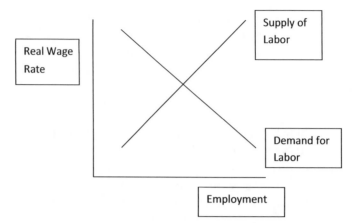

FIGURE 2.1 The Supply of and Demand for Labor

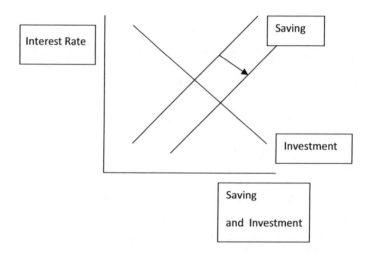

FIGURE 2.2 The Supply of and Demand for Saving

consumption and saving in real terms. The supply of savings depends upon the interest rate, and those savings are provided to firms for the purpose of purchasing real investment goods. The demand for real investment goods also depends upon the interest rate; a lower interest rate increases the amount of investment that can earn a profit for the firm. The simplified statement of the theory is "supply creates its own demand." This statement came to be known as Say's Law.

As shown in Figure 2.2, the market for savings produces a competitive equilibrium interest rate at which the supply of savings equals the demand for savings (to be used to purchase real investment goods). The interest rate always acts to equal savings and investment at the full employment level of output. To see this, suppose that the economy starts out at the full employment level of output and employment. Now assume that workers decide to save more and spend less on consumption. This is shown as a shift to the right in the supply of savings in Figure 2.2. Does the economy go into a tailspin that results in unemployment? No, because the increase in savings produces a decline in the interest rate, which stimulates spending on real investment goods. In fact, a new equilibrium is established in which the increase in savings (decline in consumption) is exactly matched by an increase in investment spending. Total income and total spending on goods and services do not fall.

So far, money has not entered into the discussion. In this simple version of the classical theory, money is presumed to be "neutral." The quantity of money has no effect on real output and employment, so there is a separation of the real and the nominal variables. This is known as the "classical dichotomy." The quantity of money determines the level of prices via the Quantity Theory of Money. In the classic quantity theory of money, the demand for money is determined by the need to conduct market transactions, and in its most basic form is simply a given fraction of the money value of aggregate income and expenditures:

$$M_d = kPY$$

Here, M_d is the demand for money (say M1), P is the overall price level, Y is aggregate income (in "real" terms), and k is the fraction of aggregate nominal income and expenditure that households and firms need to hold in the form of money. Money demand is aggregate income times the price level times k. Money is supplied by the monetary authorities in the amount M_s. Setting money demand equal to money supply and rewriting, we have:

$$P = M_s/kY$$

As we have seen, real aggregate income Y is set in the "real" economy. Technology and convention set k, the fraction that translates aggregate nominal income and expenditures into the demand for money. Therefore, the overall level of prices depends directly on the supply of money. Increases or decreases in the supply of money are matched by changes in the level of prices, with no impact on the real variables.

An alternative version of the Quantity Theory of Money can be stated as:

$$MV = PY$$

where M is the generic stock of money and V is called the velocity of money. The velocity of money is the number of times in a year that the stock of money is used to handle transactions for final goods and services. In this version, the velocity of money is simply equal to (1/k).

Keynes himself worked extensively with the Quantity Theory of Money. One of his influential early studies is *A Treatise on Money* (1924), which showed that variations in the money supply and the price level can cause substantial mischief. An increase in the general price level helps debtors (people who owe money) and hurts creditors (people who made the loans) because, when the money is paid back, it will purchase fewer real goods and services. Reverse the argument for a declining general price level.

This book is not intended to be a treatise on classical macroeconomics, but a couple of complications to classical theory are worth mentioning. First of all, as

Baumol (1999) indicated, J. B. Say was an early-19th-century economist who probably never (in French) said "supply creates its own demand." Say's comments were not very clear. Baumol referred to a more complex set of ideas known as the Law of Markets, which can be summarized as follows:

■ Production (supply) does generate the income sufficient for the demand for those products. There cannot be a general failure of demand.

■ Saving is essential for economic growth and is channeled into spending on commodities that will satisfy future demands (i.e., investment). The economy cannot save too much.

■ Overproduction of some commodities is possible when "mistakes were made." This misallocation of resources will be eliminated quickly by market forces, but unemployment is possible during the period of adjustment.

■ Unemployment can occur when labor-saving technology is adopted, and a great deal of suffering can ensue. Baumol (1999, p. 198) noted that Say even advocated public works to reduce unemployment at such times.

In short, classical economists such as J. B. Say did not deny the possibility of unemployment, and even believed that there were times when government spending should be used to alleviate unemployment. But Say and the other classical economists did deny that there could be a general failure of demand.

Knut Wicksell was another notable classical economist who thought deeply about the theory illustrated in Figure 2.2. He proposed that there exists a "natural rate of interest," the interest rate at which the supply of savings by the society just equals the demand for investment to produce goods in the future. The rate of interest just equals the real rate of return on new capital assets. The standard quantity theory of money states that the supply of money determines the overall price level. Wicksell (1906) expanded on the quantity theory by adding an indirect effect of the supply of money on the market interest rate. In particular, if banks increased the supply of money and drove the market rate of interest below the natural rate of interest, then investment would increase and saving would decrease, producing an overall increase in spending. Overall demand would exceed currently available supply. The increase in spending that came with the increase in the supply of money would be one cause of inflation. Wicksell provided a mechanism through which an increase in the supply of money produced an increase in prices.

So classical economics was more complex than "supply creates its own demand," unemployment cannot exist, and the real and monetary economies can be separated using a simple quantity theory of money. But classical economics had no real answer for the Great Depression.

Pre-Keynesian macroeconomics also included data-driven analyses of business cycles. A leading and perceptive example of this approach is Wesley Clair Mitchell's *Business Cycles and Their Causes*. The original version of the book was published in 1913, and an abbreviated version was published in 1941. The later version became a popular item on the economist's reading list. Professor Mitchell was for many years the Director of the National Bureau of Economic Research, an organization known for dating recessions and for empirical work on business cycles (and many other topics).

Mitchell explained how:

- Prosperity accumulates,
- Prosperity breeds crisis,
- Crisis unfolds and leads to depression, and
- Depression leads to a revival of economic activity.

Here is a very brief summary of the story. Prosperity arises from a depression because the costs of doing business and interest rates are low. Some industries will begin to expand, and this leads to expansion in other industries and a general improvement overall. However, expansion will generate higher costs of doing business in comparison to prices, and interest rates will rise. Profits begin to fall, and the security of outstanding debts comes into question. A crisis ensues when some important enterprises declare bankruptcy. A sudden demand for the repayment of loans can cause a panic. Employment declines, so consumer demand falls. The demand for investment declines as well because future prospects do not appear to be promising. A depression is the outcome. And so and so on. Mitchell's book includes a detailed empirical examination of the panic of 1907 in the United States that concentrates on the banking system. At this time, there was no central bank in the United States charged with the mission to keep banks from failing (and therefore wiping out the funds of depositors). This incident was one reason the nation created the U.S. Federal Reserve System.

Mitchell's approach was to develop a detailed empirical history of business cycles so that the public could understand and anticipate the ups and downs of the economy. But his is not a macroeconomic theory, and his book does not provide policy recommendations for an economy in depression. Let us now turn to Keynes.

Introduction to the general theory of employment, interest, and money

The *General Theory* was written during the depths of the Great Depression of the early 1930s. It is a product of its time, to be sure. As noted in Chapter 1, Keynes believed that useful economics is a product of its time. His purpose was to develop a theory that explained the obvious facts that the capitalist economies of the day were not generating anything close to full employment, and that this state of affairs had existed for several years. The economic theory of the time, as outlined in the previous section, which Keynes called the postulates of classical economics and dismissed in a few pages, was not capable of providing an explanation of these overwhelming facts.

Keynes did not invent his theory out of whole cloth. He used ideas that he and others had been formulating in the 1930s, added some new ideas, and produced a new and coherent theory of a national economy. His introductory summary of the theory (1936, Ch. 3) recalls his Marshallian supply-and-demand roots at Cambridge and is called the "Principle of Effective Demand." Keynes starts with the concept of aggregate supply, in which the total output of the national economy is a function of employment. The aggregate supply function is

$$Q_s = \varphi(N).$$

Here, Q_s is aggregate output and N is employment. The notation $\varphi(N)$ means "is a function of N." The other half of the story is aggregate demand (1936, p. 25), "the proceeds which entrepreneurs expect to receive from the employment of N men." The aggregate demand function is written

$$Q_d = f(N).$$

Aggregate demand is also a function of employment (i.e., the number of people earning money) but a different function than aggregate supply. The volume of aggregate employment is given by the intersection of the aggregate supply function and the aggregate demand function. The value of Q_d, aggregate demand, at this point is called *effective demand*. Keynes asserted that the classical economists believed that supply creates its own demand through the earning of wages, interest, and profits so that $Q_s = Q_d$ for all levels of employment.

For Keynes, the notion that supply creates its own demand was absurd. In Keynesian theory, demand consists of two components – goods for consumption (denoted C) and output devoted to new investment (denoted I). Indeed, entrepreneurs respond to and base employment on the *expected* amounts of these demands. The demand for consumption goods is called the propensity to consume, and is written

$$C = \chi(N),$$

which states that this component of demand increases with employment – more employed people consume more goods. Because

$$Q_d = C + I = Q_s,$$

we can write

$$Q_s - C = \varphi(N) - \chi(N) = I.$$

As aggregate supply Q_s depends upon employment N, Keynes (1936, p. 29) states that,

> Hence the volume of employment in equilibrium depends on (i) the aggregate supply function, Q_s, (ii) the propensity to consume, $\chi(N)$, and (iii) the volume of investment, I. This is the essence of the General Theory of Employment.

As Keynes explained, the problem is that as N increases, the gap between aggregate supply Q_s and consumption C will become larger and larger. Supply does not create its own demand. The increase in supply, as employment increases, is larger than the increase in consumption demand because only a fraction of income is spent on consumption, and there is no guarantee that investment spending will be sufficient to fill the increasing gap. If equilibrium employment falls short of full employment, then either the propensity to consume or the volume of investment needs to increase, but there are no mechanisms to ensure that either increase will occur in sufficient amount. Most of the remainder of the *General Theory* is devoted to full explanation of this summary. But before we examine the theory in greater detail, one technical matter needs to be explained in case you are motivated to study Keynes in the original.

Keynes chose to measure output in what he called "wage units." As he put it (1936, p. 41), he proposed "to make use of only two fundamental units of quantity, namely quantities of money-value and quantities of *employment*." Economists are often guilty of this sort of thing – beginning a discussion with a confusing definition that puts the reader off. Keynes chose not to measure output as the money-value of real output (i.e., nominal gross domestic product) divided by a price index. No price indexes existed at the time. Instead, he confined the theory to the case in which capital and technology are held constant so that output in real terms would vary only with employment. If all labor is of identical skill, then output can be measured as the total hours of employment per year. However, labor is not homogeneous. For Keynes, then, a "labor unit" is an hour of labor of the lowest skill level. An hour of special labor paid at double the rate of the lowest-skilled labor counts as two labor units. The wage unit is the money wage of a labor unit – the money wage paid for an hour of unskilled labor. Effective demand is thus measured as its money-value divided by the wage unit. So, if total demand in money terms is $15 trillion per year and the minimum wage is $15 per hour, the Keynesian measure of effective demand is 1 trillion hours (of *employment*) per year. In other words,

$$(\$15 \text{ trillion/year}) \text{ divided by } (\$15/\text{hour}) = 1 \text{ trillion hours/year}.$$

The dollar units cancel, and the hours move up into the numerator. If the money-value of effective demand and the wage unit happen to increase by the same percentage, the real amount of effective demand has not changed. Nowadays the theory uses a price index, not the rather quaint notion of the wage unit. This was one Keynesian idea that did not catch on.

The propensity to consume and the inducement to invest

Keynes hypothesized that consumption (measured as real consumption in wage units, of course) is a relatively stable function of the income (also measured in wage units) that corresponds to a particular level of employment. Consumption could have been made a function of employment, but Keynes decided to switch the variable to income because he thought that it is a good approximation to regard income as determined uniquely by employment. We shall use the conventional notation of C for consumption and Y for income, both in real terms, so consumption is a function of income:

$C = c(Y).$

Keynes asserted (1936, p. 96) that this function followed a "fundamental psychological law . . . that men are disposed, as a rule and on the average, to increase their consumption as their income increases, but not by as much as the increase in their income." For example, a linear function with a slope less than 1.0 matches this psychological law:

$$C = a + bY, \quad \text{with b less than 1.0 and greater than 0.}$$

An increase in Y of 1 wage unit increases C by b wage units, a number less than 1.0 that is known as the *marginal* propensity to consume.

In Keynesian theory, saving is just the income not spent on consumption, so

$$S = Y - C = Y - (a + bY) = Y(1-b) - a.$$

Figure 2.3 depicts this saving function. Note that saving increases with income at the rate of $(1-b)$. In Figure 2.3, if Y increases by 1.0, saving increases by 0.25, and therefore consumption increases by 0.75.

Keynes recognized that the position of the consumption function can be altered by several factors, including:

■ Windfall changes in capital values (such as the value of one's house);
■ Changes in the rate of interest, which is both the cost of consumer borrowing and the return to saving;
■ Changes in income taxes – fiscal policy; and
■ Social incentives for saving.

Keynes (1936, pp. 92–95) thought that the first and third of these factors are potentially important in the short run but that the effect of changes in the rate of interest on consumption is relatively unimportant and that the social incentives for saving change slowly over time. In the end, Keynes believed that the demand for consumption was a stable function of current income. This conclusion led him to emphasize the famous multiplier, which was first introduced by his colleague R. F. Kahn in 1931.

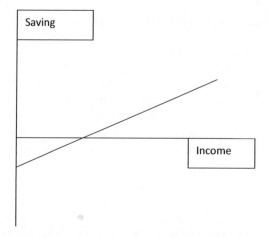

FIGURE 2.3 Income and Saving. Income equals consumption plus saving. Both consumption and saving are positive and stable functions of income

As we saw, effective demand consists of consumption and investment. If the consumption is stable, then an increase in the demand for investment will increase employment and income, which will in turn increase consumption demand and employment and income. How large are the increases in employment and income generated by an increase in investment? The answer can be found by noting that, at the equilibrium employment level, total income equals the sum of consumption and investment demanded. In symbols,

$$Y = C + I.$$

But we also know that $Y = C + S$; total income is divided between consumption and saving. Thus, investment demand equals saving at equilibrium employment and income. The linear model can be solved very simply. Set $I = S$ and solve for Y as follows:

$$I = Y(1 - b) - a, \text{ so}$$
$$Y = (a + I)/(1 - b).$$

What happens when I (investment) increases by 1 wage unit? Total income increases by $1/(1 - b)$, which is the multiplier. How large is the multiplier? Well, if $b = 0.75$ as in the example, then the multiplier is 4.0! Keynes thought that the multiplier effect of changes in investment demand is very important, because a decline in investment demand would have large effects on employment and income. Furthermore, if investment demand could somehow be stimulated, the positive effects on employment and income possibly would be large as well.

Keynes (1936, p. 119) discussed a very revealing numerical example. Suppose that "a Government employs 100,000 additional men on public works, and if the multiplier (as defined previously) is 4, it is not safe to assume that aggregate employment will increase by 400,000." Why not?

1   The government must finance the additional employment somehow. If government borrowing can be done only by increasing the interest rate, other components of investment demand may be retarded unless offsetting steps are taken by the monetary authority.

2   Confused psychology may undermine "confidence" and retard investment.

3   Some of the additional income may be spent on imports from abroad, which Keynes called a "leakage" that diminishes the full multiplier effect.

Keynes proposed a numerical example in which the marginal propensity to consume is 0.8 and the propensity to spend on imports is 0.2. If the propensity to spend additional income on domestically produced goods is 0.6, then the multiplier is only

$$1/(1 - 0.6) = 2.5.$$

Furthermore, in his example, the unemployed are assumed to purchase (out of loans or other sources) 50 percent of their normal consumption when employed. This means that providing employment for the unemployed will produce an even smaller multiplier effect. Keynes (1936, p. 128) reviewed data provided by Simon Kuznets for the United States during 1925–1933 and concluded that the multiplier for investment demand in the country was "fairly stable in the neighborhood of 2.5."

Given that consumption demand is stable and predictable, the level of employment and income for the macro economy depends critically upon the level of investment demand. The first part of the Keynesian analysis of the demand for investment states that investment is greater if the interest rate on loans is lower. What Keynes called the *marginal efficiency of capital* is just the rate of return for an investment. The marginal efficiency of capital is compared to the interest rate, which is the opportunity cost of the investment, i.e., what could be earned by investing in some other asset such as a loan to someone else. Keynes presumed that, if the interest rate is lower, more potential investments pass the test of marginal efficiency of capital greater than the interest rate. In short, just remember that the demand for investment is a negative function of the interest rate in the economy. The idea is really the same as the demand for investment depicted in Figure 2.2.

For Keynes, the more important insight is that the demand for investment depends upon prospective returns. As he put it (1936, p. 149), "The outstanding fact is the extreme precariousness of the basis of knowledge on which our estimates of prospective yield are to be made." The general state of confidence in the future of the economy plays a crucial role, as does (1936, p. 161) "spontaneous optimism," or "animal spirits." Rational calculation takes the potential investor only so far. The demand for investment depends upon the willingness of people to take action rather than remaining passive. Keynes had some hope that managing the rate of interest can serve to smooth out the demand for investment, but he believed that there would be times (such as the 1930s) when direct government action would be needed. His policy conclusion (1936, p. 164) is clearly stated.

> For my own part I am now somewhat skeptical of the success of a merely monetary policy directed towards influencing the rate of interest. I expect to see the State, which is in a position to calculate the marginal efficiency of capital–goods on long views and on the basis of general social advantage, taking an ever greater responsibility for directly organizing investment; since it seems likely that the fluctuations in the market estimation of the marginal efficiency of different types of capital, calculated on the principles I have described above, will be too great to be offset by any practicable changes in the rate of interest.

This is how Keynes saw it in 1935, but he did not give specific examples of how the State would be directly organizing investment.

Interest rate theory

The remaining piece of Keynesian theory is his theory of the interest rate, the rate at which funds are supplied to those who would demand investment goods. His basic point is that the interest rate is the price of holding a portion of one's assets in the form of cash or checking deposits, i.e., money (which earned no interest in those days). He called the demand for money *liquidity preference*. The Keynesian world has two assets – those that earn interest and the one that does not earn interest, called money. He believed that liquidity preference consisted of three parts. Money was demanded because of:

- The transactions motive (need for cash to carry on current exchanges), which is the basic motive assumed in the Quantity Theory of Money;
- The precautionary motive (desire for cash for security); and
- The speculative motive (desire for cash because the individual thinks he/she can outguess the market and make a profit from buying assets later at a lower price).

Consider this last motive, the speculative motive, a little more. People will hold money if they expect that the interest rate will increase (asset prices will fall). Why do asset prices fall when the interest rate rises? Suppose you own a $10,000 bond that pays $300 in interest per year (3 percent). Suppose the general interest rate rises to 4 percent. Now an investor can earn $300 by investing less than $10,000 ($7,500 actually), and so now that investor is not willing to pay $10,000 for your bond.

Keynes thought that, at some very low rate of interest, nearly everyone would expect that the interest rate will rise, asset prices will fall, and nearly everyone would demand money for speculative purposes. In this situation, any increase in the supply of money will simply be held by the public for speculation. Monetary policy is ineffective in this case. As Keynes (1936, p. 207) expressed:

> There is the possibility . . . that, after the rate of interest has fallen to a certain level, liquidity preference may become virtually absolute in the sense that almost everyone prefers cash to holding a debt which yields so low a rate of interest. In this event the monetary authority would have lost effective control of the rate of interest.

This situation is known as the liquidity trap, although Keynes himself did not use the specific term. However, one might add that it is not clear why, in the middle of a depression, people would think that the interest rate will increase – even if it is at a very low level. In any case, Keynes believed that the speculative demand for money is an important part of the total demand for money.

The interest rate is determined by the demand for and supply of money. Clearly the quantity of money demanded depends upon its price, the rate of interest, but what other variables determine the demand for money? The other variable that clearly determines the demand for money is income. The quantity theory of money in its simplest form, as described earlier, states that the demand for money in nominal terms is

$$M_d = kPY,$$

Where k is some constant, P is the general price level, and Y is income in real terms. Money income (GDP) is PY, and k is the number that says how much money is needed

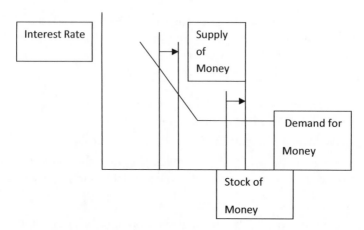

FIGURE 2.4 The Supply of and Demand for Money. The supply of money is fixed by the central bank. The demand for money declines with the interest rate because the interest rate is the cost of holding money, an asset which does not earn interest. At some very low rate, the interest rate no longer has any effect on the amount of money demanded.

to support the market transactions associated with any money income level. The demand for money in real terms in the simple quantity theory is $M_d/P = kY$. Keynes (1936, p. 199) wrote down the demand for money in *real* terms in two parts as:

$$M_d/P = M_t + M_r = L_1(Y) + L_2(i).$$

Here, M_t corresponds to the demand for money for transactions and precautionary motives, M_r is the speculative demand, and i is the interest rate in the economy (the opportunity cost of holding money that earns no interest). The total demand for money thus depends upon both income and the interest rate. Equilibrium in the market for money is established where the supply of money equals the demand for money.

The Keynesian demand for money is illustrated in Figure 2.4. Note that the demand function becomes roughly horizontal at a very low interest rate. This reflects the hypothesis that, at this very low interest rate, nearly everyone expects the interest rate to rise and values of assets other than money to fall, so assets can be purchased at lower prices. Figure 2.4 includes the supply of money and the resulting equilibrium interest rate. Two cases are shown; in one, an increase in the supply of money reduces the interest, and in the other, the interest rate does not change.

The Keynesian system according to Keynes

We now have all of the elements of the Keynesian system. Keynes restated the basic theory in Chapter 18 of the *General Theory*. As any good economist does, he began by stating his assumptions that the following elements of the economy were taken as given:

■ The quantity and quality of labor and capital;
■ The tastes and habits of the consumers;

- The degree of competition; and
- Other factors having to do with the nature of employment and how it is organized by firms.

So, now we are ready. Keynes's first summary of the model is that the independent variables are the propensity to consume, the schedule of the marginal efficiency of capital, and the rate of interest. Given a rate of interest, the level of investment demand is determined by the schedule of the marginal efficiency of capital. The level of investment determines the level of income and employment through the propensity to consume by establishing the income level at which investment equals saving. A reduction in the interest rate causes an increase in investment and therefore an increase in income via the multiplier effect.

Keynes (1936, p. 246) went on to say that

> the rate of interest depends partly on the state of liquidity-preference (i.e., on the liquidity function) and partly on the quantity of money measured in terms of wage-units. Thus we can sometimes regard our ultimate independent variables as consisting of the three fundamental psychological factors, namely, the psychological propensity to consume, the psychological attitude to liquidity, and the psychological expectation of future yield from capital–assets.

Note the word "sometimes" in this statement. Sometimes we can take the interest rate as given, and sometimes we work back to the demand for and supply of money to determine the interest rate. This version of the model is shown in Figure 2.5.

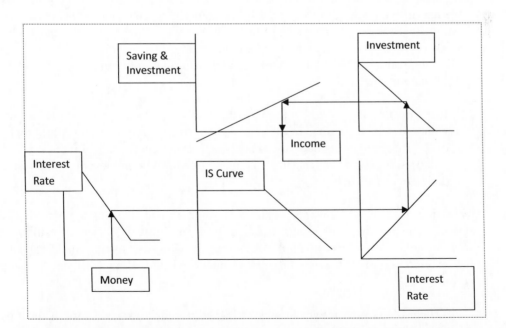

FIGURE 2.5 The Keynesian System. The supply of and demand for money determine the interest rate, which in turn determines the amount of investment spending. Investment spending determines income and output through the multiplier effect. The IS (investment equals saving) curve shows that output is greater at a lower interest rate

The interest rate is determined in the diagram on the lower left. The diagram on the lower right simply makes the interest rate switch from being a vertical to a horizontal variable. This interest rate determines the rate of investment in the diagram in the upper right, and investment determines income. The diagram at the middle bottom of Figure 2.5 shows how income varies with the interest rate. A lower interest rate means a higher level of income. This curve is known as the investment equals saving curve (IS curve).

John R. Hicks (1937) pointed out that Keynes did not include the effect of total income on the demand for money. The full-blown Keynesian model must have an interest rate that is consistent with the supply of money and total income. This complication is discussed in Chapter 3.

It is important at this juncture to understand the Keynesian philosophy towards the construction of a theoretical economic system. His words of wisdom (1936, p. 247) are:

> The division of the determinants of the economic system into the two groups of given factors and independent variables is, of course, quite arbitrary from any absolute standpoint. The division must be made entirely on the basis of experience, so as to correspond on the one hand to the factors in which the changes seem to be so slow or so little relevant as to have only a small and comparatively negligible short-term influence on our *quaesitum*; and on the other hand to those factors in which the changes are found in practice to exercise a dominant influence on our *quaesitum*.

For those of you who are not sure what our *quaesitum* is, as I was – it is our inquiry. One reasonable reading of this quote is that sometimes, changes in the interest rate have little effect on investment and little short-term influence on our *quaesitum* – namely, what determines income and employment in the short term.

Keynes dismissed Wicksell's theory of the natural rate of interest. Keynes (1936, p. 243) stated:

> I am now no longer of the opinion that the concept of a 'natural' rate of interest, which previously seemed to me a most promising idea, has anything very useful or significant to contribute to our analysis. It is merely the rate of interest which will preserve the *status quo*; and, in general, we have no predominant interest in the *status quo* as such.

Why did he say this? Consider Figure 2.5. Employment depends upon aggregate output, which is the same as aggregate income. In Figure 2.5, there is a different interest rate for each level of aggregate output (the IS curve for I = S). There is an interest rate consistent with full employment output. Keynes (1936, p. 243) continued:

> If there is any such rate of interest, which is unique and significant, it must be the rate which we might call the *neutral* rate of interest, namely, the natural rate in the above sense which is consistent with *full* employment, given the other parameters of the system; though this rate might be better described, perhaps, as the *optimum* rate.

It is critical to remember that Keynes was concerned with the depression-era here and now. Unemployed resources mean output lost forever. Wicksell (and many economists who followed) was concerned with the longer-run tradeoff between current and future consumption. Real investment should be made up to the point at which its real rate of return was just equal to the willingness of people to give up current consumption for future returns. Keynes thought that it was foolish to worry about longer-run efficiency during a depression, because an economy with high unemployment was operating in a massively inefficient manner.

One final point about the Keynesian system according to Keynes: Some classical economists had counted on reductions in nominal wages and prices to bring about full employment. Reductions in nominal wages and prices increase the *real* supply of money, which will tend to reduce the interest rate and stimulate investment and income and employment. Keynes did not deny that this is a theoretical possibility, but he thought that relying on this mechanism was foolish. First of all, prices and wages had declined in nominal terms during the depression with little effect on real income. Wages fell by 21 percent in the United States. Workers could agree to cuts in nominal wages, but there was no guarantee that there would be a decline in real wages needed to increase employment. Secondly, somehow it would be necessary to orchestrate reductions in all wages and prices at the same time. Otherwise, who would volunteer to go first? To use the modern language, a general reduction in nominal wages and prices is a public good. The problem with public goods is that people will try to be "free riders" to get the benefits without paying the cost. Instead, according to Keynes, why not just increase the money supply – and support investment directly if necessary? For Keynes, stable nominal wages were a policy recommendation, not a statement of empirical fact. His basic conclusion is that a government operating according to Keynesian recommendations can be much more effective at restoring employment and income than is the unaided private market.

A more complete Keynesian model

This section provides the algebra for a more complete Keynesian model as depicted in Figure 2.5. This section is optional, but it does provide a more realistic picture of how Keynesian models are formulated for forecasting and analysis purposes. The model is based on the fundamental equation from Chapter 1:

$$Y = C + I + G + X.$$

All variables are in real terms. The Keynesian model includes an equation for each of the four components of real GDP. Simple versions of the equations are used for illustration.

Consumption function $C = C_0 + b(Y - T)$, where T is taxes paid.
　　Consumption is a linear function of income after taxes.
Tax function　　　　　　$T = tY$, where t is the tax rate.
　　Taxes are a constant fraction of income.
Investment function　　$I = I_0 - hr$, where r is the interest rate.

Investment is a negative function of the interest rate. How is the interest rate determined? In Figure 2.5, it is determined by the supply of and demand for money. The supply of money is a given (by the monetary authorities) and the demand for money is

$$M_d = M_0 - mr.$$

So with money demand equal to money supply, $M_d = M_s$,

$$r = (M_0 - M_s)/m.$$

An increase in the money supply reduces the interest rate by $1/m$, the inverse of the slope of the money demand function. In this version of the Keynesian model, the solution for the interest rate will be plugged in.

Government spending on goods and services $G = G_0$

Government spending is taken as given outside the model.

Net exports $X = E - F$, where E is exports and F is imports.

Exports $E = E_0$

Exports are taken as given outside the model.

Imports $F = F_0 + f(Y - T)$

Imports increase with income after taxes, where f is the marginal propensity to import.

A Keynesian model that can be used for forecasting and analysis purposes includes empirical estimates of these equations.

All of these equations can be inserted into the equation for total income.

$$Y = C_0 + b(Y - tY) + I_0 - h_r + G_0 + E_0 - [F_0 + f(Y - tY)].$$

This equation can be solved for Y by moving all of the terms containing Y to the left-hand side and factoring out the Y from each of these terms.

$$Y[1 - b + f + t(b - f)] = C_0 + (I_0 - h_r) + G_0 + E_0 - F_0.$$

The solution for Y is

$$Y = [C_0 + (I_0 - h_r) + G_0 + E_0 - F_0]/[1 - b + f + t(b - f)].$$

The terms in the numerator include the constant terms from the equations for each of the components of GDP; C_0, I_0, G_0, E_0, and F_0. The Keynesian multiplier that applies to all of the constant terms from the equations is:

$$1 / [1 - b + f + t(b - f)].$$

What is the numerical value of the multiplier? For that, we need to have empirical estimates of b (marginal propensity to consume), f (marginal propensity to import), and t, the tax rate. An estimate of the multiplier can be based on data for the United States from 2014.[1] The average propensity to consume from after-tax income is 82.4 percent (b = 0.824), the average propensity to import out of after-tax income is 19.8 percent (f = 0.198), and the tax rate is 28.6 percent (t = 0.286).

If the marginal propensities are equal to the average propensities, the multiplier is $1/0.553 = 1.81$. An exogenous increase of $1 in any of these – consumption, investment, government spending, or exports – increases total income by $1.81. An increase of imports of $1 reduces total income by $1.81. This multiplier is not impressively large, and rather less than the guesstimate that Keynes made in 1936 of 2.5. Keynes left out the tax rate from his calculation, but his estimates for the propensities to consume of 80 percent and to import of 20 percent are remarkably similar to the current values.

The final equation for Y also shows how total income varies inversely with the rate of interest. Write the collection of constant terms as $Z = [C_0 + I_0 + G_0 + E_0 - F_0]$ and $\mu = [1 - b + f + t(b - f)]$. Now,

$$Y = (Z - hr)/\mu.$$

This is the IS curve for the model (as from Figure 2.5). And an increase in the interest rate reduces Y by h/μ. Recall that $\mu = 0.51$ in the numerical example and h is the impact of an increase in the interest rate on investment.

One more thing. The government deficit in the model is $G_0 - tY$. The model permits the government to fund a deficit or a surplus depending upon the level of total income. A more complex model would permit government spending to vary with the level of total income.

Summary of Keynesian theory

This chapter has outlined Keynesian macroeconomic theory as Keynes himself presented it. Keynes's purpose was to develop a coherent theory that was consistent with the world as he found it – in severe depression with little apparent movement towards self-correction. His view was that the job of the economist is to provide the economic theory that works for the existing state of the world. He had disinterest in exploring all logical possibilities. It was apparent to Keynes that the private economy in depression was not able to bring itself back to anything close to full employment and income at its potential level. His theory shows why this was so. His theory also had clear policy implications, which he did not discuss at length in the *General Theory*. If effective demand is not forthcoming from the private economy, then the government must step in and provide the needed stimulus directly. Monetary policy might be able to bring about a reduction in the interest rate, but Keynes was not optimistic about the effectiveness of monetary policy at increasing effective demand in depression conditions. Public works expenditures would be needed. Nevertheless, as Rauchway (2015) documents, Keynes advised President Roosevelt to abandon the gold standard and pursue a policy of increasing the supply of money during the Great Depression to halt the deflation and start prices rising. And what was *not* needed was a cut in money wages and prices. For Keynes, holding money wages constant was a *policy recommendation*. A general reduction in money wages and prices would indeed increase the real stock of money, which might in turn bring about an increase in effective demand. But any such general reduction in money wages and prices was bound to be painful, contentious, and totally unnecessary.

Keynes's ability to adapt his economic thinking to the situation was illustrated brilliantly in1940 in the short pamphlet *How to Pay for the War*. Britain's budget starting in 1939 included massive expenditures for the military, so the problem was not too little effective demand, but too much. Britain had paid for World War I by printing money, and prices had quadrupled. Britain's people had paid for this war through great effort and sacrifice, and the "inflation tax." Everyone recognized that a repeat performance would not be satisfactory. A straightforward Keynesian solution was sharply higher taxes on the general public. However, Keynes recognized that simply raising the income tax rate would mean that the British people would be called upon to work much harder with no reward. His proposal was to have a graduated temporary increase in the income tax and a program of compulsory savings. The compulsory savings would be credited to interest-earning individual accounts that would be repaid after the war to reward the public and to help pull the economy through an anticipated post-war recession. The Keynes plan was widely discussed and admired, but not adopted. The Treasury opted for massive borrowing and rationing.

Note

1   After-tax income is computed as GDP minus total federal receipts and state and local government purchases of goods and services (because states must have balanced budgets) plus transfer payments. Total federal receipts pay for most of the purchases of goods and services and transfer payments, but total federal outlays also include borrowing. The tax rate is federal receipts plus state and local government purchases divided by GDP. So in 2014, U.S. governments collected 28.6 percent of GDP in taxes but spent an amount equal to 31.4 percent of GDP, with federal government borrowing an amount equal to 2.8 percent of GDP ($485 billion).

3

Keynesian theory after Keynes

Introduction

Numerous extensions to Keynesian theory have been made over the previous 80 years. This chapter provides an introduction to topics that appear to be important for understanding some of the macroeconomic episodes discussed in the second half of this book, especially the financial crisis and deep recession of 2008–2009. We begin with an immediate reaction to Keynes.

Paul Samuelson weighs in (at age 23)

Paul Samuelson, who is regarded generally as the most important academic economist of the 20th century, was an early convert to Keynesian theory. He set out a reasonably complete viewpoint on macroeconomics (1940) that was presented at a conference in 1938. The purpose of the article was to discuss the effects of fiscal policy on national income and employment. In order to discuss these effects, it was necessary to describe the essential features of the macro economy. Samuelson's list of essential features (1940, pp. 492–493) is revealing, and is as follows:

- The economic system is not perfect and frictionless so that there exists the possibility of unemployment and under-utilization of productive resources.
- Cumulative movements of a dis-equilibrating kind are possible.
- The propensity to consume is less than 1.0, so net investment of sufficient magnitude is needed to reach full employment. Insufficient net investment produces a downward spiral.
- In addition, *"even in a perfect capital market there is not tendency for the rate of interest to equilibrate the demand and supply of employment."* (Italics in the original.) Net investment is volatile, and the schedule of the marginal efficiency of capital may be inelastic with respect to the interest rate.
- The government has no difficulties financing deficits.

Samuelson regarded these features as a summary of the business cycle literature of the day, including Keynes' *General Theory*, of course.

Samuelson considered two related questions: the timing of public expenditures and the optimal amount of cumulative public deficit over a period of time. He favored prompt deficit spending when there is a downturn arising from a lack of investment opportunities and also when firms have accumulated excessive inventories. However, he pointed out that an increase in income that results from a sustained increase in public expenditure will not have a multiplier effect immediately; he suggests there is a one-period lag between an increase in household income and an increase in consumption, followed by additional effects in subsequent periods. In addition to this Keynesian-type multiplier, Samuelson accepted the notion of the acceleration principle, in which an increase in consumption produces an increase in private net investment. But his detailed technical analysis of the interaction between the multiplier and accelerator (1939) showed that an initial amount of public spending ("pump priming") is unlikely to set off forces that return the economy to full employment.

As for the second question, Samuelson did not supply an answer, but ended with the following (1940, p. 506):

> If the real national income can be increased by five or ten percent over a long period of years only at the cost of incurring debt of some tens of billions of dollars, I for one should consider the price not exorbitant.

The Hicks–Hansen version of Keynesian theory

John R. Hicks (1937) read the *General Theory* carefully and invented the graphical presentation that has been used to teach Keynes to students ever since. This Hicks–Hansen version of Keynesian theory is known as the neoclassical synthesis. The neoclassical synthesis combines Keynesian and classical theory. You know that Keynesian theory shows that the government must provide fiscal and monetary stimulus to bring an economy to full employment. However, once full employment has been reached, the economy can rely on market forces to allocate resources efficiently, as argued by the classical economists.

For Hicks, the critical feature of the Keynesian theory is the demand for money (in wage units), which as we have seen, is assumed to depend upon the interest rate and real income. But Hicks asserts that Keynes introduced a "special theory" in which the demand for money does not depend upon income – only the interest rate. In this case, the interest rate is determined as shown in Figure 2.4, and investment, employment, and income are determined in sequence. As Hicks (1937, p. 153) put it,

> It is this system of equations which yields the startling conclusion, that an increase in the inducement to invest, or in the propensity to consume, will not tend to raise the rate of interest, but only to increase employment.

Rather, the "general theory" should include income as a determinant of the demand for money. Equilibrium in the market for money must be consistent with the level of income determined in the model. An increase in income caused by, for example, an increase in the propensity to consume will in general cause the interest rate to increase as well – which in turn will reduce investment, and so on.

Hicks invented a graphical device that is known as the IS-LM model. The price level is assumed to be constant in this model. The full model is shown in Figure 3.1. The diagram on the left shows the demand for and supply of money. The demand for money (at a given interest rate) is presumed to shift upwards when income rises, so three alternative demand schedules for money are shown. The diagram in the middle bottom includes the IS curve from Figure 2.5. It shows the combinations of income and interest rate at which investment and saving are equal. The other curve, labeled the LM curve, shows the combinations of income and interest rate at which the demand for and supply of money are equal. As the diagram on the left shows, for a given supply of money, an increase in income requires that the interest rate must be higher. An increase in income means that more of the money stock must be used to handle transactions and satisfy the precautionary demand for money. Less money is available to satisfy the speculative demand for money, so the price of holding money – the interest rate – must rise so that households and firms will be content with smaller money balances held for this purpose. LM stands for liquidity-money, and the LM curve has a positive slope because a higher level of income is consistent with a higher interest rate (except in the range where the interest rate is so low that it does not change with changes in the supply of money).

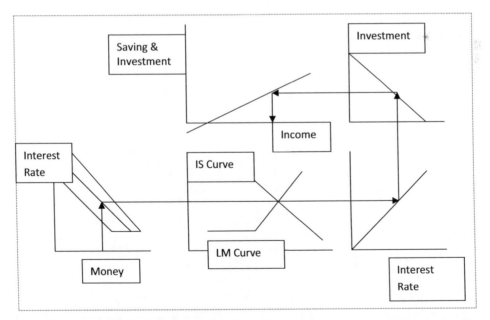

FIGURE 3.1 The Hicks Version of Keynesian Theory. Hicks added the LM (liquidity-money curve) to the Keynesian model. The LM curve shows the interest rate and real output combinations at which the supply of and demand for money are equal. A higher level of output (i.e., income) requires a higher interest rate because the demand for money for transactions purposes is greater, leaving less money available for speculative purposes. People are content to hold less money for speculative purposes because the cost of holding money has increased. Overall equilibrium output and rate of interest occur where the IS and LM curves cross

Equilibrium in the economy, as depicted in Figure 3.1, occurs when both investment equals saving and the demand for and supply of money are equal. This occurs where the IS curve and the LM curve intersect. The rate of interest and income are determined. The level of income shown is consistent with equilibrium in the market for money on the left side of Figure 3.1. Suppose that total income was somehow (tentatively) set at a level higher than equilibrium. For example, firms assume a low interest rate and plan for a high level of investment. The implied interest rate for the income level at the high level of investment, given the supply of money, will be too high to sustain the high level of investment. Investment plans will be scaled back, the income level implied will drop, and the interest rate will fall as well. The process continues until equilibrium is reached.

Consider shifts in the IS and LM curves. An outward shift in the demand for real investment (positive animal spirits) shifts the IS curve to the right because investment equals saving at a higher level of income at any given interest rate. This shift is shown in Figure 3.2. For a given supply of money and therefore a given LM curve, the new equilibrium has a higher level of income and a higher rate of interest. In Figure 3.2, the higher rate of interest "chokes off" some, but not all, of the potential increase in investment.

An increase in the supply of money at a given interest rate shifts the LM curve to the right because the greater supply of money is consistent with a higher level of income at a given interest rate. The shift in the LM curve also is depicted in Figure 3.2. The results of the increase in the money supply for a given IS curve are an increase in income and a reduction in the interest rate. In other words, for a given demand curve for investment, a reduction in the rate of interest generates more investment and income, unless the rate of interest is so low that an increase in the supply of money has no impact on the interest rate.

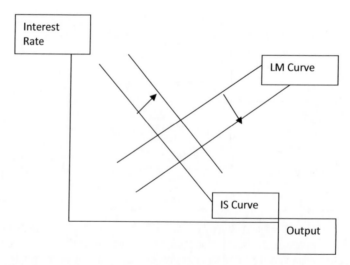

FIGURE 3.2 Two Cases of Keynesian Theory. An increase in aggregate demand is represented by a shift outward in the IS curve, and results in an increase in the interest rate and real income and output. An increase in the money supply shifts the LM curve to the right and produces a decline in the interest rate and an increase in real output

Figures 3.1 and 3.2 are generally regarded as the correct presentation of Keynesian theory – although the discussion in Chapter 2 suggests that Keynes might not have agreed. Skidelsky (1992, pp. 614–616) looked into the matter and concluded that the Hicksian version did not interest him very much. Hicks had pointed out a logical possibility and had brilliantly formulated a nifty general equilibrium model that remains the principal device for the teaching of Keynesian macroeconomic theory. But according to Skidelsky, Keynes never much cared for general equilibrium models and was more concerned with formulating a model that captured the essence of the world in which he lived. Skidelsky's conclusion (1992, p. 616) is that "he let the Hicks 'generalization' of the *General Theory* through on the nod."

Keynes gained disciples immediately. The chief Keynesian in the United States was Professor Alvin Hansen of Harvard University. Hansen wrote many books in the Keynesian mode, including a chapter-by-chapter explanation of the *General Theory* with the title *A Guide to Keynes* (1953), a book that was read by students of economics for many years as they grappled with Keynes. Hansen (1953, pp. 165–166) stated flatly that

> Keynes, in fact, makes the rate of interest an independent variable (p. 245). But this is wrong. His mistake follows from the fact that he often, perhaps generally, made the rate of interest depend exclusively on liquidity preference and the quantity of money. . . . The rate of interest and the national income are together mutually determined.

So this is the Keynesian "mistake." Was it intentional? Almost surely, because he was intent on depicting an economy in depression.

Skidelsky gets the last word on this matter. His second volume on Keynes contains a brief and brilliant summary of the controversy (1992, pp. 622–624). His interpretation is that the Keynesian theory of depression is shown in the IS-LM diagram in Figure 3.3. The Keynesian depression case is shown in the region of the LM curve where the curve is close to being flat because, at a low interest rate, any increase in the demand for money is for speculative purposes. The relevant IS curve is labeled "IS Keynes." The demand for and supply of money remain in equilibrium as income increases with very little increase in the interest rate. An increase in the supply of money has little effect on the already-low interest rate and, even if it did, Keynes thought that a decline in the interest rate would have little impact on investment during a depression – when investor confidence has been shattered. But a public works program that shifts the IS curve to the right (as shown in Figure 3.3) will raise income and employment and have little impact on the interest rate.

The alternative view of the world, which was associated with Britain's Treasury in 1929, is that the LM curve is almost vertical. This region of the LM curve has the IS curve labeled "IS Treasury" in Figure 3.3. This is the "classical" case in which money is demanded almost exclusively for transactions purposes. An increase in income is associated with a large increase in the interest rate because the increase in income requires an increase in the demand for money for transactions purposes. Any effort to shift the IS curve through tax cuts or public works expenditures (shown in Figure 3.3) will mainly cause an increase in the interest rate, which will cause a reduction in private investment. Public spending "crowds out" private

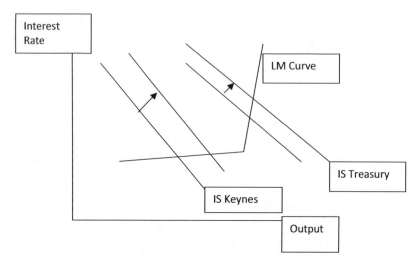

FIGURE 3.3 Keynes and Treasury Versions of Keynesian Theory. The Keynesian version depicts an economy in depression. The LM curve is horizontal (or nearly so) because the interest rate is already very low. Additions to the money supply have little or no impact on the interest rate and real output. An increase in aggregate demand through government spending (shift outward in the IS curve) is needed to increase real income, output, and employment. The Treasury version depicts an economy near full employment. An increase in aggregate demand through an increase in government spending causes the interest rate to increase, choking off part of private investment spending and leaving real output unchanged.

investment and leaves effective demand virtually unchanged. This is the classical dichotomy. It is all a matter of the actual shapes of the curves – and the actual state of the world.

The Keynesian case depicted in Figure 3.3 became known as the liquidity trap. In other words, attempting to push more money into the economy would simply mean increases in idle balances held for speculative purposes. The idle balances can be either reserves held by banks that are not used to increase loans, or as currency, and bank accounts of the public (or both). For example, firms that make profits do not reinvest those profits to expand the business or pay out dividends. They are waiting for the upturn that, according to Mitchell (1941), is supposed to come. But when?

External and internal balance

It was noted in Chapter 2 that Keynes was an internationalist who worked to improve the international financial system for his entire career. He concentrated on the closed economy in the *General Theory* but afterward returned to the international economy. The Bretton Woods system he helped to establish in 1944 lasted until the 1970s and was an important factor in promoting international trade that boosted postwar economic growth. During the 1970s, the international monetary system was changed from a system of fixed exchange rates with limited flexibility to floating exchange rates. The international system was established in 1944 at a conference held at Bretton Woods, New Hampshire. The key actors at Bretton Woods were Keynes for the United Kingdom and Harry Dexter White for the U.S. Treasury. Much has been written about this conference; Rauchway (2015) provides an illuminating telling of the story. This system committed members to fixed exchange rates and required members to intervene to keep its exchange rate within a band of 1 percent up or down. The nation's central bank was to buy or sell its own currency in order to stay within the band. However, the agreement also created the International Monetary Fund to provide loans to help each country to manage its currency, and member nations were permitted to devalue by up to 10 percent one time. Additional devaluations beyond the 10 percent required a majority vote of the member nations. The exchange rates of the other currencies were pegged to the U.S. dollar, which was established as the reserve currency to be used for settling international payments. The value of the dollar was pegged in terms of gold at $35 per ounce, and the United States agreed to buy and sell gold at that price. The system was designed to facilitate international trade by ensuring stable exchange rates, but it did permit a nation to devalue its currency when necessary. The system worked well as long as the member nations had similar, low rates of inflation.

Just prior to the time of his death, Keynes was working on a theory that would solve the problem of finding the combination of domestic demand and exchange rate that is consistent with noninflationary full employment (internal balance) and exports equal to imports (external balance). The job of working out and writing down the theory was accomplished by an associate of Keynes, James Meade (1952), in a book for which he was awarded the Nobel Prize. Meade stated his indebtedness to Keynes. The basic model is shown in Figure 3.4 and follows the presentation in Temin and Vines (2014, p. 82).

The real exchange rate, as defined in Chapter 1, is shown on the vertical axis. A greater real exchange rate means a higher price for the nation's exports and a lower price for imports. The level of domestic demand (C + I + G − exports) is measured

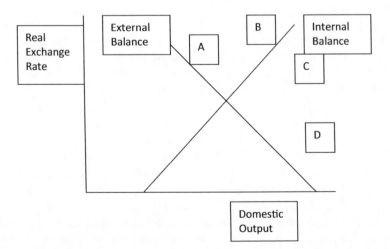

FIGURE 3.4 Internal and External Balance. The intersection of the internal balance (full employment) and external balance (exports equal imports) curves shows the combination of domestic demand and exchange rate that solves both problems

on the horizontal axis. Consider first internal balance (i.e., domestic demand consistent with full employment without inflation). A higher real exchange rate means a lower volume of exports and more imports (lower level of net exports), so full employment requires a higher level of domestic demand for goods and services produced domestically. The internal balance line has a positive slope. Next, consider external balance. As a lower real exchange rate means more exports and fewer imports, a higher level of domestic demand is required to bring imports up to equal exports. The external balance line slopes negatively. The intersection of the two curves indicates the combination of exchange rate and domestic demand that solves both the internal and external balance problems.

Each of the four areas defined by the two curves represents a particular set of problems. If the nation finds itself to the right of the internal balance curve, it experiences inflation (too much domestic demand). A position on the left-hand side of the curve indicates unemployment. A point to the right of the external balance curve is a point of deficit in the balance of payments (too many imports, not enough exports). And a point to the left of the external balance curve produces a surplus in the balance of payments (not enough imports, too many exports). Feel free to write notations of these combinations on your copy of the diagram. Make the notations lightly in pencil if you intend to sell the book. I wrote on mine.

The policy conclusions follow from the diagram, and they are complicated. For example, suppose you have domestic demand lower than required for internal and external balance and a balance of payments deficit (point A on Figure 3.4). Then you need to increase domestic demand and lower the exchange rate. But if you start with domestic demand greater than needed for internal and external balance along with the balance of payments deficit (point B on Figure 3.4), then you need to reduce domestic demand as you lower the exchange rate. A lower exchange rate by itself will not reduce domestic demand enough. Clearly, one approach is to set domestic demand at the level consistent with internal and external balance and then let the exchange rate float to the level at which exports equal imports. Milton Friedman was one who made the case for market-determined exchange rates, and his views are discussed in Chapter 4.

Two more examples: Suppose you have inflation and a surplus in the balance of payments. Domestic demand must be reduced. If the exchange rate is at a level that is greater than the rate consistent with internal and external balance (point C on Figure 3.4), then the exchange rate must be reduced. But if the exchange rate is too low for internal and external balance (point D on Figure 3.4), then it must be increased. Again, one approach is to reduce domestic demand to the level consistent with internal and external balance and let the market for foreign exchange set the correct exchange rate to have exports equal imports.

Two conclusions pop out immediately for a regime with a fixed exchange rate. If the exchange rate is fixed above the rate at which internal and external balance occurs, a full-employment level of domestic demand creates a deficit in the balance of payments. The nation must borrow or sell assets or settle for an economy with less than full employment. As discussed in detail in Chapter 15, the difficulties of some nations in the Euro zone are related to a balance of trade deficit coupled with an inability to devalue. Alternatively, if the exchange rate is set below the rate consistent with both internal and external balance, domestic demand for a full-employment economy (or less) produces a surplus in the balance of payments. In this case, the nation can use that surplus to loan money to, or purchase assets of, the deficit countries. Those purchased assets could include intellectual property that can enhance productivity of the export industries. Such a manipulation of the exchange rate is pretty well known. Temin and Vines (2014) argue that both Japan and China have followed this strategy of export-led growth.

The Meade model focuses on the conditions for external trade balance, i.e., balance in the current account (revenue from exports equal to revenue from imports). As discussed previously, policy implications to achieve both external and internal balance (full employment) follow. An alternative approach to the same issue starts with the assumption that the balance of payments, including both the current and capital accounts, is always in balance (money flowing out equals money flowing in). The following example is based on the work of Mundell (1963) and Fleming (1962). For purposes of discussion, assume that international capital flows are highly mobile and that a nation is under a regime of flexible exchange rates (as are the United States, the United Kingdom, etc.). Now suppose that the nation decides to stimulate the domestic economy.

First, consider the use of monetary policy. The central bank reduces interest rates and brings about an increase in the supply of money. The decline in interest rates means an increase in domestic demand for investment, capital will flow out of the country (decline in the demand for home-country money), and the exchange rate will decline. The decline in the exchange rate will stimulate the nation's exports, so aggregate demand is stimulated by both domestic investment spending and exports.

The case of fiscal policy is quite different. The government increases its spending on final goods and services. If the supply of money is constant, the increase in aggregate demand will cause an increase in interest rates (as you know), except in the case of the liquidity trap. The increase in interest rates will result in an inflow of foreign capital (greater demand for the nation's currency), which will increase the nation's exchange rate. That increase in the exchange rate will reduce exports. Some (or all) of the stimulation of domestic aggregate demand will be offset by the decline in exports. So there we have it – monetary policy is the more effective policy tool under conditions of highly mobile international capital and flexible exchange rates. Is this the world in which we live? Maybe. . . .

The addition of the price level to the Keynesian model

So far, prices have been mentioned only in passing. As noted in Chapter 2, a reduction in prices increases the real supply of money, may reduce interest rates, and perhaps may stimulate the economy. A more complete model adds the labor market, the wage level, and the price level. The simple version of the Keynesian model assumes that the wage level in money terms remains constant as prices rise or fall. This means that workers will supply more labor at the given money wage if labor demand increases, even if the real wage has been cut by an increase in prices. More realistically, we could assume that money wages do not respond to an increase in labor demand when labor demand is low but that wages respond more rapidly as the economy approaches full employment. Modern Keynesians develop models that show that some prices (in this case, the money wage rate) do not adjust quickly to changes in demand or supply.

As explained in Chapter 2 and shown in Figure 2.1, firms in competitive industries hire workers up to the point at which the marginal product of labor equals the real wage rate. Now we add the price level, so the rule now is that firms hire labor up to the point at which the marginal product MP equals the real wage rate, denoted the money wage W, divided by the price level P:

$$MP = \text{real wage} = W/P.$$

If the money wage is constant, an increase in the price level lowers the real wage (W/P) and increases employment and output. Employers wish to hire more workers, and more workers are willing to work at the same money wage W (even though the real wage has been cut). The more general statement is, if the percentage increase in the money wage is less than the percentage increase in prices, employment and output increase; or a reduction in prices increases the real wage and reduces employment and output.

Modern Keynesians have developed various formal models of firm and labor market behavior that produce slow changes in prices and wages. For example, some labor is hired subject to contracts that specify money wages over a period of several years. Such an agreement is rational for both parties, because adjusting wages is a process with a cost and generates sticky wages. Prices in perfectly competitive markets are thought to adjust quickly to changes in demand and supply. Prices for stock and agricultural commodities, for example, change continuously on organized exchanges. Labor markets are not so well organized.

The addition of this simple labor market model means that the Keynesian model can be presented as aggregate demand and aggregate supply curves, with real output on the horizontal axis and the price level on the vertical axis. Consider aggregate demand first. As stated earlier, a lower price level increases the real supply of money, lowers the interest rate, and increases real output if investment responds positively. The aggregate demand curve has a negative slope. Aggregate supply is based on the labor market model. A higher price level with a fixed money wage will increase employment and real output because the real wage (W/P) has been reduced. The aggregate supply curve has a positive slope. These two curves are shown in Figure 3.5, and they look like the familiar supply and demand model for an individual competitive market.

In this model, an increase in aggregate demand increases both prices and output in some combination. Such an increase is shown in Figure 3.5. This is regarded as the normal state of affairs as long as the economy is not in a severe recession or depression. An increase in supply, also illustrated in Figure 3.5, increases output and reduces prices for a given aggregate demand curve. A shift outward in the curve can occur through an improvement in technology, for example. Similarly, a decrease in supply (a shift inward in the curve through a natural disaster, for example) increases prices and reduces output. Do you remember that these points were made in Chapter 1?

A model of this type led to the idea that *changes* in the wage or the price level and the amount of unemployment in the economy are inversely related. The aggregate supply curve is thought to be steeper as real output is greater, as shown

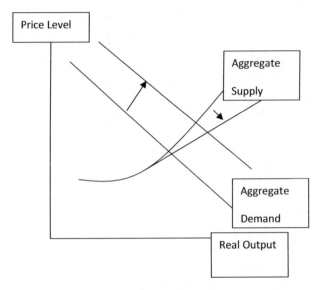

FIGURE 3.5 Aggregate Supply and Demand. Aggregate demand is a negative function of the price level because a reduction in the price level increases the real supply of money, which lowers the interest rate and increases real investment. Aggregate supply increases with the price level because money wages are fixed (by contract, for example). An increase in the price level lowers the real wage rate and increases employment and output

in Figure 3.5. Indeed, at very low levels of output and employment, the aggregate supply curve may be horizontal. An increase in aggregate demand will increase output and employment with no effect on wages or prices. But as aggregate demand approaches the full-employment level, prices (and perhaps wages) will increase with increases in demand, perhaps sharply, and continue to rise (i.e., produce inflation). Economists now talk about the noninflationary rate of unemployment (NAIRU) as a target for policy. Actually, Keynes explored this idea in *How to Pay for the War* (1940).

How exactly does inflation occur in the aggregate supply–aggregate demand model? Suppose the monetary authorities increase the money supply in order to increase aggregate demand and hit a target level of real output, as in Figure 3.5. Money wages do not adjust at first, prices and output rise, and the real wage declines. But then suppose that workers later demand an increase in money wages to compensate for the increase in prices. Any increase in the money wage increases the real wage and reduces real output below the target level. If the monetary authorities wish to maintain the target level of output, another increase in the money supply will be needed. Prices increase once again as output is brought up to hit the target. Then workers, with a lag, insist on another increase in money wages, and so on. In essence, in order to keep the economy at some high level of real output, the monetary authorities must keep increasing the money supply ahead of the demands by workers for increases in money wages. Therefore, a particular level of real output and unemployment is associated with a continuing rate of increase in prices and a lagged increase in money wages. What if the workers catch on and reduce the lag to zero? That is a topic for the next chapter.

The notion of demand-pull inflation was investigated in detail empirically first by A. W. H. Phillips (1958), who studied unemployment and the rate of change in wage rates in the United Kingdom. The curve he found, which plots wage changes on the vertical axis against the unemployment rate on the horizontal axis, became known as the Phillips Curve. Samuelson and Solow (1960) quickly adapted the idea for the United States (with some reservations). Their look at the U.S. data for the period after World War II led them (1960, p. 193) to "guess":

> In order to have wages increase at no more than the 2 ½ percent per annum characteristic of our productivity growth, the American economy would seem on the basis of twentieth-century and postwar experience to have to undergo something like 5 to 6 percent of the civilian labor force unemployed. That much unemployment would appear to be the cost of price stability in the years immediately ahead.

They also guessed that in order to have an unemployment rate of 3 percent, the price index might increase by 4 to 5 percent per year. They regarded the points on the Phillips Curve as a menu of choices. A Samuelson–Solow-type Phillips curve is illustrated in Figure 3.6.

One might ask, "How can wages and prices increase with no increase in the supply of money?" One answer is that the velocity of circulation of money increases. The purchase of goods at higher and higher prices requires that the stock of money be used more rapidly. People spend money faster before prices go even higher. Another idea is that the banks actually increase the money supply by lending to the limit (and beyond, perhaps) as unemployment falls. And yet another is that the central bank acts, as suggested previously, to increase the money supply to "accommodate" business – instead of taking away the punch bowl just as the party really gets going.

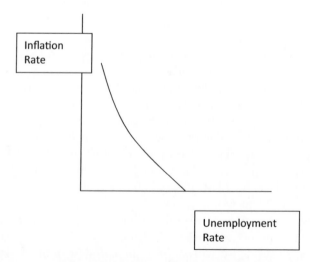

Inflation Rate

Unemployment Rate

FIGURE 3.6 Phillips Curve. High unemployment means very low inflation, perhaps zero or negative (deflation), and very low unemployment means the economy is "overheated" and inflation (continuing price increases) breaks out. Some level of unemployment is consistent with stable prices – zero inflation

James Tobin and refinements to Keynesian theory

James Tobin was a Keynesian economist and winner of the Nobel Prize. His long-term project was to further and improve upon the Keynesian theory. The maverick Keynesian Hyman Minsky, whom we will meet later in this chapter, lamented (1975) that Keynes suffered a heart attack in 1937 and was unable to participate in the refinements to his theories. However, James Tobin was there to improve upon Keynes while remaining in the same spirit. This section examines Tobin's theories of real investment and the demand for money.

Tobin's theory of real investment (1969) is now the accepted theory and is known as the Q theory of investment. Q is defined as the ratio of the market value of a real investment to its cost. For example, real estate developers compare the cost of a project to the price at which it can be sold. A ratio greater than 1.0 indicates an incentive to undertake the investment. It is understood that real estate projects take time to be completed, so a lag is built into the model. So where does Q come from?

The value of Q includes the present discounted value of the stream of outputs attributable to one unit of capital, divided by the cost of adding the unit of capital. It is assumed that capital has a rising supply price. Suppose the value of Q for the first unit of additional capital is 1.2, Q for the second unit is 1.15 because of the cost of the second unit of capital is higher than for the first unit, Q for the third unit is 1.1, etc. Investment will proceed until the last unit of capital added has a Q of 1.0. So the rate of investment depends upon Q for the first unit of additional capital and the (positive) slope of the supply curve of additional capital.

Q theory has been extended to include investments made under conditions of risk. Risk refers to situations in which future values of key variables have known probability distributions. In this case, the present discounted value of output produced by adding a unit of capital is a random variable. In the case of risk, the discount rate is adjusted for market risk. Note two things about the theory. First, the theory has been worked out for risky situations but not for situations of uncertainty when the future is just about completely unknown. Second, the value of an investment depends upon expectations of the price of future outputs. So investment decisions depend critically upon *opinions* regarding future market values. What could go wrong here?

Next consider the demand for money, the asset that earned no interest at the time Tobin (1958) formulated his theory. Keynes stated that the demand for money includes two parts – the amount needed for transactions and the amount held for speculation. His concern was with the speculative demand for money. Why would anyone hold an asset for speculative purposes when interest-earning assets are available? The demand for money in the Keynesian model (and in the standard IS-LM model) assume that the demand for money is greater the lower the interest rate is, which is the opportunity cost of holding money. The simple version of the Keynesian argument is that, if the interest rate is very low, people expect the interest rate to rise to its "normal" level. Therefore, the market value of interest-earning assets will fall. But the value of money does not fall. People are avoiding capital losses. However, critics of the model ask why people do not learn from experience and adapt expectations to current facts. Why are interest rate expectations "sticky"?

Tobin (1958) instead applied portfolio theory under conditions of risk, as developed by Harry Markowitz (1952), and considered the situation in which money is one of the available assets. It turns out that investors will choose to hold some money to avoid risk. Furthermore, the model makes sensible predictions. For example, an increase in the interest rate causes two effects – a substitution effect in favor of interest-earning assets and an income effect that may cause investors to reduce exposure to risk. The risk-aversion theory of liquidity preference largely avoids the logical weakness in the Keynesian theory regarding the stickiness of interest rate expectations. One might add that Tobin's theories of investment and money demand are important assets in a Nobel-winning portfolio.

New Keynesian economics

What is known as the new Keynesian economics started to develop during the 1970s, the period of high unemployment and inflation – a combination inconsistent with the standard Keynesian model. Keynesians adapted their models to account for the events of the 1970s, and these adaptations are described in Chapters 4 and 5. Mankiw and Romer (1991) define new Keynesian models as having these features:

■ The model violates the classical dichotomy between the real and money economies. In other words, changes in the supply of money have real economic effects.

■ The model presumes that there are real imperfections in the economy that explain the nature of economic fluctuations.

New Keynesians devised a variety of models to explain the "real imperfections."

An important part of that research agenda was providing microeconomic foundations for the stickiness of wages and prices that cause markets not to clear rapidly. In particular, the stickiness of wages leading to involuntary unemployment was a critical topic. Janet Yellen (1984) provided a good summary of the resulting theoretical research. She began (1984, p. 200) with:

> Keynesian economists hold it to be self-evident that business cycles are characterized by involuntary unemployment. But construction of a model of the cycle with involuntary unemployment faces the obvious difficulty of explaining why the labor market does not clear. Involuntarily unemployed people, by definition, want to work at less than the going wage rate. Why don't firms cut wages, thereby increasing profits?

The models she discussed are based on the efficiency wage hypothesis – the idea that labor productivity depends on the real wage paid. A firm will offer a wage rate that maximizes its profits, and that wage induces an efficient amount of "effort" on the part of the workers. The "real imperfection" idea is that worker effort cannot be monitored continuously (i.e., information is not complete), so workers are motivated by good wages. Unemployed workers would like to work at this efficient wage rate or even a lower wage, but the firm will not hire them. The firm has already set employment and the wage to maximize profits, so it will not hire more workers at that wage. Furthermore, they will not lower the wage and hire more workers because the lower wage will reduce labor productivity. In other words, the real wage rate is not flexible in the downward direction because labor productivity will fall.

Why does labor productivity depend upon the real wage rate? One idea is that workers gain valuable specific experience on the job, so the employer wishes to keep labor turnover low. New workers take time to "learn" the job. Not all employers operate using the efficiency wage notion. Now suppose that the economy consists of two sectors; in one sector, work experience increases labor productivity and workers are paid to keep turnover low, while in the other sector there is no enhancement of productivity with experience. The labor market in this other sector does clear, because anyone can get a job there. However, the wage differential between the two sectors can mean that some workers will spend their time searching for jobs in the higher-wage sector rather than working in the lower-wage sector.

Does rigidity of the real wage mean that the money wage also is "sticky" as demand fluctuates? A sticky money wage is needed to generate Keynesian fluctuations in unemployment. Suppose that demand for output declines. The nominal price of output falls. Firms reduce employment and can cut the money wage to keep the real wage constant. But firms may not cut the money wage. A decline in prices with no decline in money wages paid by the firm increases the real wage, and this appears to be a departure from rationality on the part of the firm. But the firm may not cut wages because of existing contracts, because resetting wages is a costly and contentious process, or because they do not wish to be without their best employees when demand recovers.

Another line of thinking by the new Keynesians follows the idea that an increase in unemployment will have longer-run effects. People who are out of work for an extended period of time lose skills or fail to keep up with changes in technology or how work is organized. The result may be that it is difficult to bring the unemployment rate back down to its initial level and/or that the labor force participation rate is reduced as people give up hope of qualifying for a job. One sees this point made in the press by some economists with reference to the lower rate of labor force participation coming out of the recent economic crisis. The idea that a short-run drop in aggregate demand can have impacts in the long run is called hysteresis, an infelicitous term that is borrowed from physics. Apparently, the idea has nothing to do with hysteria.

The financial instability hypothesis

Keynes included an extended discussion of financial markets and the tendency to speculate on changes in asset prices. His conclusion (1936, p. 159):

> Speculators may do no harm as bubbles on a steady stream of enterprise. But the position is serious when enterprise becomes the bubble on a whirlpool of speculation. When the capital development of a country becomes the by-product of the activities of a casino, the job is likely to be ill-done.

The late Hyman Minsky, a Keynesian who was ignored by most Keynesians in his lifetime, is now back in fashion. Minsky objected strenuously to the neoclassical synthesis of Hicks and Hansen. His chief objection is the much-too-simple model of investment spending in the Hicksian IS-LM model, in which investment is simply a function of the interest rate. He argued that Keynes without including the inherent instability of financial markets is akin to "Hamlet without the prince" – in other words, the play staged without the central character. Minsky (1975) supplemented the Keynesian approach by arguing that during a boom period, asset prices increase and, in order to take advantage of increasing values, the private sector will figure out ways and means of expanding credit and financial leverage that defeat attempts at regulation. "Animal spirits" take over. Financial bubbles can and do exist. This sounds familiar, does it not? Recall that the Q theory of investment includes the effect of expected changes in asset prices. Then, some event occurs that starts financial collapse and the process of deleveraging. In particular, increases in investment in assets such as real estate and durable equipment took place in response to the increase in their market values. Investors discover too late that they have created too many real assets. The annual incomes from those assets fall below expectations. Hedge investors (cash flow sufficient to cover all debt service) become speculative investors (cash flow covers only interest of debt, with no return to the investor), speculative investors become Ponzi investors (cash flow insufficient to cover interest payments), and Ponzi investors become zombies (walking dead). Investment collapses, and Keynesian remedies are needed. The process is inherent in the nature of a capitalist economy, according to Keynes as interpreted by Minsky.

Now let's turn to Minsky's intellectual heirs. The late Charles Kindleberger's classic book *Manias, Panics, and Crashes: A History of Financial Crises* is based on Minsky's model. This book is an encyclopedic account of financial crises through history. One can predict that Kindleberger's coauthor, Robert Aliber, will update the book soon to include the recent crisis. Similarly, Robert Shiller has gained prominence from a series of books that argues that financial bubbles are the cause of financial crises. One of his latest is *The Subprime Solution*, in which he states that the housing market bubble began in 1997 (well before the U.S. Fed cut interest rates starting in 2001), and that the actions taken by the private sector can be explained by the existence of rising housing prices. Why not make loans to anyone when the price of the house will always go up? Who cares if the borrowers are not qualified? But housing suppliers responded and the bubble burst – as it always does.

Another aspect of Minsky's work concerns the alleviation of poverty. As summarized by Wray (2016), Minsky argued that the alleviation of poverty requires putting to work everyone who is willing and able to work. This group is much larger than the number of people who are officially unemployed; it also includes those who are not working and actively seeking work. Minsky's policy recommendation is a guaranteed jobs program to employ those able and willing to work as they are, high school dropouts included, and to pay a living wage. Improvements in job skills would occur "on the job" and not in separate training programs that provide no work experience. The government-funded program would be larger during an economic downturn and would shrink naturally as the economy improved and workers were hired by the private sector from the program. One purpose of the program is to promote consumption spending to stabilize the economy. Minsky did not favor fiscal policies used to stimulate private investment through tax cuts and subsidies. Such programs would, in his view, lead to financial instability.

Conclusion

Chapters 2 and 3 have presented a variety of versions of Keynesian theory – the basic theory as formulated by Keynes himself, the theory with external balance added, the theory with an overall price level included expressed as aggregate supply and demand curves (with the Phillips Curve tradeoff between inflation and unemployment), Tobin's theories of investment and money demand, the financial instability hypothesis that Keynes and Minsky discussed at length, and the Hicks general equilibrium version of basic Keynesian theory known as the neoclassical synthesis. So we actually have a small portfolio of Keynesian models that can be applied to data. It is well to remember that Keynes developed his theory in response to the Great Depression. Does it apply all of the time? Leading Keynesian James Tobin, as quoted by Snowdon and Vane (2005, pp. 150–151), reiterated the neoclassical synthesis by saying:

> Sometimes the economy is in the classical situation where markets are clearing (demand equals supply) and the economy's ability to produce output is supply-constrained. . . . At other times the economy is in a Keynesian situation in which the constraint on actual output is *demand* – aggregate spending.
>
> (emphasis in original)

How does Tobin's view stack up against the evidence? We shall see. . . .

4

The Monetarist school of thought and monetary policy rules

Introduction

The reaction to Keynes' *General Theory* was mixed, to say the least. The book was received enthusiastically by many, especially younger economists, but as discussed in Chapter 2, some economists of the older generation were harsh in their initial judgments. Frank Knight (1937), a leading economist at the University of Chicago, wrote a review of the book in which he stated:

> It claims to be itself a theory of stable equilibrium, like the conventional systems in being free from cycles, but different in that instead of full employment a large amount of unemployment, involuntary and not due to friction, is characteristic of the equilibrium position. I may as well state at the outset that the direct contention of the work seems to be quite unsubstantiated. . . . The argument, therefore, requires extensive re-interpretation and integration with a general theory running in terms of equilibrium with full employment, before it can be accepted as sound or useful.

Professor A. C. Pigou, Keynes's colleague at Cambridge University, was a target of criticism in the *General Theory*, and clearly he was offended. The Pigou (1936) review includes:

> Einstein actually did for Physics what Mr. Keynes believes himself to have done for Economics. He developed a far-reaching generalization, under which Newton's results can be subsumed as a special case. But he (Einstein) did not, in announcing his discovery, insinuate, through carefully barbed sentences, that Newton and those who had hitherto followed his lead were a gang of incompetent bunglers. The example is illustrious: but Mr. Keyes has not followed it.

Later in the review, Pigou asserts:

> The lack of clarity in Mr. Keynes' explanation is *mainly* due, I suggest, to a lack of clarity in his thought, a lack of clarity which he now himself recognizes to have been present when he wrote the *Treatise on Money* but, naturally enough, now believes himself to have overcome.

But it was a member of the younger generation of economists who became the most influential anti-Keynesian. Milton Friedman was a graduate student in economics at the University of Chicago in the early 1930s – before the *General Theory*. His recollections are revealing. His colleague Abba Lerner was a graduate student at that time as well, but Friedman (1974) observed:

> Yet we were affected very differently by the Keynesian revolution – Lerner becoming an enthusiastic convert and one of the most effective expositors and interpreters of Keynes, I remaining largely unaffected and if anything somewhat hostile.

Friedman (1974) recalled:

> My teachers regarded the depression as largely the product of misguided governmental policy – or at least as greatly intensified by such policies. They blamed the monetary and fiscal authorities for permitting banks to fail and the quantity of deposits to decline. Far from preaching the need to let deflation and bankruptcy to run their course, they repeated pronunciamentos calling for governmental action to stem the deflation. . . . So far as policy was concerned, Keynes had nothing to offer those of us who had sat at the feet of Simons, Mints, Knight, and Viner.

I might add that "somewhat hostile" is an understatement. Once he became a faculty member at the University of Chicago in 1946, Friedman turned his energies to the construction of an alternative school of thought in macroeconomics that is based on the traditional quantity theory of money. But before we look at the details of Monetarism, it is useful to consider the larger matter of schools of thought in economics.

Schools of thought in economics

Economics textbooks as a rule avoid openly discussing different schools of thought. Controversies in macroeconomics are discussed in technical terms, and this book will do likewise. However, membership in a particular school of thought influences research and policy discussions at every turn. On the normative side, schools of thought differ in the ethical objectives that are taken as given. On the positive side, the school of thought influences the nature of the data that are gathered, the nature of the facts that are deemed important to explain, the choice of economic model to explain those facts, and the use of the models that are formed. The existence of fundamentally different schools of thought leads to competing economic models that coexist and claim to explain the facts. What is an informed observer supposed to do? The first step is to understand the basic tenets of the schools of thought, and that is the purpose of this section.

There are three fundamentally different schools of thought in economics. One is Marxism, but very few macro economists are members of this school. The overriding theme in Marxism is class struggle between the two social classes that are associated with the two primary factors of production, capital and labor. Inherent in the capitalist economy are "contradictions" that lead to the class struggle, which in turn results in major changes in society – such as revolution. Marxists exist in universities in the United States, Japan, and Europe and in other places as well, but they are not influential in the field of macroeconomics in advanced, highly developed nations. Marxism will not be discussed further in this book.

The other two schools of thought can be labeled "mainstream economics" and "conservative economics." Members of these two schools agree on some things. In particular, they agree on the usefulness of notions that people maximize utility subject to constraints on income and time, and firms maximize profits given technological constraints and the state of the market. These are, of course, the building blocks of microeconomics. Mainstream economists go one very big step further. They take the objective of utility maximization subject to constraints to the level of the society (or nation). The utility of a society is a function of the utility of its members, and the constraints are the availability of resources including land, capital, and (above all) the time of its members. Framing the economic question in this way leads to the familiar normative conclusion that the marginal benefit to society of a particular good or activity (and hence price) should equal its marginal cost to society.

Mainstream economists think that the allocation of resources to their alternative uses is, for the most part, best accomplished by the market. However, there are very important exceptions to this proposition that call for intervention into the economy by government, including:

■ Public goods
■ Monopoly
■ Externalities (pollution, congestion, and so on)
■ Information problems (such as murky accounting by firms and other situations in which some people have more information than others)
■ Macroeconomic stability and growth

Mainstream economists are in the Keynesian tradition that calls for active policy to reduce macroeconomic fluctuations. They also think that government should help provide for future economic growth. They believe that government intervention in these situations will improve matters. They think that the government is capable of using monetary and fiscal policy wisely. Government policies can be mistaken or badly timed, but on balance they think that policies of a democratic government can be made to improve society's welfare. The research agenda of mainstream economists is influenced by membership in this school of thought. A good deal of their research examines the costs and benefits of various economic policy actions or proposals. For example, think back to the previous chapters on Keynesian theory. Keynes (and many others) pointed out that unemployment imposes a huge cost on the individual unemployed person, and on the entire society in terms of real output that is lost and can never be recouped. For Keynes, returning an economy to full employment provides a great benefit for society at little or no cost.

The conservative economics school of thought has been very influential since the 1970s, but many students may not really know how it differs from mainstream economics. Most students know that the late Milton Friedman, a Nobel Prize winner and for many years a professor at the University of Chicago, was the most prominent conservative economist. But it was Friedrich A. von Hayek (another Nobel Prize winner) who wrote what conservative economists consider to be the classic statement of their values. Hayek's best-known book, *The Road to Serfdom*, was published in 1944, and it made him famous. In 1947, Hayek invited a group of like-minded intellectuals to join him in founding an organization called the Mont Pelerin Society. Milton Friedman attended the meeting and was a founding member of this society, which is devoted to human freedom, the rule of law, private property, competitive markets, and diffused power. (The Mont Pelerin Society is still in business, and it's actually fun to surf their website.)

Hayek and Keynes were contemporaries – Hayek from Austria, and Keynes from England. As you know already, Keynes and his followers believe that the government must step in to save a market economy from itself. Full employment is not automatic in a market economy, and people suffer needlessly. Keynes was responding to the situation in which he was living. Hayek was living in a different place, a place that had lost the Great War and was the home of Austrian economics. The work of the Austrian school was to counter Marxist thinking and collectivist and socialist proposals. They were strong defenders of private property and a decentralized market economy. Hayek became the leading member of the Austrian school. He and Keynes argued about basic economic philosophy throughout the 1930s. In 1944, Hayek published *The Road to Serfdom*, in which he argued that even the rather moderate Keynesian proposals will lead a nation down the path to authoritarianism.

Hayek's chief concern was the progressive replacement of competition with planning, or central direction of a nation's resources towards some objective. At the time he wrote, he was worried about the progressive advance of socialism in western nations, especially England. His concern was with the method of centralized planning, even if the goals espoused by its advocates were admirable. He saw that the ultimate effect of socialism and other forms of central planning would be a return to serfdom, the condition of ordinary people prior to their progressive liberation that began roughly with the Renaissance. For Hayek (1944, p. 14), the hallmark of Western civilization is:

> The respect for the individual man *qua* man, that is, the recognition of his own views and tastes as supreme in his own sphere, however narrowly that be circumscribed, and the belief that it is desirable that men should develop their own individual gifts and bents.

Conservatives think that the emergence of this respect for the individual was closely associated with the development of the laissez faire market economy.

For Hayek, the danger was people who advocated goals for the society other than freedom and liberty. This includes mainstream economists who advocate the maximization of utility of society's members and government policy to ensure full employment. Hayek's central point is that the pursuit of social goals (except for those that can achieve virtually unanimous agreement), even those chosen through democratic means, must inevitably sharply restrict the freedom of individuals. The democratic decision to engage in central planning of a particular sector of the economy will lead to a delegation of substantial power to planning agencies. Hayek (1944, p. 66) stated that:

> The objectionable feature is that delegation is so often resorted to because the matter at hand cannot be regulated by general rules but only by the exercise of discretion in the decision in particular cases. In these instances delegation means that some authority is given power to make with the force of law what to all intents and purposes are arbitrary decisions (usually described as 'judging the case on its merits').

The attempt to plan a substantial portion of the economy will eventually cry out for an economic dictator, someone who can get things done – make the trains run on time, and so on. Free societies are governed by the rule of law, not by administrative discretion. Or, as Milton Friedman suggested, the central bank should follow a simple, well-defined rule rather than attempt to engage in discretionary monetary policy. It should be noted that Friedman's notion of a money supply rule already had been part of the tradition at the University of Chicago for years. Surely Hayek's book and the Mont Pelerin Society enhanced Friedman's enthusiasm for such a rule, because he published his famous *American Economic Review* article, "A monetary and fiscal framework for economic stability," in 1948. Friedman's proposal was that banks must have 100% reserves against deposits, and that the money supply would increase only when the federal government ran a deficit (and would decline when the federal government ran a surplus).

University of Chicago economist Henry Simons proposed a monetary rule in 1936. Recall that Milton Friedman sat at his feet. Simons stated (1936, p. 29) the basic idea:

> The most important objective of a sound liberal policy, apart from the establishment of highly competitive conditions in industry and the narrow limitation of political control over relative prices, should be that of securing a monetary system governed by definite rule.

"Liberal" in this context means classical liberal. After considering a variety of alternatives, his proposal (1936, p. 30) was straightforward:

> A monetary rule of maintaining the constancy of some price-index, preferably an index of prices of competitively produced commodities, appears to afford the only promising escape from present monetary chaos and uncertainties.

Simons stated that the responsibility for implementing the rule would be given to a federal authority, which would be under close supervision to follow this well-defined policy. (In 2012, the U.S. Federal Reserve actually adopted a target of 2 percent inflation and has found that meeting the target requires the use of active monetary policy.) Simons was also a proponent of the 100% reserve rule for banks and thought that a rule that fixed the total quantity of money would merit consideration. Simons died in 1946, but Friedman kept trying to formulate a workable rule for monetary policy in the 1950s and 1960s. Friedman's ideas are discussed in the next section. For now, we note that the problem of finding the "right" rule for monetary policy is a research question that flows directly from membership in the particular school of thought that came to be called Monetarism, which makes the maximization of human freedom as the ethical objective that is taken as a given. Keynesians were not necessarily searching for the right monetary policy rule. They were formulating models that would help them determine discretionary monetary and fiscal policy to improve the performance of the macro economy.

Conservative economists downplay the importance of monopolies, externalities, and information problems. For example, monopoly limits alternatives for consumers, so it is an inhibition of freedom. Monopoly most often results from government policy or collusive agreements, so the first things to do are to eliminate the offending policies and to enforce the anti-trust laws vigorously. Mainstream economists agree with this point; both schools of thought supported the deregulation of the airline, trucking, and electric power industries. For monopolies that occur naturally from technological factors, the choices are government regulation, government operation, or private monopoly. For Friedman (1962, p. 28), permitting private monopoly "may be the least of the evils." And externality problems can be solved by private negotiations more often than one might think. Besides, the attempt by government to regulate externalities may make things worse. Mainstream economists largely do not follow the conservatives on this point; pollution and traffic congestion are two serious problems that cannot be solved by private negotiations. Both schools of thought include the proposition that information problems can be attacked by rules requiring transparency.

Monetarism

The Monetarism of Milton Friedman and his colleagues is a coherent body of thought that produced a huge body of research that includes numerous doctoral dissertations written at the University of Chicago. Recall that the Quantity Theory of Money that can be stated as:

$$MV = PY = GDP,$$

where
M = the stock of money however measured;
V = the velocity of circulation of money, i.e., the number of times the stock of money is used to purchase final goods and services in a year;

P = the overall price level; and
Y = the real level of output of final goods and services.

The equation can be stated in alternative forms:

P = MV/Y,
M = PY/V, and
V = PY/M.

The Quantity Theory of Money provides a convenient explanation for inflation, which is the *continuing* increases in prices. The basic idea is that if the supply of money keeps rising, so will prices. Money supply increases are directly linked to inflation, provided that real output and the velocity of money do not change (or change very little). The empirical evidence for the hypothesis linking money and inflation is voluminous. As Milton Friedman said often, "Inflation is always and everywhere a monetary phenomenon."

Consider the American Civil War. The Confederate side had very little ability to finance the war other than by printing money. Further, states, local governments, and private firms printed money too. By the end of the war in 1865, consumer prices had increased by 9,000 percent. Confederate money was worthless, and people were carrying on routine transactions by barter. Then there is Weimar Germany. Saddled with unrealistic reparation payments after World War I, the government printed money instead of imposing taxes or borrowing. The price of a gold Mark in terms of paper Marks at the end of various years were: 10 in 1920, 100 in 1922, and 1 trillion in 1923 (that is 1,000,000,000,000). A recent example is the nation of Zimbabwe. The government printed money to pay for wars against other African countries and to pay corrupt officials. The official exchange rate against the U.S. dollar was 1,000 to 1 on January 1, 2004, $10^{7.5}$ to 1 on January 1, 2008, and 10^{23} to 1 on January 1, 2009. That rate on January 1, 2009 is 100,000,000,000 trillion (1 hundred million trillions). By comparison, the GDP of the United States is about 20 trillion dollars. The people of Zimbabwe were using other currencies or barter.

The Quantity Theory of Money also provides a neat explanation for deflation, continuously *decreasing* prices. A good example is the United States in the decades after the end of the Civil War in 1865. The North had experienced inflation during the war of about 75 percent, because much of the war was financed by taxation and bond sales rather than printing money. However, the postwar government wished to avoid inflation and decided to return to the gold standard at the prewar rate. The government stopped printing the Greenbacks used during the war and also stopped minting silver coins. The growth of the money supply fell well short of the growth in real economy, which was booming in the industrializing North. Data for money, income, and prices for 1869 and 1879 are shown in Table 4.1.

In percentage terms:

%ΔM + %ΔV = (2.7% + 0.4%) = 3.1% and
%ΔP + %ΔY = −3.8% + 6.8% = 3.0%.

In short, the real economy grew rapidly and the money supply did not, so prices fell. The nation failed to provide a flexible money supply – on purpose.

TABLE 4.1 Money, Income, and Prices in the United States

	1869	1879	Annual Percentage Change
Money Stock	$1.3 billion	$1.7 billion	2.7%
Real Net National Product	$7.3 billion	$14.52 billion	6.8%
Price Index ($1,929)	79.1	54.3	−3.8%
Velocity of Money	4.48	4.65	0.4%

Deflation hurts debtors and helps creditors. Debtors included farmers and Southerners. Creditors included Eastern bankers. A political movement known as populism was born. Populists advocated, among many things, the monetization of silver. William Jennings Bryan, the 1896 Democratic Party candidate for President of the United States, gave the "Cross of Gold" speech at the convention in Chicago. L. Frank Baum wrote a novel in 1900 that many think is a monetary allegory pertaining to the period from 1869 to 1896. The novel is *The Wonderful World of Oz*. The hurricane (populism) sweeps through the Midwest (Kansas); Dorothy follows the yellow brick road (the gold standard) in Oz (abbreviation for ounce) and meets the scarecrow (the farmer), the tin man (the industrial worker), and the cowardly lion (Bryan himself). The little band finally meets the wizard (the chairman of the Republican Party and money power behind the party, Mark Hanna), who really cannot and will not solve anything. In the end, Dorothy clicks the heels of her silver (yes, silver, not ruby) slippers and returns to Kansas, where nothing has changed. See Rockoff (1990) for a full explanation.

Friedman (1956) provided a restatement of the Quantity Theory of Money as it was at the University of Chicago in the 1950s. His restatement is as follows:

■ The theory is a theory of the demand for money, and the standard theory of demand applies.

■ Money is one asset among several that are used to hold wealth.

■ Money as an asset provides services such as ease in making transactions and protection from uncertainty.

■ The demand for money is a function of total wealth, income, the overall price level and its expected rate of change, the price and return features of other assets, and tastes and preferences. Tastes and preferences are assumed to be constant over the relevant time period.

■ Standard consumer theory states that, if all prices and income are doubled, quantities of goods and services demanded by consumers are not affected. Therefore, the demand for money can be stated in "real" terms (M/P) as a function of wealth and income in real terms, the expected rate of change in prices, and the real returns to other assets (with tastes and preferences held constant); $M/P = Y/V$.

If the Quantity Theory of Money is a theory of the demand for money, how does money influence total income? William Fellner wrote a survey of macroeconomic theory as of the immediate post–World War II period in which he stated (1948, p. 51):

> Theories of money income based on the quantity theory approach argue from the supply of money to income. Income is what it is because a certain amount of money is available and because this money is being spent at a certain rate.

In other words, (p. 52), "individuals and institutions aim at some relationship between their cash balances and their money expenditures, that is, at some rate of spending their cash balances." Fellner (p. 52) goes on to say:

> The contemporary theories of employment have been developed mainly in terms of the savings-investment approach, rather than the quantity theory approach, because it is widely believed that the propensity to consume part of one's *income* is a truer (more "dependable") propensity than the propensity to hold some definite amount of *cash* in relation to one's expenditures. Obviously, any completed economic process can be expressed just as easily with the aid of the one as with the other.
>
> (emphasis in original)

In other words, the Keynesians think that the consumption function (or updated versions thereof) is a more stable basis for macroeconomic modeling than is the demand for money. Milton Friedman (1956, p. 12) countered with:

> The quantity theorist accepts the empirical hypothesis that the demand for money is highly stable – more stable than functions such as the consumption function that are offered as alternative key relations.

Friedman did not mean that the real quantity of money demanded (or the velocity of circulation, $V = PY/M$) is a constant over time. Rather, the money demand is a stable function of the variables stated previously. And he set out to show that the empirical hypothesis was correct.

It is reasonable to question whether money is an independent variable, or whether the holdings of money are decided because the decision has been made to spend. Recall from Chapter 1 that the supply of money is largely in the form of bank deposits, which increase primarily because of the actions of borrowers (firms and households) to obtain loans – provided that the bank possesses excess reserves. An increase in the stock of money precedes an increase in income, but correlation does not mean causation. Indeed, James Tobin (1970) demonstrated that such evidence on timing can be derived from a Keynesian-type model, and accused Friedman of falling for the "post hoc, ergo propter hoc" fallacy (i.e., before this, therefore because of this).

Friedman's own empirical studies of the demand for money culminated in the publication with Anna J. Schwartz of *A Monetary History of the United States, 1867–1960* in 1963. This massive study is regarded as a landmark in monetary economics and economic history, and some of its findings are discussed in later chapters of this book. Friedman (1959) provided a summary of the main findings of the book. He divided the findings into long-run (secular) and short-run (cyclical) outcomes.

The long-run changes in the real stock of money (M/P) per capita are correlated highly with long-run changes in real income per capita. An increase in real income per capita of 1.0 percent was associated with an increase of 1.8 percent in the per capita real supply of money, and thus a reduction in the velocity of money of 0.8 percent. This suggests that money is a "luxury" good that increases more rapidly than income. Long-run movements in money income (PY) were related to long-run change in the nominal stock of money (M) and in velocity (V), but the movement in the nominal stock of money is the dominant factor. Long-run changes in money income are dominated by changes in prices. In short, long-run movements in prices are related to the nominal stock of money.

In the short run (cyclical episodes), the real stock of money (M/P) rises during expansions and falls (or rises less) during downturns in the economy. However, the fluctuations in the real stock of money are small; a 1.0 percent change in real income (Y) is associated with a change in the real stock of money of only 0.2 percent. This means that, since

$$(M/P)V = Y,$$

the velocity of money (V) tends to rise during cyclical expansions and falls during contractions. Cyclical movements in money income (PY) are attributed to movements both in the nominal stock of money (M) and the velocity of money (V) in the same direction at roughly equal magnitudes. The short summary is that, over the long period, the movement of money income (largely movement in the price level) is mainly attributed to movement in the nominal stock of money, while in the short (cyclical) period the fluctuations in money income are larger than fluctuations in the stock of money because of pro-cyclical variations (movement in the same direction as the total economy) in the velocity of money. As we are mainly concerned with cyclical episodes in this book, we will see whether fluctuations in GDP are discernibly greater than fluctuations in the supply of money (but the two variables move together).

The most famous portion of *A Monetary History of the United States, 1867–1960* is the 120-page chapter titled "The Great Contraction," the Friedman–Schwartz analysis of the Great Depression of 1929 to 1933. Their conclusion, stated at the beginning of the chapter, is as follows (1963, pp. 300–301):

> The contraction is in fact a tragic testimonial to the importance of monetary forces. True, as events unfolded, the decline in the stock of money and the near-collapse of the banking system can be regarded as a consequence of nonmonetary forces in the United States, and monetary and nonmonetary forces in the rest of world. Everything depends on how much is taken as given. For it is true also, as we shall see, that different and feasible actions by the monetary authorities could have prevented the decline in the stock of money – indeed, could have produced almost any desired increase in the money stock. The same actions would also have eased the banking difficulties appreciably.

Prevention or moderation of the decline in the stock of money, let alone the substitution of monetary expansion, would have reduced the contraction's severity and almost as certainly its duration. The contraction might still have been relatively severe. But it is hardly conceivable that money income would have declined by over one-half and prices by one-third in the course of four years if there had been no decline in the stock of money.

It is almost needless to say that this is one of the most noteworthy conclusions ever stated in economics. Ben Bernanke, then a member of the Federal Reserve Board, gave a talk at the celebration of Milton Friedman's 90th birthday (2002) in which he said:

> Let me end my talk by abusing slightly my status as an official representative of the Federal Reserve. I would like to say to Milton and Anna: Regarding the Great Depression. You're right, we did it. We're very sorry. But thanks to you, we won't do it again.

How were Friedman and Schwartz convinced that changes in the stock of money caused changes in the macro economy during the Great Depression, and not the other way around? A downturn in the economy causes banks to reduce lending, so the volume of bank deposits falls. Their method was to look for times when the Fed brought about a change in the stock of money for reasons that were independent of the trend in the domestic economy. For example, when the United Kingdome left the gold standard in September 1931, there was fear that the United States. would follow suit (which it did later, in 1933). The gold standard is a monetary system in which the money supply is backed by gold. Holders of dollars could demand gold for those dollars. In practice, countries held a gold reserve that was small compared to the stock of money. Hence, a drain on the gold reserve was seen as a serious problem. Investors began to demand gold for their dollars because it was feared that the price of gold in terms of dollars would increase sharply when the gold standard was ended. The gold reserve was falling rapidly. In October 1931, the Fed raised the interest rate it charges banks to borrow in order to increase interest rates in general and persuade investors to continue to invest in the United States. Recall from Chapter 1 that foreigners who invest in the United States must purchase dollars. A wave of bank failures ensued as a result of this tightening of policy, causing the money supply to contract sharply and the decline in output and prices to became worse. In short, a policy move for reasons other than domestic economic stability produced the expected economic impacts.

Exchange rate policy

Monetarists favor floating exchange rates. Obviously, they favor prices that are determined in competitive markets, but they also point out that permitting the exchange rate to float permits monetary policy to concentrate on the domestic economy. A floating exchange rate is an integral part of the Monetarist program. Milton Friedman made the case for flexible exchange rates soon after the adoption in 1944 of the Bretton Woods system for international finance of fixed exchange rates (with limited devaluation possibilities). Friedman's famous essay (1953) originated in a memo written in 1950 for an agency of the federal government.

Friedman (1953) began, oddly enough, by considering a nation with a surplus in the balance of payments. There are five ways to bring the demand and supply of the nation's currency into balance:

- Permit the market to adjust the exchange rate continuously;
- Make jumps in the official exchange rate;
- Permit prices within the nation to rise;
- Impose direct controls such as export licenses; or
- Use the nation's reserves to supply the needed currency.

A nation with a deficit in the balance of payments also has five options: let the exchange rate float, do an official devaluation of the fixed rate, permit domestic prices to fall, impose direct controls such as tariffs on imports, or reduce the nation's reserves (i.e., ship the gold). Friedman then proceeded to argue against all of the options that are not floating exchange rates.

Friedman (1953, p. 164) had a particularly harsh critique of making jumps in the official exchange rate. He stated:

> In short, the system of occasional changes in temporarily rigid exchange rates seems to me the worst of two worlds: it provides neither the stability of expectations that a genuinely rigid and stable exchange rate would provide in a world of unrestricted trade and willingness and ability to adjust the internal price structure to external conditions nor the continuous sensitivity of the flexible exchange rate.

Friedman was prescient in pointing out that "occasional changes" would be anticipated and lead to large amounts of speculative sales of currencies expected to be devalued.

The strategy of relying on falling domestic prices and wages to correct a balance of payments deficit was discounted because of inflexible prices and wages and because economies in the modern era try to ensure full employment.

Of course, Friedman opposed imposition of direct controls on exports and/or imports on the grounds that inserting the government controls into markets causes mischief. Efficient production and distribution of goods is interrupted. Lastly, use of the nation's reserves does not work well. Eventually, a nation in deficit will run out of reserves, and speculators will have a field day with the expectation of an "emergency" devaluation. And will a nation with a surplus be willing to continue to accumulate reserves as they ship their products abroad?

Inflationary expectations and monetary policy rules

Freidman's presidential address to the American Economic Association (1968) introduced the idea of rational expectations to macroeconomics. He pointed out that you can't fool all of the people all of the time. People form expectations about the economy in a rational manner – which includes the anticipation of changes in monetary and fiscal policy. For example, if people correctly anticipate that the monetary authorities will increase the supply of money, they will increase prices and wages so that monetary policy will have no impact on the real economy. There is no tradeoff between inflation and unemployment, unless you "fool" the people by increasing the supply of money when it is not expected. This point debunked the notion of a stable Phillips Curve – the tradeoff between inflation and unemployment. People catch on and, in the longer run, there is no tradeoff between inflation and unemployment. There is only the "natural" rate of unemployment. Actually, Keynesians conceded the point and acknowledged a role for expectations and switched to talking about the noninflationary rate of unemployment (NAIRU), but they still maintained that the economy will not quickly return to some sort of natural rate of unemployment.

Kydland and Prescott (1977) gained fame by pointing out the "time inconsistency" problem. If policy makers say one thing (money supply will increase modestly), and then do something different (big increase in money supply), the private economy will have undertaken actions that turned out to be mistakes. Policy makers need to follow rules that make them predictable. As noted earlier, Friedman had been advocating a simple rule for monetary policy since the 1940s. He recognized that 100 percent reserve currency was not about to be implemented, so he revised his rule to state that the money supply should increase by a stable rate per year. He stated the rule as some number between 3 and 5 percent in his popular book, *Capitalism and Freedom* (1962). Friedman had two compelling reasons for advocating this rule. In addition to the argument that society should be run by rules rather than men (and women), his research on monetary history led him to think that changes in the rate of increase in the money supply have effects that play out with a "long and variable lag." In other words, changes in monetary policy have effects – the timing of which is not predictable with much accuracy.

The rule that the money supply should increase at a constant rate fell out of favor because, in reality, the Fed does not control the supply of money directly. Recall the point made in Chapter 1 that private banks and borrowers must act to increase the supply of money. The Fed cannot make banks increase lending and cannot order borrowers to borrow. And besides, the Friedman rule permits no response to fluctuations in the macro economy. Perhaps a better rule would stipulate *how* the Fed will respond to economic fluctuations.

A famous rule is called the Taylor rule (after John Taylor), which stipulates that the federal funds rate should increase when inflation increases and should decrease when the economy is operating below capacity. The Taylor rule pertains to the federal funds rate (FFR), the rate on short-term government bonds that *is* controlled by the Fed through its bond purchases and sales. The rule is:

$$FFR = 1 + 1.5 \text{ (inflation)} - 0.5 \text{ (percentage that GDP falls below potential).}$$

Compute the federal funds rate as the rate of inflation (past four quarters) times 1.5, minus 0.5 times the percentage shortfall of GDP below its full–employment potential, plus 1.0. Taylor (2009) has provided evidence that, if the U.S. Federal Reserve had followed the Taylor rule during 2002–2004, the federal funds rate would not have been so low for so long and housing starts would not have ballooned.

Along with Robert Lucas, Kydland and Prescott are also among the originators of the real business cycle school, which argues that variations in real output stem from shocks on the supply side – rather than shocks on the aggregate demand side. They have returned to the classical economists' view that the market economy will react efficiently to these shocks, and that public policy should not be used to attempt to mitigate their effects. This theory is the topic of Chapter 5.

A monetarist model

This section provides an example of a Monetarist model that was used for forecasting and analysis purposes. The model was developed by Anderson and Carlson (1970), economists at the Federal Reserve Bank of St. Louis. It is known as the St. Louis model, and it was influential during the 1970s.

The model consists of three equations that describe the behavior of the economy and three identities. These six are:

Spending equation	Change in nominal spending is a function of the change in the money supply (M1) and the change in high employment government expenditures.
Demand pressure identity	Demand pressure is the change in nominal spending minus the difference between real full employment output and actual real output from the previous year.
Price equation	Change in nominal spending due to inflation is a function of demand pressure and anticipated inflation. Empirically, the effect is smaller in the short run and larger in the longer run as expectations of inflation adjust.
Real output identity	Real output level is the change in nominal spending minus the change in nominal spending due to inflation plus the real output level from the last year.
Real output gap identity	Real output gap is full employment output minus actual real output, expressed in percentage terms.
Unemployment equation	The unemployment rate is a function of the real output gap.

The exogenous variables in the model are the change in the money supply, the change in high employment government expenditures, and the full employment level of real output.

High employment government expenditures consist of government purchases of goods and services plus transfer payments (social security, welfare, etc.). Note that, following Friedman (1968), the model includes anticipated inflation as a determinant of the change in nominal spending due to inflation. This variable is a function of previous rates of inflation and past values of the unemployment rate.

See how the model flows from a change in the supply of money (or from a change in the amount of high employment government expenditures, for that matter). An increase in the supply of money increases nominal spending, which increases demand pressure. An increase in demand pressure increases the change in

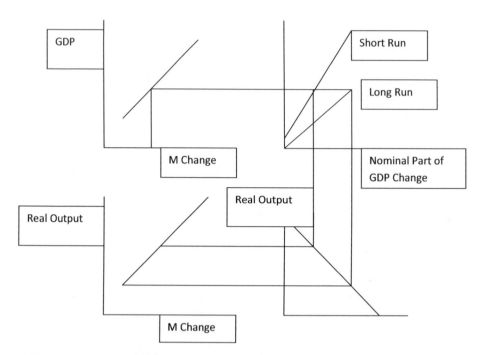

FIGURE 4.1 A Monetarist Model. A change in the money supply leads to a change in nominal output (GDP), which is divided into the nominal and real parts of the change in GDP. In line with the Monetarist view, in the short run the effect includes an increase in real output, but in the long run most (nearly all) of the effect comes in the form of inflation

nominal spending due to inflation, which in turn determines the increase in real output. The increase in real output reduces the real output gap, which lowers the rate of unemployment. These changes affect the anticipated rate of inflation for the next year.

The model can be depicted graphically. The diagram in the upper left of Figure 4.1 shows how total nominal output (GDP) changes as the supply of money changes. This change in total nominal output is split into its nominal portion in the diagram on the upper right (using what is called the price equation, noted previously). Recall from earlier in this chapter that the nominal portion of the change in total nominal output is larger in the long run than in the short run because expectations of inflation adjust. In other words, the effect of an increase in the supply of money on real output is greater in the short run than in the long run. Figure 4.1 depicts both the short-run and the long-run versions of the impact of an increase in the supply of money. Given the nominal portion of the change in total nominal output, the change in real output is given in the diagram on the lower right of Figure 4.1. The last diagram, on the lower left, shows the relationship between the change in the money supply and the change in real output. A final diagram (not shown) would depict the unemployment rate as a function of the gap between full employment real output and actual real output.

Conclusion

The Monetarist school of thought looks at the economy through the lens of the Quantity Theory of Money. Money matters – it matters a lot. Pumping more money into the economy will produce inflation in the long run. In the short run, a change in the nominal money supply leads to inflation if the economy is at full employment or to changes in real output and prices in roughly equal percentage amounts if the economy is not at full employment. Monetary policy is a powerful tool, and serious mistakes have been made by the Fed (the Great Depression being the leading example). The addition of the notion of rational expectations to the analysis leads to the conclusion that there is no tradeoff between inflation and unemployment. An unexpected increase in the money supply will increase employment for a time, but the public will catch on to the game and start to expect when money supply increases are going to happen. We are now quite familiar with the practice of "Fed watching" and attempts to discern the real meaning of statements made by the Fed chair. Monetarists think that the Fed policy should be governed by an explicit rule, such as the Taylor rule, because discretionary monetary policy is a dangerous toy, and because society should be governed by rules and not at the discretion of bureaucrats. In addition, permitting the exchange rate for the nation's currency to float permits the rule for monetary policy to be in pursuit of domestic economic stability.

5

Austrian capital and business cycle theory

Introduction

This chapter is a basic introduction to the Austrian theory of capital and business cycles as developed principally by Ludwig von Mises and most prominently by Friedrich A. von Hayek (1931) in a series of lectures at the London School of Economics. This theory has continued to have a following among the relatively small group of Austrian economists, who are politically very conservative. The sources for this chapter are the books by Skousen (2005) and Woods (2009) and the collection of articles by Caldwell (1995). As you will see, the Austrian theory has regained some prominence because of its apparent ability to match up with many of the facts of the 2008 financial crisis and severe economic recession. However, other conservative economists (such as the late Milton Friedman) think that the Austrian theory is not correct. Keynesians generally have ignored the Austrian theory, although Keynes discussed it (and argued with Hayek), as detailed later. Joseph Schumpeter was another prominent Austrian economist. He is best known for the term "creative destruction" – the idea that an economy progresses and grows through the process of technological change that results in the destruction of old products and processes as new ones are invented and take over.

In 1974, the Royal Swedish Academy of Sciences awarded the Prize for Economic Science in Memory of Alfred Nobel jointly to Gunnar Myrdal and Friedrich von Hayek "for their pioneering work in the theory of money and economic fluctuations and for their penetrating analysis of the interdependence of economic, social, and institutional phenomena." The Academy attached great importance to Myrdal's monumental work, *An American Dilemma: The Negro Problem and Modern Democracy*. In Hayek's case, the Academy first cited his work on economic fluctuations, noting that he was one of only a few economists who warned of the great crash of 1929. The Nobel Prize citation includes the following:

von Hayek showed how monetary expansion, accompanied by lending which exceeded the rate of voluntary saving, could lead to a misallocation of resources, particularly affecting the structure of capital. This type of business cycle theory with links to monetary expansion has fundamental features in common with the postwar monetary discussion.

Let us explore this statement in some depth.

We met Hayek in Chapter 4 as a philosophical antecedent of the monetarist school led by Milton Friedman. The debate between Hayek and Keynes during the 1930s and 1940s regarding the proper role (or non-role) of government in a market economy had attracted a great deal of attention, including among those at the University of Chicago economics department. Other economists might say that *The Road to Serfdom*, even if paved with good intentions, is not a good road upon which to travel. Now we turn to the basics of the Austrian economic theory based on Hayek and others.

Basic Austrian capital theory

The theory begins with a version of classical free-market economics as applied to real investment, which involves giving up current consumption to be able to produce more goods and services in the future. This discussion is similar to the presentation of classical economics at the beginning of Chapter 2. The interest rate (or rather, the complex structure of interest rates in which risk and term of a loan matter) is the price that induces consumers to give up current consumption for future consumption. It is also the price that those who would purchase investment goods must pay for funds that give them command over current resources to be used to produce goods and services in the future. Investment goods include goods such as factories and computers – and also includes time spent investing in education and training. (In the case of investment in human capital, the person who gives up current consumption is the same person who engages in investment in education and training.) The basic classical proposition is that, left to its own devices, a free-market economy does an efficient job of allocating available resources to these two fundamental demands – consumption now and consumption later. The interest rate is established in the market that just balances the value of current consumption goods with the value of investment goods. The basic result is shown in Figure 5.1. In a nutshell, the Austrians were concerned with the long run, while Keynes was famously focused on the short run. In the long run we are all dead, after all.

Figure 5.1 illustrates two ideas: the demand for resources for investment is greater at lower interest rates, and the supply of resources for investment is greater at higher interest rates. The market equilibrium equates demand and supply at the efficient price – the interest rate (the payoff to postponing consumption) that just balances society's demands for current and future consumption. Society's level of voluntary saving, as mentioned previously, has been determined. As advocates of the free market, Austrian economists believe that we alter this efficient tradeoff through public policy at our peril. Recall that Wicksell referred to the interest rate shown in Figure 5.1 as the natural rate of interest.

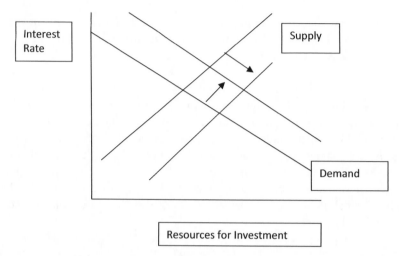

FIGURE 5.1 The Market for Resources for Real Investment. The demand for resources for real investment increases as the interest rate declines, and the supply of resources (i.e., saving for the future by households and firms) increases with increases in the interest rate

The Keynesian critique

Keynes (1936, Chapter 14) showed that because saving increases with income, the supply function in Figure 5.1 is drawn for a *given* level of aggregate income and employment. Recall from Chapter 1 that the factors that stand behind given supply and demand curves are held constant. Keynes (1936, p. 179) stated that:

> But, in fact, the classical theory not merely neglects the influence of changes in the level of income, but involves a formal error. For the classical theory . . . assumes that it can then proceed to consider the effect on the rate of interest of (e.g.) a shift in the demand curve for capital, without abating or modifying its assumption as to the amount of the given income out of which the savings are to be made.

Suppose that there is a new invention that leads to one of Schumpeter's waves of creative destruction. The demand for resources for investment shifts to the right (as shown in Figure 5.1). Investment increases. What happens next? According to Keynes, the increase in investment spending increases aggregate income (and has a multiplier effect). The supply of saving shifts to the right (as shown in Figure 5.1) because aggregate income has increased. Both investment and aggregate income increase, and the interest rate may wind up higher or lower, depending upon the extents to which demand and supply have shifted to the right. In other words, the demand for investment determines aggregate income, which determines the position of the saving curve. There are equilibrium levels of income, saving, and rate of interest given a demand for investment.

In the basic Keynesian model, the supply of savings shifts to the right by an amount that is equal to the shift in the demand curve, leaving the interest rate unchanged. To see this, write (from Chapter 2):

$$Y = C + I,$$
$$C = a + bY, \text{ [consumption function]}$$
$$\text{so } Y = a + bY + I.$$
$$Y(1 - b) = a + I, \text{ and}$$
$$Y = (a + I)/(1 - b), \text{ [multiplier} = 1/(1 - b)].$$

The increase in Y as I increases by 1 is $1/(1 - b)$. Next,

$$S = Y - C = Y - a - bY = -a + (1 - b)Y \text{ [saving function]}.$$

When Y increases by 1, S increases by $(1 - b)$. Now consider the change in S as I increases by 1. An increase in I increases Y, which increases S. All of this can be written, where Δ means "chance in,"

$$\Delta S/\Delta I = (\Delta S/\Delta Y)(\Delta Y/\Delta I) = (1 - b)[1/(1 - b)] = 1!$$

The increase in saving equals the increase in investment, leaving the interest rate in Figure 5.1 constant. In this example, the same rate of interest occurs regardless of whether the economy is at full employment or at some lower level of output.

If investment is insufficient to bring the economy to full employment, then Keynes would say that the interest rate should be reduced through monetary policy in order to stimulate more investment. See Figure 5.2. The cut in the interest rate engineered by the monetary authorities moves investment along the given demand curve. The increase in investment will increase income and saving, shifting the supply curve of savings to the right. Any shift of this supply curve to the right means that the interest rate at a given amount of saving is at a lower level than before, even though a lower interest rate tends to reduce saving (at a given income level). For Keynes, who was concerned with the here and now of a downturn, the problem was to find the interest rate that corresponds to full employment, given the level of investment demand.

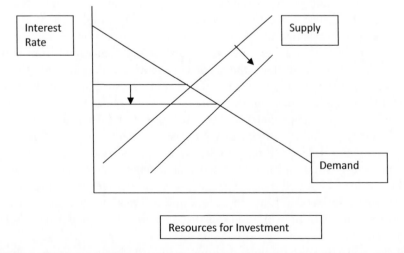

FIGURE 5.2 The Market for Resources for Real Investment. A cut in the interest rate engineered by the monetary authorities increases investment, and saving increases because income increases

Schumpeter on creative destruction

Joseph Schumpeter was a most prominent Austrian economist, along with Hayek, during the Keynesian era of the 1930s and 1940s. Schumpeter's 1942 book, *Capitalism, Socialism, and Democracy,* has been a big seller and a staple of college reading lists since the 1940s. Schumpeter has been justifiably renowned for what he called the process of creative destruction inherent in the capitalist economy. Schumpeter's (1942, p. 32) summary of this process states that:

> Possibilities of gains to be reaped by producing new things or by producing old things more cheaply are constantly materializing and calling for new investments. These new products and new methods compete with the old products and old methods not on equal terms but at a decisive advantage that may mean death to the latter. This is how "progress" comes about in a capitalist society.

Schumpeter built his work on business cycles around creative destruction and how it disrupts existing production methods with the investment in new technologies. These concepts are taught in today's schools of business administration (along with the related product cycle framework). But, with good reason, those schools rarely teach the second half of Schumpeter's story – that capitalism was being killed by its own success. We shall tell the whole story here because you should know it, and because it may have been the case that Schumpeter made his arguments to fit his end result. Economists no longer take the second part of Schumpeter's story seriously, or do they? See what you think.

Schumpeter recognized that modern capitalism produces industrial enterprises that operate at a very large scale and have some monopoly power, but this monopoly power is not of great concern because of the "perennial gale of creative destruction." Indeed, those large firms are the ones with the wherewithal to turn the process of creating new products and new processes into a routine function. In short, Schumpeter believed that the existence of large firms would increase the rate of product and process innovation. He did not stop there but went on to state that the people who made the innovations would be employees of large firms. In this process, the class of entrepreneurs and small business owners are largely wiped out. As firms become larger and larger, ownership is divorced from control. The owners of these firms lose their entrepreneurial function, and the firms are operated by professional managers. In addition, the success of the large firms will drive many smaller firms out of business. Few people are vitally concerned with the sanctity of private property and the freedom of private contracting. With fewer people left to defend the institution of private property, its opponents win the day. The opponents include intellectuals, who will persuade the mass of workers through the written and spoken word that socialism will improve the conditions of the working class and that the grossly unequal income distribution produced by capitalism is not needed to ensure economic progress. Capitalism thus destroys its own institutional framework and sets the stage for the socialistic takeover of those large firms.

What a prophecy! Schumpeter thought that the balance of forces he described would lead to the advent of socialism in the United States in about 50 years from the time he issued the third edition of his book (in 1947). Clearly, his prophecy was wrong in its timing. By the way, Schumpeter died in 1950, shortly after he reiterated his prophecy at the American Economic Association meetings.

Austrian business cycle theory

We shall now walk through the chain of logic of Austrian business cycle theory, with the assistance of Woods (2009, pp. 74–75).

1   We begin by positing a decline in the rate of interest, which can occur through (at least) two mechanisms: the public decides to save more at a given rate of interest, or the interest rate is reduced artificially by the central bank through monetary policy.

2   Businesses respond by starting new investment projects, which means purchasing current resources to be used for construction, capital equipment, and so on. Resources are diverted from current consumption.

3   If the interest rate has declined because the public has decided to save more, the market works well. The decision to reduce current consumption means that resources are available for investment goods, and firms can carry out the projects to completion.

4   On the other hand (a favorite phrase for economists), if the interest rate has been cut by an increase in the supply of money engineered by the central bank, not all of the investment projects can be completed because not all of the necessary resources have been released by the public. Indeed, low interest rates induce the public to save less. The prices of resources needed for investment projects (construction workers, capital goods) have increased. As Woods (2009, p. 74) puts it, "Investors have been misled into production lines that cannot be sustained." The economy has been stretched in two inconsistent directions. One has the image of condominium developments begun but not completed.

5   In the latter case, some new investment is inefficient use of resources. Some of those investments will not pay off in the longer run – which is the relevant time horizon for investment projects such as real estate construction. The cost of the investment projects may have turned out to be greater than expected, and the demand for the future output has been overestimated.

6   The market eventually catches on to the fact that "overinvestment" has occurred, and the demand for investment goods collapses as the prices of real capital assets (and the paper claims to them) fall. The end of the boom also may be initiated by an increase in the interest rate engineered by the monetary authority in order to tamp down the inflation that its previous interest rate cut has created.

7   One implication is that capital-intensive industries are more cyclical than other industries, but this is not the only business cycle theory with this implication. Another important implication of the theory is that the sooner the artificially low interest rate environment can be ended, the shorter and less painful the

subsequent economic downturn will be. Attempts to prop up the situation will only lead to a worse crash. **In other words, a decision by the monetary authorities to reduce the rate of interest during a recession is exactly the wrong thing to do**.

Caldwell (1995, p. 16) summarizes the theory:

> A typical cycle unfolds as follows. Banks expand credit, lowering the market rate of interest to induce firms to borrow. Firms use their newly created purchasing power to begin lengthening the process of production, just as if there had been a fall in the natural rate [as shown in Figure 6.1]. In a world in which all resources are fully utilized, this bids resources away from consumers. However, unlike the example in which the natural rate had fallen (because consumers decided to save more), consumers have not voluntarily reduced their real desired consumption. They are forced to consume less than they desire; Hayek accordingly attached the term "forced savings" to this phenomenon. The partially unmet demand for current consumption goods begins to push up the prices of such goods relative to future goods, or, put another way, the market rate of interest begins to rise. This signals firms that their previous decisions to undertake more roundabout investment projects had been incorrect, that the demand for future goods had not truly risen. The more roundabout projects are no longer profitable and must be abandoned before they come to fruition. This initiates the crisis, or slump, phase of the cycle.

As noted earlier, Keynes showed that there is a "formal error" in this scenario. A reduction in the interest rate through an increase in the supply of money will increase investment, which increases aggregate income and aggregate saving. The additional saving is not "forced saving" but rather comes from the increase in aggregate income. If the economy is operating below full employment, the reduction in interest rates moves the economy towards full employment. Of course, if the economy is at full employment, the increase in the money supply will produce inflation. The increase in saving brought about by the increase in investment spending just equals the increase in investment (in the simple Keynesian model shown previously).

The road to serfdom

Hayek was opposed to the whole idea of "top–down" macroeconomics as an approach to "managing" the economy. He believed that the economy is too complex for anyone (or small group of officials) to understand, and that an attempt of government to manage it is the "road to serfdom." As discussed in some detail in Chapter 4, Hayek is most famous for his 1944 book, *The Road to Serfdom*, which warns of the dangers of central planning and rule by men rather than by rules clearly stated. This view is in sharp contrast to both Keynesians and Monetarists. Keynesians think that fiscal and monetary policies skillfully used can smooth out business cycles. Monetarists such as Milton Friedman think that monetary policy should be conducted according to a clear–cut rule, because unexpected changes and mistakes in monetary policy cause great harm. Hayek believed that money should be issued by private firms and that the supply of money should not be under the control of a central bank. Former congressman and failed 2012 presidential candidate Ron Paul advocated abolishing the Federal Reserve in his 2009 book, *End the Fed*. The Austrian economists are his inspiration.

Woods (2009, p. 75) relates the Austrian theory to the financial crisis of 2008:

> The housing boom is a classic example of this theory in action.
>
> Artificially low interest rates misdirected enormous resources into home construction. We now know that was unsustainable. There were only so many $900,000 homes that the public, which had been saving very little, was in position to buy.

However, there is no evidence that the shift of production to housing resulted in "forced saving" on the part of consumers. The reduction of interest rates engineering by the Federal Reserve (the effects of which were magnified by the loosening of credit standards and financial engineering) had been designed to stimulate economic activity and employment coming out of the recession of 2001. Indeed, the policy succeeded only too well. The actions of the Federal Reserve contributed to a bubble in housing prices that further stimulated housing construction, which led to the crash in housing prices.

End the fed?

One modern Austrian economist, Roger Garrison (2005, p. 516) stated:

> The Austrians' policy advice to the central bank consists of prevention rather than cure: do not engage in credit expansion – not even if ongoing economic growth is causing some index of output prices to fall. Abiding by this imperative is not only politically difficult but also technically difficult, because the central bank cannot know what the natural rate of interest is and how it might be changing. The difficulties (both political and technical) of the central bank's avoiding a credit-inducing boom suggest that what is needed is fundamental reform rather than a policy prescription. Subsequent writings by contemporary Austrians . . . have made the case that a thoroughly decentralized banking system, one in which the market rate of interest is an unbiased approximation of the natural rate, may be the ultimate solution to the problem of boom and bust.

In other words, abolish the U.S. Federal Reserve System and other central banks.

As noted earlier, one public official, former congressman Ron Paul, has taken up the call and wrote a book titled *End the Fed*. Paul (2009, p. 141) stated:

> The Federal Reserve should be abolished because it is immoral, unconstitutional, impractical, promotes bad economics, and undermines liberty. Its destructive nature makes it a tool of tyrannical government. Nothing good can come from the Federal Reserve. It is the biggest taxer of them all. Diluting the value of the

dollar by increasing its supply is a vicious, sinister tax on the poor and the middle class.

Well, nobody's perfect.

Paul advocates the gold standard with no central bank, as opposed to fiat currency controlled by the central bank. The gold standard works as follows. Banks accept customer deposits and issue currency, both backed by gold held in reserve. Banks make loans by crediting the borrower's account and/or handing out the bank's currency. The prudent bank will hold enough gold reserves to satisfy its customers that the bank is safe and sound. The supply of money is constrained by the stocks of gold and by the prudent management of the banks. As Paul (2009, p. 190) put it, "Markets are self-regulating, responding to the wishes of consumers. It would be the same in banking." What could go wrong? He dismissed the thought that banking during the period of "wildcat banking" in the United States from 1830 to 1860 was unstable and unsafe. However, he did not mention the fact that the bank notes issued by the various state banks carried different values in actual trade based on the reputation of the individual bank. People had to carry around the latest version of the booklet that indicated the rates of exchange between the different bank notes. You might have a $10 bank note from Bank X, but it really would be worth only $9.

Congressman Paul was a member of the U.S. House Financial Services Committee, and he questioned the Federal Reserve chairmen frequently. He dug up an article written by Alan Greenspan (Fed chairman from 1987 to 2006) in 1966 in which Greenspan stated, "In the absence of the gold standard, there is no way to protect savings from confiscation through inflation. There is no safe store of value." Paul asked Greenspan whether he had this view. As recounted by Paul (2009, pp. 87–88), Greenspan said that he would not change a word of the article, but when asked whether monetary policy is needed, Greenspan responded:

> Once you decide that a commodity standard such as the gold standard is, for whatever reasons, not acceptable in a society and you go to a fiat currency, then the question is automatically, unless you have government endeavoring to determine the supply of the currency, it is very difficult to create effectively what the gold standard did. I think you will find, as I have indicated to you before, that most effective central banks in this fiat money period tend to be successful largely because we tend to replicate that which would probably have occurred under a commodity standard in general.

In other words, the nation had decided to go to a fiat currency and Greenspan was serving as the chairman of the central bank charged with the job of managing the nation's currency in the public interest, as defined by Congress in legislation. He answered questions from that perspective.

Paul found that Fed Chair Ben Bernanke (2006–2014) was less forthcoming in answering his questions about Austrian economics, the gold standard, and more current topics. Paul's conclusion (2009, p. 110) is that "If Greenspan was cocky about the genius of central bankers, Bernanke is even more so." Bernanke (2015, p. 450) stated that Paul "veered toward conspiracy theories." He notes that Paul pushed to have the Fed audited by the General Accounting Office as a step towards having Congress influence monetary policy. Bernanke's (2015, p. 451) conclusion on Ron Paul is that he lacked an understanding of how the gold standard actually had worked and that, "He was certainly sincere, but his thinking was dogmatic."

In the category of "the apple does not fall far from the tree," consider a column in *The Wall Street Journal* by Rand Paul, Ron's son and one of several candidates for President in 2016. The title of the article is "If only the Fed would get out of the way." He and coauthor Mark Spitznagel (2015) stated:

> The Austrian diagnosis leads to an unorthodox prescription: Rather than provide "stimulus" to boost demand during a slump, the Federal Reserve and Congress should stand aside. Recessions are a painful but necessary corrective process as resources – including labor – are guided toward sustainable niches, in light of the errors made during the giddy boom period.

Recessions are necessary. What about depressions?

Critics of Austrian theory

As noted previously, Keynes (1936, Chapter 14) devoted an entire chapter to criticizing the Austrian theory of saving and investment as depicted in Figure 5.1. The nub of the argument is as follows (1936, p. 179):

> The classical theory of the rate of interest seems to suppose that, if the demand curve for capital shifts or if the curve relating the rate of interest to the amounts saved *out of a given income* shifts or if both these curve shift, the new rate of interest will be given by the point of intersection of the new positions of the two curves. But this is a nonsense theory. For the assumption that income is constant is inconsistent with the assumption that these two curves can shift independently of one another. If either of them shift, then, in general, income will change; with the result that the whole schematism based on the assumption of a given income breaks down.
>
> (emphasis added)

In other words, the classical theory of interest tells us (1936, p. 181) "what the rate of interest will have to be, if the level of income is to be maintained at a given figure (e.g., the level corresponding to full employment)." For Keynes the rub is, of course, that the economy does not automatically get back to full employment during a depression.

Keynes (1936, pp. 192–193) also briefly mentions the Austrian theory of capital later in the *General Theory*. He argues that the theory confuses the prices of consumer and investment goods and the rate of interest. The decision by consumers to save more and spend less on consumer goods will tend to lower the prices of consumer goods relative to the prices on investment goods. The decision to save more will also tend to lower the rate of interest. Keynes pointed out that, with the combination of price declines for consumer goods and an interest rate decline, the net effect on the incentive to invest is not clear. However, it seems to me that Keynes neglected to include the idea that the demand for consumer goods will be greater in the future. That is why consumers have decided to save more now. Keynes was concerned with the here and now and the fact that the economy was stuck in an underemployment equilibrium. Austrian theory is concerned with the long run for an economy that tends to operate under conditions of reasonably full employment.

Milton Friedman was a conservative who had common cause with the Austrians on many issues of human freedom and free markets. But for Friedman, the ultimate test of an economic model is how well it works, and he believed that the Austrian business cycle theory outlined earlier does not pass the empirical test. Friedman (1993) reported on a series of empirical studies that he conducted over the years on whether a larger boom is followed by a larger contraction. His summary statement (1993, p. 171) is that "There appears to be no systematic connection between the size of an expansion and of the succeeding contraction, whether size is measured by physical volume or by dollar value." He goes on to note (1993, p. 172) that:

> For one thing, it would cast grave doubt on those theories that see as the source of a deep depression the excesses of the prior expansion (the Mises cycle theory is a clear example).

"Grave doubt" is not good. A recent book by Skousen (2005 p. 161) captured Friedman's conclusion but misquoted the Friedman article: "The Hayek–Mises explanation of the business cycle is contradicted by the evidence. It is, I believe, false. – Milton Friedman (1993, p. 171)."

Skousen (2005) responds to Friedman by citing some recent examples. The high-tech boom and bust of the late 1990s and early 2000s is a good example of investment that was based on real innovations but that ran far ahead of demand as the Federal Reserve increased the money supply in response to Y2K fears and financial problems abroad. The Japanese economy experienced rapid monetary growth in the late 1980s and asset price increases that defied reason, and this was followed by a severe crash and the "lost decade" of the 1990s.

As noted previously, Woods (2009) argues that the facts of the boom and crash of 2008 match the Austrian model well. We shall see about that in Chapter 14.

6

Real business cycles and supply-side economics

Introduction: the supply side

The supply side of the macro economy has been considered only briefly thus far (with the aggregate supply curve in Chapter 3). The basic idea is that an economy has a real potential output level (Y_p) at full employment that depends upon the existence of basic inputs into production and the efficiency with which those inputs can be combined to produce output (i.e., the level of production technology). Often economists refer to the extent to which the economy is operating below its potential. After all, that is what Keynes was all about. And recall that the Taylor rule for monetary policy makes the federal funds rate that is controlled by the U.S. Federal Reserve depend upon the shortfall in output below its potential level. Economists who study economic growth usually concentrate on ways and means to increase potential output. What are those ways and means? What are the factors that contribute to economic growth?

Economic growth is central to the entire discipline of economics. Adam Smith thought about it deeply in the book that many consider the founding document of economics, *An Inquiry into the Nature and Causes of the Wealth of Nations*. What is the nature of the wealth of nations? It is the ability to produce goods and services for the people of the nation, not the amount of gold piled in a vault. What are the causes of the wealth of nations? The causes are many and Smith discussed them, and the factors that inhibit productive economic activity, in over 900 pages. Smith's prescription (1937, p. 423) was a market system in which the individual "by directing industry in such a manner as its produce may be of the greatest value, he intends only his own gain, and he is in this, as in many other cases, led by an invisible hand to promote an end which was no part of it." This is the famous "invisible hand" passage.

Modern analysis of economic growth began after World War II when the field of economic development was founded. This field began by concentrating on the problems of economic growth in less-developed countries, but the field expanded to consider economic growth in all nations. Robert Solow is the most prominent contributor to the theory of economic growth, and he received the Nobel Prize for this work in 1987. It is fair to say that most subsequent research on economic growth either builds upon Solow's analysis or attempts to criticize his framework. Solow's (1957) basic framework is to state that the real output is a function of the economy's labor and capital inputs and an autonomous technological factor. In equation form,

$$Y = A\ f(L,K),$$

where L is an index of the labor input, K is an index of the capital input, and A is the autonomous technological factor that converts function f(L,K) into output. Solow stated that the growth of real output depends upon the growth of the labor and capital inputs employed and the autonomous factor, and that growth in real output per worker depends upon the growth of the capital input and the autonomous factor. Since the 1950s, much of the debate about economic growth has centered on the autonomous factor. Of what does it consist, and how can it be increased? Other debates focus on how to improve the quantity and quality of the labor and capital inputs.

Progress has been made in quantifying the sources of national growth. Solow's original study (1957) found that gross output per man hour (not value added), a measure of labor productivity, can be attributed primarily to the autonomous technological factor (87.5 percent), and the remaining 12.5 percent can be attributed to the increased use of capital. This justifiably famous study had one unintended consequence. It left the impression that economists had no coherent explanation for economic growth, and one sometimes still hears this stated. Numerous studies followed Solow. For example, Edward Denison (1985) estimated the sources of U.S. real economic growth for 1929–1982, which averaged 2.92 percent per year, as shown in Table 6.1. This study attributes 26 percent of economic growth to

TABLE 6.1   Sources of Growth: United States, 1929–1982

Factor	Contribution to U.S. Growth 1929–1982
Labor	34%
Education per worker	13%
Capital	17%
Advances in knowledge	26%
Improvements in resource allocation	8%
Economies of scale	8%
Other factors	−6%
Total	100%

Source: Denison (1985)

advances in knowledge but increases in labor and capital, and improvements in education, also figure in prominently.

A major puzzle arose when the rate of growth for the United States, which had been 2.5 percent per year from 1948 to 1973, fell to just 0.7 percent per year from 1973 to 1989. One result from this growth slowdown was that household incomes stagnated, and inflation-adjusted average hourly earnings in the private sector declined by 0.7 percent per year. Several possible causes for the slowdown in labor productivity have been advanced, and include:

- Decline in the average quality of the labor force;
- Failure to invest in public capital, the infrastructure;
- Increasing cost of raw materials (oil, etc.); and
- Increases in government environmental and safety regulations.

Researchers have not reached a consensus on the relative importance of these factors. Paul Krugman's (1990, p. 15) conclusion was:

> So we really don't know why productivity growth ground to a near-halt. That makes it hard to answer the other question: What can we do to speed it up?

The good news was that U.S. GDP growth was 3.55 percent per year from 1993–2001 as the result of the widespread adoption of computer technology. Since then, the growth of potential real output has returned to a slower pace of about 2.0 percent per year. Japan has experienced slow economic growth since 1990, a topic that is discussed in Chapters 12 and 14.

Solow imagined that advances in technology are public goods – goods that are available to anyone who cares to take the time to learn. Some advances in technology, such as math theorems published in academic journals, are public goods. However, modern growth theory, which is now 30 years old, imagines that technological progress is, as stated by Paul Romer (1990, p. 75), "a nonrival partially excludable" good. It is nonrival because everyone potentially can use it simultaneously, but partially excludable because it is possible to exclude some (perhaps most) from using it. Exclusion is done through patents and copyrights, which provide the incentive to invent new and/or improved technologies. The study of the economics of technological change is its own important field of study. (Economic growth theory is a public good, by the way, but not easy to learn.)

Real business cycle theory

The theory of real business cycles, which also is called the new classical theory, is an outgrowth of economic growth theory. It began with the observation that a modern economy such as that of the United States grows at a fairly even percentage rate, with some randomness around the long-run trend. In particular, the theory posits some randomness in the rate of technological progress. In contrast to the single-period model of the *General Theory*, the theory of real business cycles is about an economy that evolves over time. The theory is very mathematical – far more technical than the other macroeconomic theories discussed in the book. Fortunately, Snowdon and Vane (2005, p. 308) lay out the basic model with the following points.

- The economy consists of representative households and firms that maximize utility and profits, respectively, and operate in a perfectly competitive market economy.
- Rational expectations prevail.
- Prices are fully flexible so that market equilibrium always exists.
- Fluctuations in output and employment are caused by random changes in available production technology (the impulses).
- Impulses are carried forward by propagation mechanisms such as lags in investment ("time to build") and decisions of workers to supply more labor in certain time periods than in others.
- Fluctuations in employment are voluntary adjustments in labor supply. Work and leisure are assumed to highly substitutable over time.[1]
- The model is entirely in real terms. Money does not matter.

Snowdon and Vane (2005) provide a nifty example that permits us to get a sense of the model. Suppose a Robinson Crusoe economy (i.e., one person who both produces and consumes). Mr. Crusoe grows crops for food and clothing; some of the crops can be stored for next year, and clothing can be worn for more than one year. His choices for labor, leisure, production, and consumption are set at standard amounts for an average year. Suppose there is unusually good weather that makes Mr. Crusoe more productive, but just for one year. Mr. Crusoe takes advantage by working more, consuming more, and producing much more because he wants to be able to consume in the future. He works less during the next year because the weather is only average (and he has more goods stored from the good year). Output and employment have fluctuated. The variation in labor supply was completely voluntary, and there was no money in this little economy. Crusoe's labor and leisure are substitutable over time.

The other side of the story is what happens during a year with bad weather. Crusoe has stored up enough food to survive, and he knows that his labor for that year will be less productive. He cuts back on work, increases leisure, and cuts back some on consumption. He knows that the bad weather is temporary. Most likely, the weather will be average next year. So there it is – labor supply, output, and consumption vary together. During bad years he voluntarily increases leisure time, and in good years he spends more time working.

A very basic version of the model with markets and money can be depicted in the aggregate demand and supply diagram from Chapter 3 (but with different interpretation). Figure 6.1 shows aggregate demand and aggregate supply for a given stock of money and a given production technology. Aggregate demand has a negative slope for Keynesian reasons; a lower price level means an increase in the real supply of money (M/P) and a lower interest rate and greater investment. Aggregate supply is fixed by the available capital and technology and by the labor supply, i.e., Solow's equation. All markets clear. There is no involuntary unemployment. Now suppose that there is a positive shock to technology that makes labor more productive. The supply of labor shifts, and output expands as

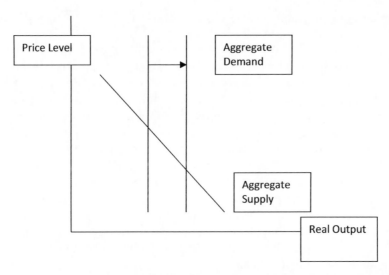

FIGURE 6.1 Aggregate Supply and Aggregate Demand. In real business cycle theory, aggregate demand increases as the price level declines because the real supply of money increases. The money wage moves with the price level to keep the real wage constant. Aggregate supply is fixed by the fixed supply of capital and the supply of labor at the equilibrium real wage. Shifts in aggregate demand have no impact on real output

shown. Prices fall because the supply of money is fixed and prices are completely flexible. A negative supply shock reduces output and increases prices. Negative supply shocks in the 1970s (increases in the price of oil) are prominent features of that decade. Real business cycle theory has the implication that the price level moves in the opposite direction from real output in response to shocks on the supply side. The theory also shows what happens if there is a shock on the demand side; a positive shock increases prices and a negative shock reduces prices, but aggregate supply does not change.

Real business cycle theory has been subjected to a hail of criticisms:

■ The theory requires that workers have a high degree of willingness to substitute work and leisure over time in response to temporary wage changes. There is little evidence that this is true.

■ The model depends upon unobservable shocks to technology. What are those shocks? (Shocks to the weather do not matter very much in a modern economy.)

■ All unemployment is voluntary, so recessions (and especially depressions) should be a time during which a lot of workers quit their jobs voluntarily because wages are reduced. In fact, empirical evidence shows the opposite. People do not quit much during a recession or depression.

■ Money is irrelevant, but both Keynesians and Monetarists contend that changes in the supply of money have effects on the real economy, at least in the short run.

■ The real business cycle economy is always operating at the optimum. There is no role for discretionary stabilization policy. There is nothing to be gained by acting to reduce "unemployment." Presumably government is supposed to collect taxes in order to supply public goods, but that is all.

Supply-side economics

Supply-side economics comes in two versions. Both versions state that economic growth is a good thing for many reasons. A larger pie means that everyone can have more (at least hypothetically). Work can be less onerous. Poverty can be reduced; lives can be prolonged and made more pleasant. People can have a wider range of choices regarding work, leisure, and consumption. Environmental impacts can be mitigated. One version is one with which all economists agree. That version states that economic growth depends upon many factors, such as those listed in Table 6.1. Society needs to figure out how to enhance the quality of the labor force, increase the rate of technical progress, make needed public infrastructure investments, stimulate private investment, and so on. Much research is devoted to these issues, and these goals are pursued through a variety of programs and incentives.

The other version of supply-side economics concentrates on a narrower range of public policies. Supply-siders such as Arthur Laffer and the late congressman Jack Kemp focused on cutting income tax rates on individuals and businesses in order to stimulate growth. Laffer argued that cutting tax rates, especially the tax rate on higher incomes, would actually increase tax revenue collected because of the incentive to produce more, hire more workers, and to engage in less tax avoidance and sheltering of income from taxes. Tax revenue equals the tax rate times the tax base. The idea is that the tax base will expand with a reduction in the tax rate enough to increase tax revenue. Laffer hypothesized that there is a marginal tax rate at which tax revenue is maximized. Tax revenue is less if the tax rate is higher or lower. The famous Laffer curve is shown in Figure 6.2.

This idea supposedly fit well with the conservative political agenda in favor of less government interference in the economy and reduction in government deficits. It is less clear that successful implementation of Laffer's proposal would mean cuts in

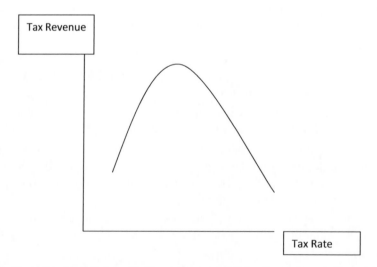

FIGURE 6.2 The Laffer Curve. Tax revenue equals the tax rate times the tax base. Laffer hypothesized that there is a tax rate at which further increases in the tax rate will cause the tax base to shrink so much that tax revenues fall

government spending. After all, the cut in tax rates was supposed to produce *more* tax revenue, and legislators can think of more ways to spend money. Laffer served as an adviser to U.S. President Ronald Reagan, and major tax cuts were made during the Reagan administration (1981–1989). The income tax rate on income in the highest bracket was cut in successive stages as follows:

Year	Top Tax Rate	Top Tax Bracket
1981	70 percent	$200,000 and up
1982	50 percent	$106,000 and up
1987	38.5 percent	$90,000 and up
1988	28 percent	$29,750 and up

The tax cuts resulted in a decline in tax revenue, not an increase. Apparently, the tax rate for the highest bracket that maximizes tax revenue is higher than 70 percent. Congress increased military spending in accordance with the President's plan and did not match the cuts in revenue with cuts in spending on other programs, so the federal deficit increased substantially. The total federal debt increased from $1.0 trillion in 1981 to $2.1 trillion in 1986. President Reagan's budget director from 1981 to 1985, David Stockman, was "taken to the woodshed" for pointing out the facts. His book *The Triumph of Politics: Why the Reagan Revolution Failed* (1986) was a best seller. The "triumph of politics" was that Congress resisted cutting spending, but who would have expected otherwise? Today, few argue that cutting the federal tax rate will increase tax revenue. The economy did grow nicely during the Reagan years. Keynesians argued that the large government deficits provided stimulus, while supporters of Reagan and Laffer argued that the tax cuts did it. The point is that a true "supply side" experiment was not run because tax cuts were not combined with cuts in government spending.

Subsequently, the income tax rate on the top bracket has been adjusted upward as follows (with a tax cut under U.S. President George W. Bush):

Year	Top Tax Rate	Top Tax Bracket	President
1991	31 percent	$82,150 and up	G. H. W. Bush
1993	39.6 percent	$250,000 and up	W. Clinton
2003	35 percent	$311,950 and up	G. W. Bush
2013	39.6 percent	$400,000 and up	B. Obama

Conclusion

Real business cycle theory grew out of economic growth theory and concentrates on the supply side of the economy. Economic fluctuations are the result of shocks to the supply side of the economy. The theory posits an economy of perfect markets and workers who substitute labor and leisure over time in response to incentives. There is no involuntary unemployment. The theory makes a contribution by bringing the supply side front and center. As we shall see, there are times when shocks to the supply side matter.

Supply-side economics focuses on the sources of economic growth, of which there are several. The version of supply-side economics that was influential during the Reagan administration emphasized cutting income tax rates to stimulate growth. While this idea still is influential in some quarters, including Republicans in the United States, the hypothesis remains unproven.

Note

1   Yes, this means that 10% of the labor force decided to take time off at one point during the financial crisis of 2008.

7 Modern Monetary Theory

Introduction

Modern Monetary Theory (MMT) is the newest member of the portfolio of macroeconomic theories. Some of its policy ideas date back to Abba Lerner (1947), but the current version of MMT dates back just to the 1990s. However, the ideas of the proponents of MMT in recent years hark back to notions about money that originated early in the 20th century. The main source for this chapter is the textbook by Wray (2015).

MMT rests on two basic propositions. The first is that fiat money, money with no "backing" such as gold, is the system we have. We accept fiat money because everyone else accepts it. In particular, the government issues fiat money and accepts it for payment of taxes. People need to accumulate fiat money in order to pay their taxes, and the government itself supplies that money. Article 1, Section 8 of the U.S. Constitution states that

> The Congress shall have Power To lay and collect Taxes. . . .
> To coin Money, regulate the Value thereof . . . .

In short, the government issues the means used to pay the taxes it imposes.

The second proposition is that financial wealth can be broken down into three basic categories representing three sectors of the economy. These are:

- Financial wealth of the government;
- Financial wealth of the domestic private sector (firms, households, nonprofit organizations, etc.); and
- Financial wealth of the nation's trading partners in international trade and other transactions.

Given this breakdown, the *change* in aggregate financial wealth over a time period, such as a year, must sum to zero. This proposition is not so easy to grasp, so follow along.

The change in the financial wealth of the government consists of income minus expenditures. Denote this change as $(\$ - E)_g$.

The change in the financial wealth of the domestic private sector simplifies to income minus expenditures also, denoted as $(\$ - E)_p$.

Now comes the harder part. The change in the financial wealth of the nation's trading partners (other nations) as it pertains to us is the net effect of their transactions with us; income minus expenditures involving us on the other side of the transactions. Denote this change for the financial wealth of the rest of the world as $(\$ - E)_{row}$. In simple terms, the value of our imports from trading partners minus our exports to the trading partners.

These definitions imply that

$$(\$ - E)_g + (\$ - E)_p + (\$ - E)_{row} = 0.$$

Financial transactions that take place within one of the sectors are called inside transactions, and transactions between sectors are known as outside transactions. For example, I own some shares of stock and you buy them from me. That is an inside transaction within the domestic private sector and has no effect on the total wealth within that sector.

Consider an example of an outside transaction. Suppose I receive my Social Security payment of $1,000 from the government. This amount is sent electronically to my bank account. My bank notifies the Federal Reserve Bank that this amount has been added to my account. The Federal Reserve Bank adds that amount to my bank's reserves held in its account at the Fed. The Federal Reserve subtracts the amount from the account of the U.S. Treasury, which is held at the Fed. The private sector has gained $1,000 in financial wealth, and the U.S. Treasury has a reduction in its financial wealth (the Social Security fund) of $1,000. The bank has no change in its financial position; liabilities are up $1,000 (my bank account), and assets are up $1,000 (reserves in its account at the Fed). Note that the government has created money out of thin air, because the Treasury has been given the authority to "coin Money." The Treasury does not really need a Social Security fund; it can just make a deposit to my bank account. If I want "real money," I can obtain ten $100 bills, which are also legal tender but are the same thing as a bank deposit.

Consider another example, this time including a foreign country. Say I own a government bond issued by Canada. During this year, I receive an interest payment of $100 from the Canadian government, and suppose the payment is in the form of a check. I deposit the check in my bank account. The check is cleared through the system operated by the Federal Reserve. The Canadian government has an expenditure of $100 and I have added $100 to my financial wealth. My bank has no change; liabilities are up $100, and assets are up $100 (reserves at the Fed). The Fed has added $100 in liabilities (my bank's reserve account) but has also received payment from the government of Canada of $100 when the check clears. (Central banks hold funds to be used in international transactions.) So no change in financial wealth for the Fed has occurred. The wealth of Canada has declined by $100 to match my increase.

Some background

In 1909, a German economist named Georg Knapp coined the term "chartalism," which is the idea that money originated with a government's effort to influence the amount of economic activity. For Knapp, fiat currency created by the government has value because the government accepts the currency in payment of taxes. His ideas differ from the more traditional idea that money either actually is gold or silver, with intrinsic value, or paper money that is backed by specie. Fiat money is created by law; money created by the government is "legal tender" that can be used to pay taxes, and therefore is accepted by all. Indeed, the use of "tax-driven" paper money had been around since Roman times.

The principle that the changes in the financial wealth of the three sectors must add to zero is based on the method of flow-of-funds accounting. The basic idea here is that double-entry bookkeeping is used to keep track of financial transactions. Two examples were outlined earlier. In the 1940s, an economist at Cornell University named Morris Copeland developed a system of flow of funds for the national income accounts, and the Federal Reserve produces a detailed report on the flow of funds for each quarter.

Flow-of-funds accounting has been adapted to the Keynesian model. Here is how it works. The adaptation is not perfect, as explained next. As you know, the Keynesian model is a model of real GDP (final output) and its components. Those components are consumption, investment, government purchases, and net exports:

$$C + I + G + (X - M) = GDP.$$

Now consider the three sectors – government, domestic private sector, and the foreign sector – in terms of the components of GDP.

The government sector collects taxes and spends on final goods and services (including the salaries of employees); the net change in GDP terms is $T - G$.

The private sector earns income from providing real capital and labor resources, and then spends some of the income, saves some, and pays taxes. The net change in GDP terms is the amount saved minus the amount spent on real investment, $S - I$.

Lastly, the foreign sector sends its imports and receives exports from the nation in question. The net change for the foreign sector is income minus expenditures, or $M - X$ (home country imports minus home country exports).

The flow-of-funds rule for GDP is therefore government balance plus private balance plus foreign balance:

$$(T - G) + (S - I) + (M - X) = 0, \cdot$$

which can be rewritten to say that total income equals total expenditure for the three sectors:

$$T + S + M = G + I + X.$$

At this point you may be asking, what happened to consumption in this equation? Here is the answer. We know that the private sector receives all of the income generated in the economy, and then spends on consumption, pays taxes, and saves. There is no other use for income. In equation form:

$$Y = C + T + S.$$

Total income is also equal to the GDP, so write:

$$Y = C + I + G + (X - M).$$

Substitute $C = Y - T - S$ for C in the equation for GDP to obtain

$$Y = Y - T - S + I + G + (X - M),$$

which can be rewritten as

$$T + S + M = I + G + X.$$

Consumption did not disappear, but it is lurking behind the flow of funds.

What is the difference between the GDP accounts and the flow-of-funds accounts? The main large difference involves amounts in GDP that are imputed and do not involve actual flows of funds. One large item in this category is the imputed rental value of owner-occupied housing. The GDP accountants estimate the rent that, in effect, a homeowner pays to himself or herself for the services rendered by the housing capital stock. This is such an "inside" transaction that it really does not occur. No actual transaction is involved. Nevertheless, the MMT proponents go ahead with the principle that the net changes for the three sectors in GDP terms sum to zero.

What use is made of the basic equation that

$$(T - G) + (S - I) + (M - X) = 0?$$

MMT analysts draw charts that show these three net items as they change over time. These charts show, for example, that when the private sector is running a big deficit (I greater than S), then either the government or the foreign sector, or both, are running surpluses.

MMT and economic policy

MMT has important policy implications. Those policies begin with the Keynesian Abba Lerner, and have been extended by the modern MMT economists.

Abba Lerner (1947) combined chartalism with Keynesian theory to develop his theory of functional finance. Functional finance includes these principles:

- The national government must accept responsibility for the prosperity of the economy, because market economies do not achieve full employment on their own. Such is a primary function of government. The United States adopted this principle with the Employment Act of 1946.

■ The government creates money, and money must be managed.

■ Fiscal policy should be directed by the goal of ensuring the prosperity of the economy. Balancing the government budget is not important. A nation that borrows only in its own currency does not face a debt constraint. The government can always print more money to service the government debt.

■ Government spending should be set to manage the economy – to achieve a certain desired level of aggregate demand. Taxes should be set according to their impact on economic activity, rather than to balance the government budget.

■ Sound finance, i.e., having a balanced budget, applies to all economic entities (households, firms, lower state and local governments, etc.) except for the national government, which issues money.

■ Interest rates in the economy should be set to produce the desirable level of investment.

Paul Krugman (2020b), a modern Keynesian economist and a winner of the Nobel Prize, thinks that Lerner was on the right track but was not entirely correct. He points out that Lerner did not say what the "desirable" level of investment would be and therefore what levels are correct for interest rates. Lerner was writing immediately after the Great Depression, a time during which very low interest rates had not succeeded in stimulating much real investment. But in more normal times, interest rates are not extremely low, and monetary policy can be used to raise and lower interest rates and have some impact on investment. In other words, during normal times, there is a tradeoff between fiscal and monetary policy.

According to standard modern Keynesian theory, increases in government deficits do cause interest rates to increase and therefore tend to "crowd out" private investment. Therefore, there is no unique level of the government deficit when the goal is to reach the full-employment level of aggregate demand. During normal times, the levels of government spending and taxes are determined by political forces, and monetary policy is used to adjust interest rates to achieve full employment without inflation (or just low inflation). Furthermore, Krugman (2020b) points out that the size of the government debt can become a problem if the interest rate on the debt exceeds the growth rate of the economy. Interest on the debt can require printing more and more money in relation to the size of the economy.

MMT economists reach nonstandard conclusions and make policy proposals that include Lerner's functional finance and more. Nonstandard conclusions include:

■ It is wrong to think that the government imposes taxes and/or sells government bonds in order to fund government expenses. Rather, the government issues money to pay for its expenses and requires that taxes are to be paid using that same money, so people will accept the money as legal tender for all debts public and private.

■ Demand can be insensitive to interest rate changes, so lowering interest rates is questionable policy.

■ Creating money by itself does not cause inflation, but spending the money when the economy is at full employment can cause inflation.

- Creating money and adding it to the domestic private sector bank accounts adds to bank reserves and can lower interest rates.
- Raising rates can be a form of stimulus, because money is deposited in bank accounts and the banks have more excess reserves with which to make loans.

MMT policy proposals include:

- Use functional finance, as described earlier. Set expenditures and taxes so as to achieve the level of aggregate demand consistent with full employment.
- Do not generate too much aggregate demand and cause inflation.
- Use a federally funded job guarantee (JG) as an automatic stabilizer. When jobs in the private sector are lacking, federally funded jobs are greater; when private sector jobs are sufficient to produce full employment, the JG program falls close to zero. Pay a living wage in the JG program.
- Permitting labor to be idle is immoral. Use functional finance and the JG program.

MMT overlaps with the work of Hyman Minsky. Wray (2015) wrote the book that is the source of much of this chapter, and he also wrote the book (2016) explaining *Why Minsky Matters*. In particular, as noted in Chapter 3, the JG proposal comes straight from the writings of Minsky.

Is MMT a new theory?

As this chapter has shown, MMT starts with some interesting observations about the macro economy; governments issue fiat money and people pay taxes with the same money, governments need not worry about the size of the budget deficit or the size of the national debt, and changes in net financial wealth sum to zero. We have also seen that MMT includes sizable elements of Keynesian theory, including the theory as applied to depression conditions. The Keynesian system of aggregate demand is used, and MMT economists think that an economy is often in a liquidity trap in which investment does not respond to monetary policy.

A new theory must have new hypotheses that can be tested empirically and possibly rejected. Does MMT meet this test? I hope that a lively discussion will be had about this question. I would make the following observations:

- MMT follows Keynesian theory in presuming that expenditures by the private sector depend upon income. This is not new and has been tested for decades with considerable success (and numerous caveats).
- MMT hypothesizes that issuing money to pay for expenditures can lower interest rates rather than raise interest rates (as hypothesized by Keynesians).
- MMT also hypothesizes that an increase in interest rates paid on the national debt generates more money in the private economy and can therefore be stimulative.
- The equation stating that $(\$ - E)_g + (\$ - E)_p + (\$ - E)_{row} = 0$ is correct.

Wray (2015, p. 35) includes a chart showing these figures as a percentage of total spending. Table 7.1 shows the figures for three representative years.

TABLE 7.1 Sector Financial Balance as a Percentage of GDP

Year	$(\$ - E)_g$	$(\$ - E)_p$	$(\$ - E)_{row}$	Sum
1982	−7%	6%	1%	0
1999	1%	−5%	4%	0
2009	−12%	8%	4%	0

Source: Wray (2015, p. 35)

We see that the three changes in financial wealth do indeed sum to zero as posited. However, the equation in question is really an identity. It is true by definition. The data in Table 7.1 are not an empirical test of the theory in which there is a hypothesis that can be found to fail.

Robert Murphy (2019), an Austrian economist, makes a basic point. To simplify, eliminate the foreign sector and write in GDP terms:

$$S - I = G - T.$$

This is a tautology. One can say that if government spending increases with taxes constant, saving will increase. As MMTers would say, private sector saving depends on government spending. However, as Keynesians or Austrians would say, increasing government spending leaving taxes constant reduces private investment, i.e., government spending crowds out private investment. Or private saving can increase *and* investment can decrease. Take your pick. The tautology is consistent with any story you wish to tell.

The other two hypotheses listed previously regarding interest rates are testable, and efforts should be undertaken to conduct the required empirical tests.

Summary of macroeconomic theories

Macroeconomic theories have been presented in Chapters 2 through 7. I do not expect you to remember them all. Well, not at first. So for your convenience, I have summarized them for you in Table 7.2. Refer to this table as often as you need. I suggest you attach a paper clip to the page.

Now, we go on to the Great Depression.

TABLE 7.2 Macroeconomic Theories and Facts

Theory	Important Propositions and Facts
Keynesian	Aggregate demand drives economy. Investment is volatile. Economy does not recover quickly from severe downturn. Monetary policy may not work in severe downturn. Unemployment–inflation tradeoff. Prosperity leads to financial instability (Minsky version).

(Continued)

TABLE 7.2 (Continued)

Theory	Important Propositions and Facts
Monetarist	Money supply drives prices in the long run.
	Money supply drives prices and output in the short run.
	Monetary policy needs a clear rule because serious mistakes have been made.
	No long-run unemployment–inflation tradeoff.
Real Business Cycle	Negative supply shocks start downturn.
	Prices adjust and markets clear quickly.
	If money supply is constant, prices fall with positive supply shock and rise with negative supply shock.
	Involuntary unemployment does not exist.
Supply-Side	Tax cuts, matched by government spending cuts, stimulate the private economy.
	Tax cuts increase tax revenue (maybe).
Austrian	Prices adjust and markets clear quickly.
	Lowering of interest rate below that which is determined in the private market leads to overinvestment and eventual downturn.
Modern Monetary Theory	Government issues fiat money, which everyone accepts because it is used to pay taxes.
	Use functional finance to attain full employment.
	The size of the government deficit does not matter.
	Do not create so much money so as to generate inflation.
	Use fiscal policy. Monetary policy may not work.

8

The Great Depression

Introduction

The Great Depression of the 1930s was both the deepest and longest depression in U.S. and European history. This chapter provides a brief review of the facts and theories that have been advanced as explanations for this economic disaster. The focus of the chapter is on the U.S. and U.K. economies, but briefer discussions of other European economies are included. Some of the same themes are pertinent to the first decade of the 21st century. A great number of economists and historians have weighed in on the Great Depression, of course, and there is no consensus on a single main cause of the depression. However, there does appear to be agreement that there were several causes and exacerbating factors.

The English classical economist A. C. Pigou published a book titled *Industrial Fluctuations* in – of all years – 1927, in which he examined six possible fundamental reasons for economic fluctuations. These are errors of optimism and pessimism, agricultural fluctuations caused by weather, new inventions, monetary instability, changes in tastes, and industrial strikes. But Pigou argued that, in all cases, the economy would return to full employment quickly. As noted in Chapter 2, Pigou served as the main example of outmoded thinking for Keynes.

As you know already, most macro economists divide into three main schools of thought – Keynesian, Monetarist, and real business cycle. (The Austrians are a small group among professional economists.) According to Keynes (1936), a depression is the result of aggregate demand that is deficient to employ the resources of a nation. Demand consists of four categories: private consumption, private investment, government purchases of goods and services, and net foreign trade in goods and services. These four add up to the gross domestic product (GDP), the total measure of the value of all final goods and services produced during a year. In a nutshell, Keynes thought that private investment was the volatile component of aggregate demand because it depended on expectations of future profits, and those expectations can change abruptly according to "animal spirits," the willingness (or unwillingness) to take risks. If firms look ahead and conclude that future profits are not there, then investment spending on plants and equipment will drop quickly.

Likewise, builders of housing (also a component of investment) decide to cut back based on their expectations. Employment falls, so household income falls, which in turn causes declines in consumption spending and further declines in employment and income. This process is the Keynesian multiplier.

When the economy turns down, Keynes insisted, the government must step in to stimulate investment through monetary policy and to stimulate demand directly by increasing government purchases of goods and services. Monetary policy is used to lower interest rates in an attempt to induce investment spending, but Keynes also believed that sometimes this effort will be ineffective. If firms are very pessimistic about the future, lower interest rates may not matter much at all. Indeed, Keynes thought that such was the situation in the Great Depression. Fiscal policy (cutting taxes and increasing government spending) was the effective policy tool. Keynes thought that there was no automatic mechanism that would return the economy to full employment.

Advocates of Modern Monetary Theory go even further than the Keynesians in arguing that budget deficits and debt of the national government do not matter. Fiscal policy, in the form of functional finance, should take the lead in stabilizing the economy. State and local government must maintain balanced budgets, but the national government issues the currency, which is used to pay taxes. The national government does not collect taxes to pay for public expenditures. Rather, taxes are assessed in government currency so that people will accept the fiat currency.

Monetarists think about the essential role of money in a market economy. Their basic framework says that:

$$\text{Money Supply} \times \text{Velocity of Money} = \text{Real Output} \times \text{Price Level (GDP)}.$$

This basic framework is called the Quantity Theory of Money. The money supply consists of the bank accounts of households and firms plus the amount of currency in circulation. The velocity of money is the ratio of GDP to the money supply. For example, if the money supply is $4 trillion and the velocity of money is 3, then GDP is $12 trillion. The velocity of money is the number of times the money supply is used to buy final goods and services in a year. Here is the catch: Suppose the money supply falls to $3 trillion and the velocity of money remains 3. Then the GDP will fall to $9 trillion. This decline consists either of a fall in real output or a decline in the price level (or both). On the other side of the coin, so to speak, if the money supply increases to $5 trillion with a constant velocity of money, then GDP increases to $15 trillion – accomplished by an increase in real output or the price level or both. If the economy is at full employment, only the price level increases. As the leading Monetarist Milton Friedman said on occasions too numerous to count, "Inflation is always and everywhere a monetary phenomenon."

The real business cycle group thinks that economic fluctuations are caused primarily by shocks, both negative and positive, to the supply side of the economy. Also, they think that markets adjust quickly so that there is no involuntary unemployment. Workers adjust their work and leisure over time in an optimal manner given the wages and employment opportunities. The Austrians agree that the economy will recover on its own. And they warn against using monetary policy to stimulate the economy by lowering interest rates, thereby (according to them) creating a misallocation of resources in favor of investment that leads to trouble.

Views regarding macroeconomic policy vary. Monetarists, the real business cycle group, and the Austrians believe that a market economy, if left to its own devices, would return from a downturn to full employment. An automatic adjustment mechanism – market incentives – would do the trick. Macroeconomic policy, if exercised by fallible humans, could disrupt this mechanism. Therefore, the basic policy conclusion of the Monetarists was that the money supply should increase automatically at a rate just slightly above the rate of real economic growth, say 3 percent. Instead, a massive wave of bank failures and a huge decline in the supply of money occurred in the United States from 1929 to 1932, and the Federal Reserve Bank did nothing to prevent this disaster. Discretionary monetary or fiscal policy likely would be badly timed or just plain mistaken.

So there you have it. Keynesians look to a drop in aggregate demand – investment spending in particular – as a basic cause of the depression, and they look to fiscal policy to bring the economy back to full employment. Note that the Keynesian remedy includes a sustained increase in the level of public spending until private investment recovers, not a "one-shot" increase to "prime the pump." Oh, and "jump start" and "economy" do not belong in the same sentence, in my opinion. In contrast, Monetarists look for a decline in the supply of money as the major cause of a depression. As it happened, both aggregate demand and the supply of money fell – a lot. The real business cycle group looks for shocks on the supply side, while the Austrians blame the central bank.

The U.S. and U.K. economies in the 1920s

The U.S. economy had emerged from World War I intact and the largest in the world. President Woodrow Wilson represented the United States at the Versailles Treaty negotiations, and the League of Nations was founded. But the United States did not join the League. The United Kingdom, France, and Italy had borrowed a great deal of money from the United States and were supposed to get reparations payments from Germany. Germany printed money like crazy and had hyperinflation and resorted to barter. The allies continued to borrow from the United States to pay for imports. The United States had positive balance of trade with high tariffs and low interest rates. Borrowed money paid for the imports from the United States and paid war debts.

Macroeconomic data for the 1920s show strong growth in real gross national product (GNP) and employment in the United States after the 1921 downturn. Over the years 1923 to 1929, real GNP increased by 22 percent (about 3 percent per year), and non-farm employment increased from 32.1 million to 37.1 million (a 15.6 percent increase) as the population increased by 8.9 percent. The unemployment rate varied between 4.2 percent and 5.5 percent from 1923 to 1928 and reached a low of 3.2 percent in 1929. However, the stock market took off into bubble territory after about 1925. The Dow Jones index hit a high of 105 in 1923, 155 in 1925, and 200 in 1927, and then ballooned to 381 just prior to the crash in 1929.

J. K. Galbraith's *The Great Crash* (1954) provides an entertaining recounting of the period. The 1920s were good times for most of the U.S. population, except for farmers, blacks in the South, and whites in Appalachia and in urban slums. Farmers suffered from the extension too far into the Great Plains and mechanization, all of which produced a large increase in supply and declining prices.

The land bubble in Florida gave a taste of how a bubble works. The Florida land boom of 1924–1925 was fueled by easy credit, with 10 percent down. People bought swamp land and land far from the ocean at inflated prices. The increase in land value when land was resold was the profit to that 10 percent equity. Huge returns were made until a 1926 hurricane gave people pause. A man named Ponzi was involved. . . .

What set off the stock market? One cause was the revaluation of the British pound to its prewar value of $4.86 per dollar and fixed value in terms of gold. This increase in value was engineered by Winston Churchill, then Chancellor of the Exchequer. This made British exports expensive and imports cheap and created a large current account deficit. Also, interest rates in the United States were relatively high. Gold flowed to the nation. At the request of Britain, the Fed lowered the discount rate. Funds available at a low interest rate were invested in stocks. Did the Fed cause stock speculation? Well, maybe it added to it.

The system for buying stocks: banks borrow from the Fed and make loans to stockbrokers, and stockbrokers make loans to customers to buy stocks. Margin requirement at first was only 10 percent. Banks could borrow at maybe 5 percent from the Fed and earn 12 percent on the call loan market. A call loan is a loan that requires some payback if the value of the collateral (stocks) falls below the outstanding balance on the loan. This is a margin call. Investment trusts were created to own stocks so customers could buy shares in the investment trust (sort of like mutual funds). Banks made loans to the investment trusts, which made loans to customers – all call loans with relatively low margin requirements. Dividends on stocks pay the interest on the loans made to investment trusts. What if dividends decline? This is a house of cards (my words) that has to rely on increasing stock values.

What about the Fed? Galbraith says it was startlingly incompetent, but in fact it had few bonds to sell to reduce bank reserves. It could increase the discount rate, but that would have had little effect because of the huge profits banks were making in the call loan market. Besides, non-banks were making call loans too. The Fed could have asked Congress for permission to set margin requirements, but it did not. C. Mitchell, CEO of National City Bank and a member of the Federal Reserve Board, said he would make loans to offset any Fed policy. In effect, the Fed acted to evade responsibility.

Some signs of economic slowdown were taking place in the first half of 1929. In fact, home building had peaked in 1926, and banks were failing in the farm sector. Consumption spending had leveled off; auto production peaked in June and steel peaked in July. Inventories were accumulating. The Fed lowered the discount rate in 1927 but increased in April 1928 in an attempt to tamp down the bubble. M2 fell by 1 percent from then to November 1929.

The actual stock market crash began on September 3, 1929, when a man named Babson wrote an article saying that the stock market could fall at any time. He had been saying this for months (years?), but this time he was right. Increases in stock values came to an end, and they had started to fall by early October. October 24, 1929 is called Black Thursday, but stock values were falling during all of October and November. Major banks attempted to support the market but gave up. (Banks could buy stocks at that time.) The Fed lowered the discount rate and purchased bonds from banks, but to no avail. The Dow fell from 381 in September to 199 in November, and then came back to 250 in December.

When stock values are declining, investors try to leave the market. When they leave in large numbers (frantic selling), stock values fall a lot, which leads to more selling. . . .

What is short selling? It is making a bet that values will fall. You borrow some stock with a promise to return it at some later date. Then you sell it immediately. When you return the stock at the later date, you buy stock at a lower price and net a pile of money. The "shorts," as they are called, were having a field day.

The stock market had a classic bubble fueled by easy credit, optimistic mood, and prosperity with ample savings by the well-to-do. Minsky argued that prosperous times can lead to asset price increases, which can breed further increases that get out of hand. But this is not always the case, and the trick is to know when it's happening. Only about 1 million were invested in stocks.

It is useful to know some of the details about the United States in the years prior to the Great Depression:

- Increased productivity and overexpansion in agriculture caused prices to fall in the late 1920s, which caused loans to farmers to go bad, which in turn made banks in the agricultural areas insolvent. These insolvent banks weakened the rest of the financial system. Banks failed in large numbers from 1929 to 1933 as the depression deepened (and the Federal Reserve did not step in to prevent these failures), which caused a large drop in the supply of money – bank accounts in particular.

- Both consumption and investment boomed in the 1920s, but spending on consumer durables leveled off starting in 1926 and residential construction began to decline after 1926. However, firms continued to issue stock and borrow money in 1928 and 1929 and to produce more consumer durables in the face of the leveling of consumer demand and falling prices. Auto production peaked in June 1929, iron and steel peaked in July 1929, and construction already had peaked in April or May of that same year. Consumption did not increase in 1929, so inventories increased sharply. In short, there was overinvestment. Investment spending plummeted by 90 percent from 1929 to 1932.

- Consumer credit was used extensively for the first time in the 1920s. Households undertook historic levels of debt. Home mortgages were of short duration, many just five years, and monthly payments just covered the interest on the loan, so homeowners had to refinance upon expiration of the loan. When the economy went into recession and incomes declined and unemployment increased, the house values fell. Many homeowners were unable to refinance their home loans and defaulted.

- The stock market boomed as investors borrowed to buy stocks "on margin." The stock market is regarded as a "leading indicator" of the economy. The crash of the stock market in October 1929 was a strong signal of trouble in the real economy. But note that the stock market crash came after the real economy had begun to decline.

■   The Fed had cut the discount rate in 1927 but later was concerned about the speculative boom in stock prices and moved to tighten credit starting in 1928. One measure of the money stock (currency, demand deposits, and time deposits – M2) declined at a rate of 1 percent per year from April 1928 to November 1929. This policy ended in the wake of the stock market crash.

The hypotheses are that the recession that began in 1929 was caused by these factors: problems in the agricultural sector (which was still a pretty large part of the economy), too much credit, overinvestment by firms (especially those producing durable goods), and a stock market bubble that ended, partly by actions of the Fed to tighten credit.

The story of the U.K. economy in the 1920s is quite different from the "roaring twenties" experienced in the United States. The United Kingdom experienced a decade of deflation and stagnant growth. First let us take a quick look at the data, and then we will consider causes of the stagnant economy.

After a postwar recovery in which the unemployment rate was 1.8 percent in 1920, unemployment jumped to 9.5 percent in 1921 and remained at 7.8 percent or higher until 1926. The average unemployment rate for 1927 to 1929 was 7.3 percent (with 7.8 percent in 1929). Wholesale prices fell by 25 percent from 1921 to 1929, but wages did not follow suit. The increase in real wages tended to reduce employment. British exports were concentrated in heavy industries such as coal, shipbuilding, and steel. Unions opposed cuts in nominal wages, and a general strike took place in 1926. Coal miners had bitter disputes with the mine owners over pay and working conditions, and other unions joined the strike. However, other unions did not join the strike and the miners were defeated. U.K. industries were slow to switch out of old industries such as cotton, iron and steel, and coal, and move into the newer growth industries such as chemicals and automobiles.

Macroeconomic policy in the United Kingdom bears considerable responsibility for the problems. Fiscal policy provided no help; the government ran a budget surplus for most of the 1920s. One big decision was to return to the gold standard at the prewar rate of $4.85 per pound. In other words, consumers in the United States who wished to import goods from the United Kingdom had to pay $4.85 for one pound to pay for the imports. The exchange rate also meant that products exported from the United States to the United Kingdom were relatively cheap. This pound was substantially overvalued, and this meant that the United Kingdom would run a sizable deficit on current account in the balance of payments (see Chapter 1, right?). How could the United Kingdom overcome the deficit on current account? The answer is high interest rates to attract foreign capital. So the over-valuation of the pound meant that the Bank of England had to maintain high interest rates, which naturally had a depressing effect on the economy. Furthermore, the deflation meant that the real interest (corrected for deflation) was even higher! Keynes famously argued that the exchange rate decision was a big mistake. Winston Churchill, the national hero of course but no economist, was the Chancellor of the Exchequer who made the fateful decision. The exchange rate remained at $4.85 per pound until the United Kingdom went off the gold standard in 1931. We will have much more about going off the gold standard later in this chapter.

Data and narrative for the United States

Table 8.1 shows the severity of the depression in the United States in numerical form. Table 8.2 is a display of similar date for the United Kingdom In the United States, GDP fell by 45.6 percent from 1929 to 1933 (26.6 percent in real, deflation-adjusted terms); consumption spending fell by 40.8 percent, and investment fell by 90 percent in nominal terms (not adjusted for inflation or, in this case, deflation). Government purchases of goods and services actually increased in 1930 and 1931 but as of 1933 had fallen by 7.4 percent compared to its 1929 level. President Hoover (1932) stated, in a speech given during his campaign for reelection in 1932,

> The federal government has been forced in this emergency to unusual expenditure, but in partial alleviation of these extraordinary expenditures the Republication administration has made a successful effort to reduce ordinary running expenses of the government.

Atack and Passell (1994) walked through the four categories of aggregate demand. The decline in consumption in nominal terms was 40.8 percent from 1929 to 1933, and some of that decline took place early on during these years. Atack and Passell (1994) note some reasons for the decline in consumption besides

TABLE 8.1 U.S. Macroeconomic Data, 1929–1940

Year	GDP $ bil.	Con- sump. $ bil.	Invest- ment $ bil.	Gov't Pur- chases $ bil.	M1* $bil.	Real GDP $1996 bil.	Non-farm Empl. million	Manuf. Empl. million	Unem. Rate Pct	Darby Unem. Rate Pct	Price Index Whls.
1929	103.7	77.5	16.5	9.4	26.1	822	31.3	10.7	3.2	3.2	52.1
1930	91.3	70.2	10.8	10.0	25.7	752	29.4	9.6	8.7	8.7	47.3
1931	76.6	60.7	5.9	9.9	24.6	704	26.6	8.2	15.9	15.3	39.9
1932	58.8	48.7	1.3	8.8	21.5	612	23.6	6.9	23.6	22.9	35.6
1933	56.4	45.9	1.7	8.7	20.6	603	23.7	7.4	24.9	20.6	36.1
1934	66.0	51.5	3.7	10.6	19.7	668	25.9	8.5	21.7	16.0	41.0
1935	73.3	55.9	6.7	10.9	23.6	728	27.0	9.1	20.1	14.2	43.8
1936	83.7	62.2	8.6	13.1	27.1	822	29.1	9.8	16.9	9.9	44.2
1937	91.9	66.8	12.2	12.8	30.6	866	31.0	10.8	14.3	12.5	47.2
1938	86.1	64.2	7.1	13.8	29.3	836	29.2	9.4	19.0	11.3	43.0
1939	92.0	67.2	9.3	14.7	31.7	904	30.6	10.3	17.2	9.5	42.2
1940	101.3	71.2	13.6	15.1	36.5	981	32.4	11.0	14.6		43.0

Sources: Historical Statistics of the United States, Friedman and Schwartz (1963), Darby (1976), and NBER Macrohistory Database

* M1 is the supply of money consisting of currency held by the public and demand deposits. Figures are for January of each year. The low point of $19.4 billion was reached in April 1933.

TABLE 8.2 U.K. Macroeconomic Data, 1929–1940

Year	Real GDP £bil. (2013)	Real Con- Sump.	Real Invest- ment	Real Gov't Purchse	Real Export	Real Import	M1 (£mil.)	Employ- Ment (mil.)	Un-emp. (Pct.)	Whsl Price (2010 =100)	Bank Rate (Pct.)
1929	245	169	19.4	46.6	38.4	39.3	1438	19.4	7.18	1.76	5.50
1930	243	172	19.5	47.8	33.0	38.9	1489	19.1	11.10	1.48	3.38
1931	232	174	19.1	48.8	26.6	40.3	1383	18.6	14.88	1.28	4.67
1932	232	173	16.7	48.8	26.0	36.0	1483	18.7	15.39	1.24	2.83
1933	239	180	17.3	49.5	26.5	35.9	1571	19.1	13.73	1.23	2.00
1934	254	184	21.0	50.6	27.5	37.5	1619	19.6	11.73	1.26	2.00
1935	263	189	21.8	54.1	31.0	39.4	1750	20.0	10.87	1.30	2.00
1936	276	196	23.9	59.1	30.1	40.3	1913	20.6	7.25	1.37	2.00
1937	285	199	24.7	65.8	31.6	41.8	1955	21.3	7.70	1.58	2.00
1938	288	198	25.0	78.5	29.5	41.0	1919	21.4	9.20	1.41	2.00
1939	300	197	22.4	119.1	27.4	44.4	2093	22.2	5.68	1.48	2.25
1940	330	172	19.4	274.9	18.6	46.5	2529	23.0	2.99	1.98	2.00

Source: Thomas, Ryland, and Dimsdale, Nicholas, Three Centuries of Macroeconomic Data, Version 2.3, available online

simple reaction to rising unemployment. These include declining incomes among farmers as prices of farm products fell as a result of oversupply, loss of wealth because of the stock market crash, and general deflation that made debtors worse off because they had to pay off debts using dollars that had appreciated in real value. The drop in nominal consumption spending in 1932 of 19.8 percent is especially notable. Perhaps one quarter of the decline in consumption can be attributed to these factors.

The decline in investment was so large that investment spending in 1932, 1933, and 1934 was insufficient to cover the depreciation of the capital stock. The stock of capital in the economy was shrinking. Atack and Passell (1994, p. 598) indicated that the decline in investment spending was sufficient to explain the entire decline in aggregate demand from 1929 to 1933. Residential construction is a component of investment, and there was overbuilding in the years before 1929, in part because of a reduction in the growth in the number of households. In short, the Keynesian explanation for the Great Depression based on the volatility of investment is a dog that hunts.

U.S. exports fell as the trading partners fell into depression as well. Many of those nations, such as Great Britain, took themselves off the gold standard and devalued their currencies before the United States did so in 1933. Devaluation makes imports from the United States more expensive because British pounds buy fewer U.S. dollars, so U.S. exports fell. And the United States imposed much higher tariffs on imports by adopting the Smoot-Hawley legislation in 1931. Other nations retaliated, which made U.S. exports even more expensive in those countries. U.S. exports were $7.0 billion in 1929 and fell to $2.4 billion in 1933, a decline of 65.7 percent, and imports fell from $5.9 billion to $2.0 billion over these same years (down 66.1 percent). The system of international trade basically broke down, and really did not get going again until after World War II.

Government spending did increase during the first years of the Hoover administration but then declined. Predictably, tax revenues fell as the downturn intensified. So a tax increase was imposed in June 1932. The tax increase moved the federal government budget from deficit to surplus. Oops.

The supply of money (M1, measured as currency held by the public plus demand deposits in banks) fell by 25.7 percent from January 1929 to the low point in April 1933. As Friedman and Schwartz (1963) showed, the Fed had done nothing to prevent the massive bank failures that led to losses of bank deposits (i.e., the supply of money). Bernanke (1983) has shown that the bank failures prolonged the depression by disrupting the ability of businesses and households to obtain credit through the normal channel of bank loans. The decline in the money supply matters, but so does the condition of the financial system as the downturn unfolds. The condition of the financial system played a major role in the recent financial crisis and deep recession.

Wholesale prices fell by 31.7 percent from 1929 to 1932 (a 21.3 percent drop from 1929 to 1934). According to the National Bureau of Economic Research, nominal wages fell by 20.6 percent from 1929 to 1933. It was not true that prices and wages were inflexible. Deflation makes debtors worse off because their debt service obligations do not decline. The low point for non-farm employment was 1932, which was off by 24.6 percent from its 1929 level. Manufacturing employment was more strongly affected than was total non-farm employment and had dropped by 35.2 percent over these same years. The official unemployment rate was 23.6 percent in 1932 compared to 3.2 percent in 1929. Prices fell a great deal in both the Great Depression and in the short depression of 1921. Flexible prices helped recovery in the earlier episode but were harmful in the early 1930s. How did these episodes differ? The decline in the real economy was much larger in the Great Depression, the money supply plummeted, and the banking system was left in a bad condition. Deflation sent households and firms into bankruptcy in the early 1930s.

Recovery from the depression began in 1934, and the macroeconomic aggregates improved steadily up through 1937. However, the official unemployment rate was still a very high 14.3 percent in 1937. The number of non-farm jobs had almost regained its 1929 total, but the increase in the labor force of 9.8 percent meant that unemployment was still pervasive. Darby (1976) found what he believes to be a flaw in the official unemployment rate data, in that people who were employed on public relief jobs were counted as unemployed (presumably because they were looking for "real" jobs). Public relief jobs included the Works Progress Administration and the Civilian Conservation Corps. Darby's correction to the official unemployment rate in 1936 brought it down from 16.9 percent to 9.9 percent. Government spending did increase starting in 1934, but clearly the increased spending was not enough to offset the declines in consumption and investment from their 1929 and 1930 levels. The supply of money began to increase in 1935 as the banking sector began to recover after the adoption of the federal deposit insurance system, and wholesale prices had begun to rise in 1933.

African Americans had higher rates of unemployment than did whites during the Depression. Sundstrom (1992) showed that the unemployment rate for African-American males in the seven largest cities of the North in 1931 was 39.8 percent, compared to 31.1 percent for white males. The corresponding unemployment rates for females were 46.8 percent and 17.9 percent. In 1936, the unemployment rate for African-American male household heads in 83 cities of the North was 17.9 percent, compared to 10.8 percent for whites. Female household heads had corresponding unemployment rates of 24.4 percent and 11.5 percent. Sundstrom (1992) found that the unemployment differential by race for males could be attributed to differences in occupational status. However, for females the unemployment differential existed within specific occupations. Sundstrom concluded that racial discrimination was a factor in producing the unemployment differentials, especially in the case of woman in unskilled service sector jobs.

The bottom of the Great Depression had occurred in 1933, the same year that President Franklin Roosevelt was inaugurated. He found an economy with massive unemployment and an exchange rate that was too high. See Chapter 3; the Keynes–Meade policy prescription is to increase domestic demand and lower the exchange rate. Roosevelt took the nation off the gold standard two days after he was inaugurated – on March 6, 1933 – and devalued the dollar over the following year. His monetary policy was to increase the supply of money and turn the deflation into price increases. Rauchway (2015) provides a detailed history of FDR's monetary policy that followed the advice of Keynes and his economic advisors in the United States. Recall from Chapter 1 that adherence to the gold standard requires deflation to stimulate exports, but it was obvious that deflation was hurting debtors and not stimulating the economy. Modern research by several scholars, including Bernanke (2000) and Eichengreen (1992), shows that countries that went off the gold standard recovered from the depression earlier because monetary policy was freed from worrying about the stock of gold and could pursue a program of stimulating the economy.

The next four years, 1934 to 1937, display significant economic recovery. Growth of the money supply resumed, wholesale prices increased by 30.8 percent from 1934 to 1937, and real GDP in 1937 exceeded its level in 1929 by 5.4 percent. But the rate of unemployment was still 14.3 percent in 1937 (12.5 percent including the emergency government employment). The economy was coming back but not nearly enough for anything close to full employment.

The recovery of the economy was interrupted by a recession in 1938. Declines were recorded in GDP, consumption, investment, and employment. Government purchases declined in 1937, and the money supply declined in 1938. The Fed had shifted policy by increasing sharply the reserve requirements for the major member banks, from 14 percent to 25 percent, because of the increasing wholesale prices and fears that the large increases in the money supply in the previous three years would lead to inflation. Fears of inflation with an unemployment rate of 14.3 percent? Wow. The decline in government spending shifted the federal government from the deficits of 1931 to 1936 to a small surplus in 1937. State and local governments recorded budget surpluses throughout the 1930s. The official unemployment rate popped up to 19.0 percent and wholesale prices declined. Recovery resumed in 1939 and 1940 after the Fed resumed money growth by lowering the reserve requirement to 24 percent, lowered the rate it charged banks for loans (from 1.5 percent to 1.0 percent), and made some open market purchases of government bonds.

Data and narrative for the United Kingdom

Data for the United Kingdom for 1929 to 1940 are shown in Table 8.2. The data for the GDP components real terms sometimes do not exactly sum to the reported real GDP, but we shall persevere. We shall see that the Great Depression was less severe in the United Kingdom compared to the United States, and recovery was aided by the reversal of some unhelpful government policies. The nation went off the gold standard in 1931, government spending increased steadily after 1932, and the bank rate at the Bank of England was put at 2.0 percent in 1933 compared to 5.5 percent in 1929. However, the national budget was kept in balance with tax increases.

In real GDP terms, the low point of the Great Depression for the United Kingdom was in 1932. The decline in real GDP from 1929 to 1932 was only 5.3 percent, compared to 26.6 percent for the United States from 1929 to the bottom in 1933. The source of the decline in real GDP for the United Kingdom is identified easily. Look at exports, which fell by 14.4 billion pounds from 1929 to 1932. This decline matches the decline in real GDP of 13 billion pounds. Real consumption actually increased by 4 billion pounds and government spending was boosted by 2.2 billion pounds over these same years. Imports declined by 3.3 billion pounds; Britain had imposed increased tariffs on goods from nations other than the British Empire members. Perhaps consumers switched from imports to goods produced domestically.

The supply of money (M1, which consists of demand deposits and currency in circulation) did decline in 1931 but came back up in 1932 actually to exceed the supply of M1 in 1929. Note that the bank rate was reduced in 1930 but went up in 1931. Then that key interest rate was cut in 1932 from 4.17 percent in 1931 to 2.83 percent and then was lowered to 2.0 percent for the remainder of the decade. The other critical change in policy came in 1931, when the United Kingdom went off the gold standard and its set exchange rate of $4.86 per pound. By 1932, the exchange rate had declined to $3.50 per pound. U.K. exports did not respond immediately to the decline in the exchange rate, probably because the rest of the world was in a depression. However, exports did recover up through 1937 by 21.5 percent.

Now let's look at the employment figures. Employment declined by 0.8 million from 1929 to 1931 (4.1 percent) and then increased slightly in 1932. The decline in non-farm employment in the United States was 24.6 percent as of 1932. The unemployment rate figures for the United Kingdom appear to tell a somewhat different story. The unemployment rate stood at 7.8 percent in 1929 and hit a high point of 15.39 percent in 1932. The seeming discrepancy between the employment figures and the unemployment rates can be resolved by considering the change in the labor force. In 1929, the unemployment rate of 7.8 percent with an employment level of 19.4 million means that the labor force was 21.0 million, with 1.64 million people unemployed. In 1932, the unemployment rate was much higher at 15.39 percent but combined with the employment level of 18.7 million, the labor force implied is 22.1 million. There were 3.4 million unemployed workers, but the labor force had increased by 1.1 million. Evidently the decline in employment had induced more people to enter the labor force, i.e., they were seeking work actively. These additional workers meant that the unemployment rate increased sharply. (Recall the section on macroeconomic data in Chapter 1.) If the labor force had not increased, the unemployment rate would have been 11.05 percent. But that is not what happened. People needed work and could not find it.

What does the recovery for the United Kingdom look like? We see in Table 8.2 that real GDP increased steadily after 1932. The increase from 1932 to 1937 was 22.8 percent, which is about 2.4 percent per year. Real GDP in 1934 exceeded the figure for 1929 by 3.7 percent. All components of GDP were increasing. Government spending increased by 17 billion pounds in real terms, and real private investment increased 8 billion pounds. According to basic Keynesian theory, the increases in these two categories of 25 billion pounds would boost consumer spending, which increased by 26 billion pounds in real terms. So, 25 plus 26 equals 51, and the increase in real GDP was 53 billion pounds. Note that both exports and imports increased and the deficit on current account did not change from 1932 to 1937. The unemployment rate in 1937 was 7.70 percent compared to 15.39 percent in 1932, and employment had increased by 2.4 million to 21.3 million. These macro data depict an economy in recovery.

The discussion so far has been in real terms. Look at wholesale prices. The price index in Table 8.2 is keyed to 2013, so the numbers are very small. Nevertheless, we see that wholesale prices fell by 29.5 percent from 1929 to 1932. We have already noted that the supply of money did decline in 1931 but came back in 1932. How can it be that wholesale prices fell by 29.5 percent, but real GDP fell by only 5.3 percent and the supply of money actually had increased by 3.1 percent as of 1932? Here is one method for answering this question. Remember the Quantity Theory of Money, MV = PY; money supply times velocity of money equals price level time real output. In percentage change terms,

$$\%\Delta M + \%\Delta V = \%\Delta P + \%\Delta Y.$$

Plug in the numbers we know:

$$3.1\% + \%\Delta V = -29.5\% - 5.3\% = -34.8\%.$$

These figures mean that the percentage change in the velocity of money was – 37.9 percent. What was going on? People were not spending their money at the same rate as they did previously. For one thing, prices were declining. Waiting to spend means you get more for your money. Secondly, more people were unemployed. Will more people lose their jobs? Save some of your money for that rainy day that probably is coming. Friedman and Schwartz (1963) found that the velocity of money does slow down in a downturn.

Now let us look at 1937. Compared to 1932, the money supply is up 31.8 percent. Wholesale prices have increased 27.4 percent. As we have seen, real GDP had increased by 22.8 percent. The right-hand side of the equation has increased by 50.2 percent. What about the velocity of money in a recovery period? Velocity increased by 18.4 percent compared to 1932. Recovery was on, so people spent their money at a faster rate. Hello, Friedman and Schwartz.

The years after 1937 reflect the preparations for the war that was likely coming – and did come, in 1939. So the economy of the United Kingdom was in the doldrums in the 1920s, suffered through the Great Depression (but not as much suffering as in the United States), and then prepared for war. By 1940, the unemployment rate had dipped to 2.99 percent as the armed forces enrolled millions of Brits and government spending had shot up to 275 billion pounds. The economy in the war years will be covered in Chapter 9.

The Great Depression in France, Italy, and Germany: brief analyses[1]

The Great Depression in France started in 1931, a bit later than in the United States and the United Kingdom. The French economy had done relatively well in the 1920s, with a strong average annual growth rate of 4.4%. The economy was buoyed somewhat by reparations payments from Germany up through 1923. Also, the French economy was more self-sufficient than the U.K. economy was. France did have a positive balance of payments on current account from tourism and other "invisible" exports. The surplus in the current account produced an inflow of gold to make France the largest holder of gold in the world in 1930.

The Great Depression did arrive. The basic picture is that France did not suffer an economic decline during the Great Depression that was as great as the decline in the United States. However, the decline in French real GDP was much greater than the decline in the United Kingdom As shown in Table 8.3, real GDP declined by 14.4 percent between 1932 and 1929 (compared to the 5.3 percent decline for the United Kingdom), and nominal GDP fell by 20 percent. Recovery of GDP was slow; the level of GDP did not reach its 1929 level until 1939. However, the unemployment rate never rose above 5 percent. One major reason for the low unemployment rate was the huge loss of manpower due to World War I. France lost 1.3 million who were killed, and almost 3 million were wounded – about 4 million casualties. The unemployment rate in 1936 was only 3.6 percent. Interest rates were kept high to keep the value of the franc high, and fiscal policy was not used to stimulate aggregate demand. The French state budget was in balance. France did not devalue the franc until 1936.

The sluggishness of the recovery after 1932 produced unrest among the population, and the conservative government was replaced by the Popular Front in 1934. Political turmoil continued and the pace of recovery did not accelerate. Among other things, the unrest produced an increase in nominal wages in 1936 as demanded by unions. Growth in military spending as war approached brought GDP in 1939 to a level above the 1929 figure. Hautcoeur (1997) attributes the length of the depression in France to the overvalued exchange rate, macroeconomic policy errors, and foreign competition.

TABLE 8.3 Real GDP for France, Germany, and Italy: 1929–1940 (Purchasing Power Parity in 1990 International Dollars)

Year	France	Germany	Italy
1929	194	262	125
1930	189	259	119
1931	177	239	118
1932	166	221	122
1933	178	235	121
1934	176	256	122
1935	171	275	134
1936	178	300	134
1937	188	318	143
1938	187	342	144
1939	201	375	154
1940	166	377	155

Source: Madison Historical Statistics, University of Groningen Growth and Development Centre

As mentioned in Chapter 4, Weimar Germany experienced hyperinflation in the early 1920s, and the nation attempted to pay reparations to the victors in World War I. American loans propped up the German economy from 1924 to 1929, but those loans ended, and lenders started calling in loans as the United States slipped into depression. The Smoot-Hawley tariffs were imposed by the United States in 1930, and German companies lost access to the U.S. market. In 1931, several banks folded in the face of runs on the banks. Table 8.3 shows that German real GDP fell by 15.6 percent from 1929 to the low point in 1932. Industrial production was down by 58 percent. The unemployment rate was about 33 percent in 1932. Many households did not have the means to purchase food, so some people died from malnutrition, and some families found themselves homeless. Llewellyn and Thompson (2019) quote the novelist Christopher Isherwood, who lived in Germany at the time:

> Morning after morning, all over the immense, damp, dreary town and the packing-case colonies of huts in the suburb allotments, young men were waking up to another worthless empty day, to be spent as they could best contrive; selling boot-laces, begging, playing draughts in the hall of the Labour Exchange, hanging about urinals, opening doors of cars, helping with crates in the market, gossiping, lounging, stealing, overhearing racing tips, sharing stumps of cigarette ends picked up in the gutter.

The Weimar government had no effective answer to the Great Depression. Rather than increasing government spending, the government under Chancellor Heinrich Brüning proposed to raise taxes and cut spending to reduce the budget deficit and force wage cuts in an attempt to lower prices. The Reichstag rejected these proposals, but President Paul von Hindenburg implemented them as emergency policies. It may come as no surprise that political instability was the result.

The National Socialist Party and Adolf Hitler had little influence prior to 1930, but in that year they won 107 seats in the Reichstag. Then the elections of 1932 brought the National Socialists 230 seats in the Reichstag, the largest number of seats won by any party during the Weimar period. Hitler was appointed Chancellor by von Hindenburg in 1933. You know the rest.

Hitler's policies, among other nefarious actions, included preparing the nation for the war to gain his "lebensraum," room for living for Germans. The Rhineland was occupied in 1936. Table 8.3 shows that German real GDP began to increase in 1933 and in 1937 was 44 percent above the low point reached in 1932.

The Italian economy in 1929 was less industrialized than were the other four countries discussed in this chapter. The GDP of the economy was roughly divided into thirds for agriculture, industry, and services. However, about 50 percent of the workforce was employed in agriculture. The Fascist government of Mussolini had taken power in 1922.

The Great Depression arrived a little later in Italy than in the other countries, but Table 8.3 shows that Italian real GDP had declined by 5.6 percent from 1929 to 1931. In 1932, the real GDP was only 2.4 percent below the 1929 level. However, real GDP showed no signs of increasing at all until 1935. Giordano et al. (2013) estimate that while GDP had declined very little as of 1932, employment was down by 20 percent and industrial production had dropped by 28 percent compared to 1929. The industrial sector was in severe depression. Both employment and industrial production increased rapidly after 1932 but had not regained their 1929 levels as of 1936. Both wage rigidities and trade restrictions are thought to have played a part. Mussolini's armies invaded Somalia, Eritrea, and Ethiopia in 1936. Table 8.3 shows that as of 1939, Italian GDP was 23 percent greater than in 1929. The war was on, and Italy was allied with Germany. What could go wrong?

Assessment of the theories

Ben Bernanke, the former chair of the U.S. Federal Reserve Bank, has devoted his academic life to the empirical study of macroeconomics in general and the Great Depression in particular. After many years of research, he has reached a few conclusions. His first conclusion (2000, p. 6) is that monetary shocks were a major factor in starting the Great Depression, and that those shocks were transmitted around the world because of the gold standard. Given that conclusion, Bernanke asks why monetary shocks should have real effects. His answers are that falling money supplies produced deflation and financial crisis, and that wages adjusted slowly to changes in nominal prices. Research comparing the experience of a large number of countries during the Great Depression shows that nations that left the gold standard earlier were able to increase money supplies and prices sooner. It is interesting that Bernanke does not regard real demand shocks (e.g., sudden decline in real investment) as the prime mover for many countries. Indeed, he thinks that too much attention has been given to the U.S. case. Let us consider the U.S. case anyway.

It was clear that the economies discussed in this chapter were not returning to full employment when Keynes was writing the *General Theory* in 1934–1935, and it was clear that investment had collapsed. Score some very big points for Keynesian theory. Furthermore, the financial instability hypothesis (Minsky) contributes some explanation because of the stock market boom and crash in the United States. The collapse of the banking sector and drop in the money supply in the United States was documented in detail by Friedman and Schwartz (1963). They contended that a significant part of the decline in the supply of money was independent of the state of the macro economy, and therefore a cause of the depression (not an effect). Score a big point for the Monetarists. Indeed, recall the quote from former Fed Chair Ben Bernanke in which he blamed the Fed for at least a sizable part of the depression in the United States. Keynes was well aware of the quantity theory of money but chose to emphasize the instability of investment and the possible ineffectiveness of increasing the money supply in a depression. Nevertheless, Keynes did advise President Roosevelt to pursue a policy of increasing the money supply, and it is clear that prices and output responded starting in 1934. It is important to remember that Keynes did not have data such as Table 8.1 at the time.

Monetarism added to its credibility for the case of the United States during the recovery years of 1933 to 1937. During this time, the money supply increased by 48.5 percent as nominal GDP increased by 62.9 percent, real GDP increased 43.6 percent, and wholesale prices increased 30.7 percent. These changes are consistent with the finding by Friedman and Schwartz (1963) that the velocity of money increases during a recovery. The money supply declined during the recession of 1938 and increased during the recovery in 1939 and 1940, but the unemployment rate in 1940 was still 14.6 percent. The economy was not yet moving back to full employment.

Full employment was not achieved until the national economies were put on a wartime basis. Governments instituted massive increases in spending in advance of the war that began in 1939. Score another very large point for the Keynesians.

What about Austrian theory and real business cycle theory? Unlike the Monetarists, who blame the Fed for monetary policy that did not prevent the bank failures and provide economic stimulation at the crucial time, Hayek (1984) stated early in the depression that

> the present crisis is marked by the first attempt on a large scale to revive the economy . . . by a systematic policy of lowering the interest rate accompanied by all other possible measures for preventing the normal process of liquidation, and that as a result the depression has assumed more devastating forms and lasted longer than ever before.

As Atack and Passell (1994, p. 614) stated,

> Unanswered in the condemnation of government interference, however, is the question of whether intervention might be justified in the face of panic that threatens the sound banks and business as well as the unsound.

Real business cycle theory would point out that the economy of the 1920s had become more efficient at producing output, especially in the agricultural sector. This positive supply shock might provide some understanding but hardly seems sufficient to explain the disaster that was the Great Depression. More importantly, output and prices moved in the same direction rather than in opposite directions, as implied by shocks to the supply side.

In the end, it would seem that a combination of Keynesian and Monetarist explanations are needed to gain a reasonable understanding of the Great Depression. It is fair to say that Keynesian economics captured the imaginations of many of the generation of younger economists of the day. But then Friedman and Schwartz came along in 1963 with the Monetarist interpretation of the Great Depression. Neither theory provides a complete explanation (no theory ever does), but together they are good enough for our present purposes. The Keynesian might reply that Keynesian theory does not ignore money, and Rauchway (2015) makes it clear that President Roosevelt was rather Keynesian in his monetary policy.

OK, so what about the United Kingdom, France, Germany, and Italy? We saw that the United Kingdom was hit by a sizable drop in exports because other nations (especially the United States) were in depression. Recovery was led by government and investment spending. The supply of money did drop in 1931 but recovered in 1932. Recall that the United Kingdom left the gold standard in 1931. You can tell a pretty good Keynesian story for the United Kingdom, but the story must be supplemented with Bernanke's gold standard hypothesis.

France experienced the Great Depression to a greater degree than did the United Kingdom. France did not leave the gold standard until 1936 and kept interest rates high to keep the exchange rate at its gold standard level. Also, fiscal policy was not used to stimulate the economy. The French budget was in balance. In short, France failed to follow the advice that Keynes and Bernanke might have given.

Germany was hurt badly both by the U.S. Smoot-Hawley tariffs starting in 1930 and the stoppage of lending by the United States after 1929. The Weimar government made terrible macroeconomic policy choices – raising taxes, cutting spending, and attempting to force wages lower. As Keynes would surely have said, why make people take nominal wage cuts when monetary and fiscal policy can be used instead? Consequences for the German people were dire indeed.

The Italian economy was hit by a severe depression in its industrial sector. Scholars of the Italian case think that both trade restrictions imposed by other nations and wage rigidities were to blame.

So where are we? First of all, all five nations recovered as they all prepared for the major war that was coming. Keynesian stimulus in the form of military spending had its impact. Beyond that, each nation has its own Great Depression story that involves different amounts of the same ingredients: shocks to aggregate demand (investment or export declines and government spending cuts and tax increases), wage rigidities, deflation with the attendant bank failures, and adherence to the gold standard with the necessary high interest rates. One theory does not tell the entire story. We have a portfolio of economic theories. We need them.

James Tobin, a leading Keynesian theorist and Nobel Prize winner, had a small sign in his office with just two words – Money Matters.

Sources

Data sources and other information for France, Germany, and Italy were provided by the following publications.

Giordano, C., Piga, G., and Trovato, G., 2013, Italy's industrial great depression: Fascist price and wage policies, *Macroeconomic Dynamics*, pp. 1–32.

Hautcoeur, P., 1997, The Great Depression in France (1929–1938), in D. Glasner, ed., *Business Cycles and Great Depression: An Encyclopedia*, New York: Garland, pp. 39–42.

Llewellyn, J., and Thompson, S., 2019, The Great Depression in Germany, *Alpha History*, https://alphahistory.com/weimarrepublic/great-depression.

Mattesini, F., and Quintieri, B., 1997, Italy and the Great Depression: An analysis of the Italian economy, 1929–1936, *Explorations in Economic History*, pp. 265–294.

Note

1　Data sources for this section are listed in the appendix to the chapter.

9

The war years and postwar recovery

Recovery in the United States and the United Kingdom

This chapter is an examination of the economies of the war years and the postwar period of economic recovery. We shall examine the U.S. and U.K. economies closely, and consider the economies of France, West Germany, and Italy briefly. The role of the U.S. Marshall Plan in European economic recovery from the war is discussed. The basic conclusion is that all four of these nations of Western Europe recovered well from the war, and the Marshall Plan is given some credit for their achievements.

First, the war years. Table 9.1 shows that the U.S. economy had not really recovered in 1940. Unemployment was still at 14.6 percent, and employment figures had just barely exceeded their levels for 1929. Government purchases had not begun to increase.

The economy had not recovered fully until government spending was increased dramatically from $15.1 billion in 1940 to $62.8 billion in 1942 (using borrowed money) and the unemployment rate was down to 4.7 percent. GDP in real terms had recovered to the 1929 level in 1936, but the official unemployment rate was still 16.9 percent because the labor force had grown.

The data in Table 9.1 show that during the war years of 1942 to 1945, the unemployment rate averaged 2.4 percent (with 1.2 percent in 1944). During those four years, 44.1 percent of the GNP was government purchases of goods and services. However, personal consumption expenditures increased in each year; consumption was 47.9 percent greater in 1945 than in 1941 (but just 9.7 percent greater in real terms). Private investment spending was held back, falling from $18.1 billion to $6.1 billion in 1943. The manufacturing buildup began in 1941, and manufacturing employment of 17.6 million in 1943 was 60.2 percent higher than in 1940.

Wartime production was organized by the War Planning Board, which was led by Donald Nelson, a former executive with Sears, Roebuck and Company. Early in 1942, production of some 600 consumer goods was halted (and other goods were subjected to price controls and rationing), leaving firms with a great deal of idle capacity.

TABLE 9.1 U.S. Macroeconomic Data, 1940–1950

Year	GDP $ bil.	Con- sump. $ bil.	Invest- ment $ bil.	Gov't Pur- chases $ bil.	M1* $ bil.	Real GDP $1996 bil.	Non- farm Empl. Mil.	Manuf. Empl Mil.	Unem. Rate Pct.	Price Index Whls.
1940	101.3	71.2	13.6	15.1	36.5	981	32.4	11.0	14.6	43.0
1941	126.7	81.0	18.1	26.6	42.6	1149	36.5	13.2	9.9	47.8
1942	161.8	88.9	10.4	62.8	49.4	1360	40.1	15.3	4.7	52.7
1943	198.4	99.7	6.1	94.9	64.4	1584	42.4	17.6	1.9	56.4
1944	219.7	108.5	7.8	105.5	78.4	1714	41.9	17.3	1.2	56.9
1945	223.0	119.8	10.8	93.2	93.8	1693	40.8	15.5	1.9	57.9
1946	222.3	144.2	31.1	39.8	102	1506	41.7	14.7	3.9	66.1
1947	244.4	162.3	35.0	36.4	109	1495	43.9	15.5	3.9	81.2
1948	269.6	175.4	48.1	40.6	113	1560	44.9	15.6	3.8	87.9
1949	267.7	178.8	36.9	46.8	110	1551	43.8	14.4	5.9	83.5
1950	294.3	192.7	54.1	46.9	110	1687	45.2	15.2	5.3	86.8

Source: Historical Statistics of the United States, Friedman and Schwartz (1963), Darby (1976), and NBER Macrohistory Database

* M1 is the supply of money consisting of currency held by the public and demand deposits. Figures are for January of each year. The low point of $19.4 billion was reached in April 1933.

Wartime production was organized through the use of subcontractors as organized by the government and a lead firm. The use of many smaller firms boosted morale, used existing equipment and workers, involved shorter startup time, and made disguising the nature of the final product easier. The effects of price controls are seen in Table 8.1, in that wholesale prices barely increased in 1944 and 1945 over the 1943 level.

Military service and wartime production made for major changes in the size and allocation of the labor force. In particular, millions of men were in uniform, and millions of women joined the workforce. Data from Table 9.2 show that the male civilian labor force fell from 41.48 million in 1940 to 35.46 million in 1944, and the female civilian labor force increased from 14.16 million to 19.17 million over the same years. Males in military service in 1944 were 11.06 million. The number of women employed in civilian work increased from 11.97 million in 1940 to 18.85 million in 1944 (as the number of unemployed women fell from 2.19 million to 0.32 million). The total female population over the age of 14 years in 1944 was 52.65 million, of whom 18.85 million (36 percent) were employed in civilian work.

Government spending began to decline in 1945 and fell drastically in 1946. Real GDP in 1946 was down by 12.1 percent compared to the peak year of 1944. Many economists feared that the economy would return to depression conditions after the war. Government spending (uncorrected for inflation) remained in the range of

TABLE 9.2 U.S. Male and Female Labor Force During World War II (Millions)

Year	Male Civilian Labor Force	Female Civilian Labor Force	Male Civilian Employment	Female Civilian Employment	Male Armed Forces	Female Armed Forces
1940	41.48	14.16	35.55	11.97	0.39	0.00
1941	41.27	14.64	37.35	13.00	1.47	0.00
1942	40.30	16.11	38.58	15.17	3.81	0.01
1943	36.84	18.70	36.27	18.20	8.76	0.11
1944	35.46	19.17	35.11	18.85	11.06	0.20
1945	34.83	19.03	34.21	18.61	11.04	0.24

Source: Historical Statistics of the United States

$40 to $47 billion for the remainder of the decade, but the private economy came back strongly. Both investment and consumption were buoyed by pent-up demand from the war years. By 1950, real GDP had reached 98.4 percent of the peak level in 1944. The removal of price controls unleashed inflation, with wholesale prices jumping by 14.2 percent from 1945 to 1946 and 22.8 percent from 1946 to 1947. Inflation cooled down during the remainder of the decade, with wholesale prices up 6.9 percent in 1950. International trade resumed, with exports of about $16 billion per year and net exports that averaged $6.6 billion from 1945 to 1950.

The economy of the United Kingdom had a different experience during the war, of course. Data for the period are displayed in Table 9.3. When you read Table 9.3, it is important to remember that the GDP components do not add exactly to the GDP total reported. Indeed, the discrepancies are especially large for the war years. We shall concentrate on trends rather than levels. Government spending started to rise rapidly in 1939, and by 1941 had almost tripled the 1939 figure of 119 billion. During the war, private investment was curtailed, consumption spending was held roughly constant, and prices were controlled. While total employment did not increase by a huge amount (8.3 percent increase from 1939 to 1943), the unemployment rate reached amazingly low numbers, such as 0.28 percent in 1944. Men of working age (and women too) were in the armed forces and were not in the labor market. Real GDP increased until 1943 and then began to decline. The United Kingdom continued to run a large deficit in the current account of the balance of payments, a gap that was filled with loans from the United States.

Britain mobilized its population effectively and stood up to Hitler virtually by themselves after the disaster at Dunkirk in 1940. The economy was geared to war production and also had to import oil, munitions, and other items mainly from the United States. Britain quickly ran out of gold and dollars needed to pay for imports because exports declined. In response, the United States started to support Britain with the Lend–Lease program in which $31 billion in supplies were provided for no payment.

TABLE 9.3 U.K. Macroeconomic Data, 1940–1950

Year	Real GDP £bil. (2103)	Real Con-sump.	Real Invest-ment	Real Gov't Spend.	Real Export	Real Import	M1 (£mil.)	Empl. Mil.	Un-emp. Pct.	Price Index Whsl.*	Ave. Bank Rate
1940	330	172	19.4	274.9	18.6	23.0	2529	23.0	2.99	1.98	2.0
1941	359	167	15.6	347.2	16.0	23.9	3147	23.9	1.03	2.19	2.0
1942	365	167	13.5	364.6	14.4	24.7	3609	24.7	0.44	2.34	2.0
1943	371	166	9.3	376.0	15.9	24.9	4110	24.9	0.32	2.37	2.0
1944	355	172	7.2	351.8	20.1	24.6	4613	24.6	0.28	2.44	2.0
1945	339	186	8.0	287.5	16.5	24.1	5016	24.1	0.41	2.51	2.0
1946	331	203	20.2	156.9	27.7	22.9	5779	22.9	1.71	2.73	2.0
1947	326	212	23.6	110.8	27.7	23.0	5854	23.0	1.29	3.44	2.0
1948	337	216	25.3	106.5	33.8	23.0	5988	23.0	1.29	3.99	2.0
1949	348	222	28.7	112.7	37.5	23.0	5950	23.0	1.16	4.23	2.0
1950	360	226	31.3	112.6	42.8	23.2	6165	23.2	1.45	4.99	2.0

Source: Thomas, R., and Dimsdale, N., Three Centuries of Macroeconomic Data, Version 2.3

* Wholesale price index scaled to 2010 prices.

Some economists feared that the U.K. economy also would slip into depression conditions after the war. As we have seen, the impact of the Great Depression was less in the United Kingdom compared to the United States, but unemployment rates in the early 1930s up to 1938 were very high. The United Kingdom had suffered considerable physical damage during the war, and some of those fears were realized as real GDP declined starting in 1944 and continued through 1947. Government spending was reduced by 68.5 percent from 1944 to 1947. Private investment and exports were recovering, and consumer spending did increase. Prices were rising rapidly. Real GDP was declining.

The U.K. government was taken over by the Labour Party in 1945. Sweeping changes in the economy were introduced – tax increases, National Health Service, pensions, expansion of social security, and nationalization of industries. The railroads, the coal industry, and the steel industry were among those industries that came under public ownership and control.

Table 9.3 shows that real GDP started to pick up in 1948, and by 1950 it had increased by 10.4 percent over its 1947 level. What was happening? Government spending was no help at all. Exports and private investment led the way, and consumption spending followed along. Export industries were being promoted to earn much-needed foreign exchange. Wartime rationing continued to keep domestic demand down, and some of the rationing remained in place until 1954.

But there is one other factor that heretofore has not been mentioned – the Marshall Plan. In Britain's case, the Marshall Plan funds were not used to rebuild the economy. Rather, the money was used to service the enormous debt that had been incurred during the war. As we shall see, other recipients of the aid used the money to rebuild and modernize their economies. In the long run, other European economies surpassed Britain in world markets.

The Marshall Plan and European recovery

The Marshall Plan, officially known as the European Recovery Program, was signed into law by President Harry Truman in June 1948. The program was named for George C. Marshall, who was Chief of Staff of the U.S. Army during the war (and hailed as the "organizer of victory") and was Secretary of State when the program was proposed and adopted. The program lasted until the end of 1951 and dispensed $17 billion in grants and loans to 17 nations on Europe. The European nations had formed a committee to help get the program approved in Congress and to get the work underway. This committee became the Organization for European Economic Cooperation (OEEC), which was the beginning of the efforts that eventually produced the European Union and the European Common Market.

The purpose of the Marshall Plan was to assist with European recovery from the war. The plan consisted mainly of grants used to reconstruct cities, repair infrastructure (railways, roads, bridges, etc.) destroyed during the war, replace shipping fleets lost, rebuild industrial facilities, and purchase modern industrial equipment. Money was awarded roughly on the basis of population. Participating nations had to create plans to gear fiscal and monetary policy towards recovery, and they joined together to reduce tariffs and trade barriers. Each nation was able to design its own plan for use of the grants and loans. One specific crucial purpose was the revitalization of West Germany. Germany had been damaged badly during the war, and a revived West Germany was seen as essential for the economic stability and growth of the region. And the focus on West Germany was in answer to the communist government and economic system next door in East Germany.

The bulk of the money was granted to the largest European nations. The top four, with the amounts of grants and loans, were:

United Kingdom	$3.30 billion
France	$2.30 billion
West Germany	$1.45 billion
Italy	$1.20 billion

The list of nations in the program included all of the other European countries not under the control of the Soviet Union, with the exception of Finland. The program had been offered to the Soviet Union and its satellite nations, but that offer was refused. Joseph Stalin instead devised his own plan, with the predictable result that Eastern Europe fell behind the nations of Western Europe.

What were the results achieved by the Marshall Plan? In economic terms, the amount of money was modest in comparison to the size of the European economy.

The total money dispensed was about 3 percent of European GDP at the time, which would have boosted GDP by less than one-half of 1 percent. The United States spent about 1 percent of GDP during each year of the plan. However, some of that money came back in the form of imports of equipment from the United States. The plan also included technical advisors from the United States who helped to modernize industries and increase productivity. And it is noteworthy that the North Atlantic Treaty Organization (NATO) was founded during the time of the plan, in 1949. NATO includes Canada in North America, and it was founded for the collective defense of Western Europe against the Soviet Union and its allies. The Cold War was on. A small piece of the money was used to fund operations of the U.S. Central Intelligence Agency (CIA) in Europe.

We know that the nations of Western Europe did indeed recover and enjoyed a period of prosperity after the Marshall Plan ended. What do the data show? Table 9.4 displays data for real GDP for France, West Germany, and Italy for 1940 to 1953. Data from the same source for the United Kingdom are also included for comparison, but the data from the two sources show the same patterns. No data are available for West Germany prior to 1946, of course. The data show the devastation

TABLE 9.4 Real GDP for France, West Germany, and Italy: Data in Billions of 1990 Purchasing Power Parity International Dollars

Year	France	West Germany	Italy	United Kingdom
1940	166	377*	155	331
1941	131	401*	153	361
1942	117	407*	152	370
1943	112	415*	137	378
1944	94	425*	112	363
1945	102	302*	87	347
1946	155	143	114	332
1947	160	161	134	327
1948	181	190	142	337
1949	205	223	153	350
1950	220	265	165	348
1951	240	290	177	358
1952	247	315	191	358
1953	250	341	224	372

Source: Madison Historical Statistics, University of Groningen, Groningen Growth and Development Data

* Data for the old Germany. Data for West Germany begin in 1946.

of the economies of France and Italy during the war. France hit bottom in 1944 (down 43 percent from 1940) and Italy GDP in 1945 was 44 percent below its 1940 level. Recovery in GDP is evident in 1946 for both nations, but the recovery in France slowed down in 1947. Italy experienced a slower recovery in 1948. At the same time, West Germany seems to have been on the road to recovery in 1947 and 1948. The data for the United Kingdom repeat the trend we saw in the previous section; wartime buildup with a peak in 1943, then a continuous decline in real GDP that ended in 1948. The United Kingdom suffered plenty of war damage but nothing like the damage evident in France, Italy, and Germany. From 1947 to 1951, U.K. real GDP increased by 2.26 percent per year. In addition, real GDP for the old Germany show that GDP peaked in 1944 and declined by 28.9 percent in 1945.

The Marshall Plan started in 1948, and GDP growth for both France and West Germany was strong. Growth in France was 7.75 percent per year for 1946 to 1948 and 9.40 percent per year for 1948 to 1951. West Germany grew by 14.21 percent annually from 1946 to 1948 and 14.10 percent annually from 1948 to 1951. West Germany continued to expand less rapidly after 1951, at 8.10 percent per year to 1953. French growth tailed off in 1952 and 1953; from 1951 to 1953, it was 3.62 percent per year. The economy of Italy continued to grow as well. Annual growth was 10.98 percent from 1946 to 1948 and 7.34 percent from 1948 to 1951. But Italy beat both of those periods with growth of 11.77 percent per year from 1951 to 1953. But the bottom line is that all three grew rapidly after 1946. Overall annual growth from 1946 to 1953 was 7.28 percent in France, 12.41 percent in Germany, and 9.65 percent in Italy. The Marshall Plan is given some credit for the result. Recall that Marshall Plan funds for Britain were used to service debt.

Conclusion

The fear that the United States would slide back into depression after the war proved to be unfounded because of pent-up demand and purchasing power built up during wartime. The theory of consumption spending had to be revised to include wealth as well as current income.

The economies of the four European countries examined in this chapter (the United Kingdom, France, Germany, and Italy) suffered greatly during World War II. Recovery of real GDP after the war had begun by 1946–1947 in France, Germany, and Italy, but the United Kingdom did not see gains in real GDP until 1949. All four nations had abundant human resources, but physical facilities had been devastated. Rebuilding was needed and was helped by the Marshall Plan, grants, loans, and technical assistance provided by the United States. The Marshall Plan and its associated committee of European nations led to the Organization for European Economic Cooperation (OEEC). The Marshall Plan is also considered a catalyst for the formation of the North Atlantic Treaty Organization (NATO). But recovery of these European economies relied on the basic factors of production that survived – human capital and entrepreneurship.

Which macroeconomic theory helps to understand what happened? Keynesian theory, if supplemented by a more complex theory of consumption, helps. But a theory of economic growth is needed as well.

10

The 1950s and 1960s
A time of economic growth

Introduction

This chapter is a detailed examination of the macro economy of the United States and the United Kingdom during a period of economic growth that took place in the 1950s and 1960s. The real GDP of the United States grew at an average annual rate of 3.53 percent from 1950 to 1970, and the United Kingdom almost matched that annual rate of growth with 3.18 percent over the same 20 years. As usual, we will examine the data and compose a narrative for each nation, consider the role of macroeconomic policies, and then make a judgment about the relevance of the different macroeconomic theories.

The economy of the United States from 1950 to 1970

In 1950, the U.S. economy stood unchallenged in the world and had already entered the postwar boom period. Postwar prosperity was fueled by productivity growth. Median family income in real terms doubled between 1949 and 1969 (up 99.4 percent). As noted previously, real GNP increased by 3.59 percent per year over these 20 years. The population of the nation increased by 34.4 percent; these were the years of the Baby Boom (1947 to 1964). Non-agricultural employment increased from 45.2 million in 1950 to 70.9 million in 1970 (up 56.8 percent) as more women entered the workforce, agricultural employment declined, and the first group of Baby Boomers grew up and took jobs.

As the economy grew, its composition was changing away from the production of goods to the production of services. The percentage of employment in the goods-producing sectors (manufacturing, construction, and mining) fell from 40.9 percent in 1950 to 36.1 percent in 1970 – and would decline at an even faster rate in the subsequent decades. The share of employment in manufacturing fell from 33.7 percent in 1950 to 27.3 percent in 1970. The boom period lasted until roughly 1973 and ended with the period called "stagflation," the combination of inflation and stagnant growth.

Americans achieved higher levels of education after World War II. In 1940, 49 percent of adults had graduated from high school, but in 1970 this figure had increased to 76 percent. The GI Bill provided subsidies for veterans to attend college or technical schools, and the modern system of higher education with massive public universities was born. The boom in education was both a cause and a consequence of the rising incomes. Those rising incomes also were spent on houses, automobiles, and a vast array of new consumer products. Those new products included television sets, household appliances, Polaroid cameras, frozen foods, clothing made from new fibers, transistor radios, stereo systems and long-playing records, and many more. The transistor was invented in 1947 and was the first step toward the computer revolution in later years.

The major urban areas were suburbanizing rapidly, especially after the construction of expressway systems in the later 1950s and 1960s. The Great Migration brought millions of African Americans from the South to the northern areas of the nation. These people were confined largely to segregated neighborhoods and struggled to participate in the prosperity that the rest of the nation was experiencing. One result of suburbanization of the white majority population and employment in major urban areas was a series of urban riots that took place from 1964 to 1971. All of these developments are discussed in detail in McDonald (2015).

The changes in society in just a few years were massive. This author was 7 years old in 1950, lived in a medium-sized urban area (Decatur, Illinois), and had never seen a television program. In 1960, I was driving a car to high school and was an avid TV viewer, and in 1970 I was studying economics in graduate school.

Narrative

The 1950s and 1960s were a time of rapid economic growth and rising incomes for most of the population. The data for the two decades are shown in Table 10.1. The economy experienced brief recessions in 1954 and 1958 and a slowdown in growth in 1961. We see that the unemployment rate jumped up in these years but declined in the next year. However, the unemployment rate was never higher than the 6.8 percent in 1958.

The year 1951 saw an increase in real GNP of 7.9 percent as government expenditures in real terms increased as a result of the Korean War. The unemployment rate fell from 5.3 percent to 3.3 percent, and the price index registered an increase of 6.7 percent. The money supply (M2) increased by 5.3 percent. Real government expenditures increased in 1952 and 1953, the unemployment rate fell to 2.9 percent in 1953, and the price index increased 3.2 percent during those years as the money supply increased by 7.5 percent over the two years.

The recession of 1954 was a result of the cut in government expenditures in that year of $10.9 billion. The unemployment rate popped up to 5.5 percent, and prices fell slightly. The economy recovered in 1955 as a result of an increase in real investment, and the unemployment rate averaged just 4.3 percent for 1955 to 1957. Prices edged up by 2.9 percent per year over those two years as the money supply increased by 6.5 percent. The 1950s are known, among other things, for "car culture," and the economy was running on all cylinders.

TABLE 10.1 U.S. Macroeconomic Data, 1950–1970: Dollar Figures in Billions

Year	GNP ($bil.)	Real GNP (1958$ bil.)	Real Cons. (1958$ bil.)	Real Inv. (1958$ bil.)	Real Gov. Exp. (1958$ bil.	Federal Surplus ($bil.)	Price Index (1958= 100)	Unemp Rate Pct	Money (M2, $bil., Dec.)	Fed Disc. Rate Pct
1950	284.8	355.3	230.5	69.3	52.8	7.8	80.2	5.3	151.5	1.59
1951	328.4	383.4	232.8	70.0	75.4	5.8	85.6	3.3	159.6	1.75
1952	345.5	395.1	239.4	60.5	92.1	−3.8	87.4	3.0	167.0	1.75
1953	364.6	412.8	250.8	61.2	99.8	−6.9	88.3	2.9	171.6	1.99
1954	364.8	407.0	255.7	59.4	88.9	−7.0	89.6	5.5	178.5	1.60
1955	398.0	438.0	274.2	75.4	85.2	2.7	90.9	4.4	181.7	1.89
1956	419.2	446.1	281.4	74.3	85.3	4.9	94.0	4.1	186.7	2.77
1957	441.1	452.5	288.2	68.8	89.3	0.7	97.5	4.3	191.1	3.12
1958	447.3	447.3	290.1	60.9	94.2	−12.5	100.0	6.8	203.8	2.15
1959	483.7	475.9	307.3	73.6	94.7	−2.1	101.7	5.5	206.9	3.36
1960	503.7	487.7	316.1	72.4	94.9	3.7	103.3	5.5	211.2	3.53
1961	520.1	497.2	322.5	69.0	100.5	−4.3	104.6	6.7	n.a.	3.00
1962	560.3	529.8	338.4	79.4	107.5	−2.9	105.8	5.5	n.a.	3.00
1963	590.5	551.0	353.3	82.5	109.6	1.8	107.2	5.7	n.a.	3.23
1964	632.4	581.1	373.7	87.8	111.2	−1.4	108.8	5.2	273.8	3.55
1965	684.9	617.8	397.7	99.2	114.7	2.2	110.9	4.5	298.1	4.04
1966	749.9	658.1	418.1	109.3	126.5	1.1	113.9	3.8	314.0	4.50
1967	793.9	675.2	430.1	101.2	140.2	−13.9	117.6	3.8	345.7	4.19
1968	864.2	706.6	452.7	105.2	147.7	−6.8	122.3	3.6	378.0	5.17
1969	929.1	724.7	469.3	109.6	145.6	7.4	128.2	3.5	386.8	5.87
1970	974.1	720.0	475.9	102.2	139.4	−13.1	135.3	4.9	418.2	5.95

Source: Economic Report of the President, 1972. Figures for M2 from 1950 to 1960 are from Friedman and Schwartz (1963, pp. 719–722). The federal government did not begin to report M2 until 1964

Real investment declined by 7.4 percent in 1957 and then fell by 11.5 percent in 1958. This cumulative decline in investment of 18 percent produced the recession of 1958. The unemployment rate jumped from 4.3 percent to 6.8 percent. But the economy recovered in 1959 and 1960, although the unemployment rate fell only to 5.5 percent. The recovery of the economy can be attributed to a revival of real investment of 20.8 percent in 1959. The 1950s end with a real GNP in 1960 that was 37.1 percent greater than in 1950, an annual growth rate of 3.2 percent. Real consumption was up by 37.3 percent.

The first year of the new decade brought a slowdown in growth for 1961 to 1.9 percent and an increase in unemployment from 5.5 percent to 6.7 percent. Real investment declined slightly, and real consumption increased by only 2.0 percent, but real government expenditures increased by 5.9 percent. The slowdown appears to be related to the decision of the Fed to increase interest rates – the discount rate charged banks for borrowing from the Fed increased from 2.15 percent in 1958 to 3.53 percent in 1960, and the money supply did not increase. The economy came back strongly in 1962 as the discount rate was lowered to 3.0 percent, real investment bounced back, and government spending increased as well.

Real investment continued to grow rapidly from 1962 to 1966, and the unemployment rate fell to 3.8 percent. Government expenditures were increasing as the nation increasingly became involved in the Vietnam War. The money supply was increasing sharply during these years – up by 14.7 percent per year from 1964 to 1966. Real government expenditures continued to rise through 1969, largely because of the Vietnam War, and the unemployment rate remained below 4.0 percent. The price index began to increase at an increasing rate (i.e., accelerate). Inflation was 3.2 percent in 1967, 4.0 percent in 1968, 4.8 percent in 1969, and 5.5 percent in 1970.

The Fed increased the discount rate sharply in the second half of the 1960s from 4.04 percent in 1965 to 5.95 percent in 1970, but the money supply continued to grow at an average of 4.6 percent over those five years. Government expenditures declined in 1969 and 1970, and the sharp increase in interest rates produced a decline in real investment in that year. Real GNP fell slightly, and the unemployment rate increased from 3.5 percent to 4.9 percent.

Let's take a quick look at fiscal and monetary policy during these 20 years. We see that the federal budget was in balance for the years from 1950 to 1957. The surpluses and deficits roughly offset. Deficits occurred during the Korean War years of 1952 and 1953 and in the recession year of 1954. A sizable deficit was run in the recession year of 1958, but then the budget surpluses and deficits roughly offset again from 1959 to 1966. Another relatively large deficit was incurred in the war year of 1967, followed by a smaller deficit in 1968, a surplus in 1969, and another relatively large deficit as the economy slowed down. One can conclude that federal deficits were caused by two factors – war and recession. A deficit during a recession normally occurs because tax receipts fall and spending on income support (e.g., unemployment insurance and welfare payments) increases automatically. Therefore, it does not appear that federal government fiscal policy was being used actively to offset recessions. The federal budget was roughly in balance during 1950 to 1957 and 1959 to 1966.

Monetary policy is another story. The Fed was using its discount rate policy to manage the economy. A commitment to the U.S. Treasury to keep interest rates low ended in 1953 and the discount rate was increased. The discount rate was lowered in 1954 in response to the recession, and then increased in the next three years as the economy was growing nicely. The sizable cut from 3.12 percent in 1957 to 2.15 percent in 1958 was in response to the recession in that year. That cut was followed by (for then) a sharp increase in 1960 to 3.53 percent. As noted earlier, this increase likely contributed to the slowdown in growth in 1961. The discount rate was lowered for 1961 to 1962 but then increased steadily during the Vietnam War years. These efforts during the last years of the 1960s did not prevent the increases in the money supply and the accelerating inflation.

The economy of the United Kingdom from 1950 to 1970

Macroeconomic data for the United Kingdom. are displayed in Table 10.2. At first glance, we see some very different numbers for the United Kingdom compared to the United States. First of all, the U.K. unemployment rate was not greater than 2.44 percent during the 20 years. But it should be noted that unemployment varied

TABLE 10.2 U.K. Macroeconomic Data, 1950–1970

Year	Real GDP £bil. (2013)	Real Con- sump.	Real Invest- ment	Real Gov't Purchase	Real Export	Real Import	M1 (£mil.)	Empl- ment (mil.)	Un- emp. (Pct.)	Whsl Price (2010 =100)	Ave. Bank Rate (Pct.)
1950	360	226	31.3	112.6	42.8	37.6	6165	23.2	1.45	4.99	2.00
1951	373	223	33.4	120.9	42.3	40.3	6132	23.6	1.18	6.62	2.08
1952	379	224	37.1	132.4	46.5	37.3	6101	23.6	1.92	6.79	3.75
1953	400	234	46.6	135.9	43.2	40.2	6272	23.7	1.58	6.79	3.83
1954	417	244	51.7	135.5	45.7	41.7	6560	24.0	1.31	6.84	3.17
1955	433	254	55.9	132.2	48.8	45.8	6449	24.3	1.08	7.05	4.42
1956	440	256	60.5	130.9	51.1	46.0	6481	24.5	1.16	7.38	5.42
1957	449	261	63.8	129.2	52.4	47.2	6476	24.5	1.4	7.52	5.71
1958	454	269	67.8	125.8	51.6	47.7	6656	24.3	2.02	7.58	5.21
1959	473	280	73.2	128.0	53.0	50.9	7012	23.7	2.11	7.60	4.00
1960	503	291	85.0	130.6	56.1	57.0	6949	24.2	1.60	7.70	5.42
1961	516	297	91.8	135.3	57.9	56.6	6944	24.4	1.52	7.91	5.79
1962	522	304	92.7	139.5	58.9	57.8	7126	24.6	1.99	8.08	4.79
1963	547	318	94.9	142.4	61.7	60.0	7708	24.6	2.43	8.17	4.00
1964	578	329	110.2	145.3	63.8	66.5	8019	24.9	1.63	8.41	5.25
1965	590	334	115.4	148.9	66.6	67.2	8243	25.2	1.41	8.73	6.42
1966	599	340	115.1	153.5	70.0	68.9	8212	25.3	1.52	8.96	6.50
1967	616	349	125.2	162.2	70.4	73.8	8773	25.0	2.34	9.06	6.21
1968	649	366	138.0	164.5	79.0	79.4	9075	24.8	2.37	9.41	7.42
1969	662	363	137.7	161.8	86.8	82.0	9098	24.8	2.29	9.78	7.92
1970	680	374	142.8	164.6	91.4	86.0	9947	24.7	2.44	10.47	7.21

Source: Thomas, Ryland, and Dimsdale, Nicholas, Three Centuries of Macroeconomic Data, Version 2.3, available online

from 1.08 percent in 1955 to 2.44 percent in 1970, more than doubling the rate. Also, total employment did not increase much at all. Employment was 23.2 million in 1950 and hit a high of 25.3 million in 1966. That is only a 9 percent increase, compared to the non-farm employment increase in the United States of 57 percent from 1950 to 1970. However, the U.K. population increased by 9.7 percent (from 50.6 million in 1950 to 55.5 million in 1970), compared to the 34.4 percent increase in the U.S. population. Let us turn to the GDP data.

Table 10.2 tells us that real GDP did not decline in any year from 1950 to 1970. However, the United Kingdom did experience some slowdowns in growth that can be seen reflected in a decrease in employment and an increase in the unemployment rate. The first slowdown occurred in 1952, when real GDP increased by only 1.6 percent, employment did not change, and the unemployment rate popped up from 1.18 percent to 1.92 percent. The causes of this slowdown appear to be on the monetary side; the bank rate was increased from 2.08 percent to 3.75 percent and the money supply declined by 0.7 percent. The increase in the interest rate likely was a lagged response to the 32.7 percent jump in wholesale prices that took place in 1951. Growth in real GDP picked up to 3.39 percent per year from 1952 to 1957, employment increased, and the unemployment fell back to low levels of 1.08 percent in 1955 and 1.40 percent in 1957. Real investment increased steadily over these years, with an increase of £5.1 billion in 1953. Note that the money supply was growing slowly during these years at 1.12 percent and the bank rate increased steadily to 5.71 percent in 1957. The rate of inflation stabilized at 2.64 percent per year from 1952 to 1957.

The next slowdown occurred in 1958, as real GDP increased by only 1.1 percent. Employment declined, and unemployment increased from 1.40 percent to 2.02 percent (a 44 percent increase). Two components of real GDP declined; government spending fell by £3.4 billion, and exports declined by £0.8 billion (but net exports actually increased over 1956). These declines were more than offset by increases in consumer spending and investment. Growth resumed in 1959 as the bank rate was cut and government spending increased again. However, employment registered another decline and the unemployment rate increased slightly. The economy was back on its growth track in 1960 with an increase in real GDP of 6.34 percent over 1959. Private investment increased sharply (16.1 percent), and government spending continued to increase. The unemployment rate declined as employment increased by 500,000 workers. The Bank of England was "leaning against the wind" by increasing interest rates from 4.00 percent to 5.42 percent.

The wait for the next slowdown was not lengthy. Real GDP increased by 1.16 percent in 1962, and unemployment popped up with a lag in 1963. The slower growth can be attributed to the very small increase in real investment of 1.0 percent in 1962. The interest rate was cut in 1963, and the supply of money added 8.17 percent in that same year. The economy picked up in 1964 as real investment increased by £15.3 billion. Employment increased by 300,000, and the unemployment rate fell from 2.43 percent to 1.63 percent.

The unemployment rate shifted upward in 1967 and remained at or above 2.3 percent for the remainder of the decade. The bank rate was set at 6.42 percent in 1965 and remained above 6.2 percent (and was as high as 7.92 percent) until 1970.

Real GDP continued to grow throughout the second half of the 1960s. The rate of inflation averaged 3.65 percent per year from 1964 to 1970. The inflation rate was matched by a money supply increase of 3.59 percent over those same years. The U.K. economy had made a transition to a high interest rate, high inflation rate, and high unemployment rate (for them) state after 1966.

Real investment, government spending, and consumption declined slightly in 1969, but the data show a small gain for real GDP. There is a discrepancy in the data; the sums of the GDP components show a decline from 1968 to 1969, not an increase. Which data do we believe? I am not sure.

So what is the basic narrative for the U.K. economy during these two decades? The economy grew strongly with a few slowdowns in the rate of growth. Those slowdowns can be associated with components of real GDP and/or with changes in monetary policy. Here is a very short rundown of the slowdowns and recoveries:

1952: Interest rate increase in lagged response to inflation in 1951, increase in real investment leads the recovery.

1958: Government spending cut, followed by an interest rate cut and an increase in real investment.

1962: Small increase in investment, followed by an interest cut and money supply increase.

1969: Declines in real investment and government spending, followed by a cut in the interest rate.

Note that the story has been written in real Keynesian terms, with some monetary factors added.

Assessment of the theories

The 1950s and 1960s were the heyday of Keynesianism. Economists were busy creating ever more elaborate Keynesian models. These models essentially were very large versions of the basic equation that

$$Y = C + I + G + X.$$

Graduate students were schooled in the intricacies of developing Keynesian models. One textbook by Christ (1966) includes a detailed example of how to create a seven-equation model of the U.S. economy with equations for consumption, investment, wages, disposable income (income after taxes), and three other variables pertaining to output, income, and saving in the private business sector. The model is in real terms. No effort is made to explain prices, and the model does not include financial features of the economy. The model is built around the consumption–investment nexus. Christ (1966, p. 580) acknowledges these weaknesses of the model, and states that the model is not intended for serious analysis. But if your goal is to estimate a basic Keynesian model, Christ showed you how. Complex statistical methods are required.

Suits (1962) estimated a model of modest size for the United States consisting of 32 equations using annual data for 1947 to 1960, as follows:

Aggregate   Demand
Consumption equations   4
Investment equations   5
Imports   1
Gross national product   1
Income and employment   9
Taxes and transfer payments   12

To illustrate, the model includes an equation for expenditures for automobiles and parts that is a function of the change in disposable income from the previous year (income less taxes plus transfer payments), the stock of cars on the road, and the real value of consumer liquid assets from the prior year (basically the supply of money, M1). Note that the model does not include an equation for inflation.

The model requires known values for government purchases, the labor force, household liquid assets from the previous period, and a few other variables. The model does not require a known value for the supply of money. The model was used for forecasting and policy analysis. An increase in government purchases from private firms has a Keynesian multiplier effect of 1.3 – an increase of $1 increases GNP by $1.30. An increase in federal employment has a larger multiplier effect of 1.9.

A much more elaborate model using quarterly data was developed by a team of economists on behalf of the Brookings Institution in Washington, D.C. Private firms soon joined the business; Data Resources, Inc., a firm founded in 1969 by Harvard economist Otto Eckstein, developed a large Keynesian-type model that is still used widely in modified form (and is now owned by the firm IHS Global Insight). Another large-scale model built along updated Keynesian lines and in widespread use is offered by Moody's Analytics.

As I mentioned and you no doubt noticed, the narratives for both the United States and the United Kingdom were written largely with a Keynesian flavor. It is difficult not to do this. The short-run ups and downs in the economy during the 1950 to 1970 period appear in both nations to be driven by changes in investment and government spending. The supply of money also played the role largely in line with Monetarist thinking. Consider 1951 and 1969, two years of full employment in the United States – unemployment rates of 3.3 percent and 3.5 percent. The price index increased by 49.7 percent over those 18 years. Nominal GNP increased by 182.9 percent, and real GNP increased by 89.0 percent. The nominal and real GNP increases are consistent with the price increase. Nominal GNP increased on average by 5.9 percent per year, while real GNP increased by 3.6 percent per year and prices increased by 2.3 percent annually. Friedman and Schwartz (1963) found that, in the long run, the movements in nominal income (mainly changes in the price level) are dominated by changes in the nominal supply of money. The growth in nominal income was dominated by an increase in the supply of money, if the definition of money is M2 (M1 plus time deposits), which is the Friedman–Schwartz preferred definition of money. M2 increased by 142.4 percent from 1951 to 1969, compared to the nominal GNP increase of 182.9 percent. The annual rate of increase for nominal GNP was 5.9 percent, and M2 increased by 5.0 percent per year. The velocity of circulation for M2 increased from 2.10 to 2.40.

In the short run, we see that nominal GNP in the United States increased 19 out of 20 times during 1950 to 1970 (with no change in 1953–1954), and M2 increased every year for which we have data (16 out of 16 times). Real GNP declined three times (1954, 1958, and 1970). The increase in nominal GNP sometimes exceeded the growth in the money supply. M2 increased by greater than 3 percent 10 times out of 16 in Table 10.1, but nominal GNP growth exceeded 3 percent 14 out of 16 times (1954 and 1958 being the exceptions). All four years in which the money supply increased by less than 3 percent was a year in which the nominal GNP increased by more than 3 percent. However, during the years of accelerating inflation of 1966 to 1970, nominal GNP increased by 29.9 percent, which closely matches the money supply increase of 33.2 percent. Recall that the Fed was using discount rate policy during these years but evidently did not exercise much control of the money supply measured as M2.

Where are we then? Both basic Keynesian theory, with its emphasis on changes in investment and government spending, and Monetarism, with its emphasis on the supply of money, are supported by the data for both nations. Neither real business cycle theory nor Austrian theory appears to apply during this period. Aggregate supply was increasing relatively rapidly and steadily. No significant "shock" to supply occurred. The Fed and the Bank of England raised interest rates steadily over the period. It lowered interest rates only during the slowdowns, but the trends were strongly upward. Austrians argue that the central bank should not manipulate interest rates at all (or even exist), but it would seem that no harm was done. Indeed, during World War II and the early postwar years up to 1953, the U.S. Federal Reserve had acted to keep interest rates low to reduce the cost of borrowing for the federal government. The Fed and the U.S. Treasury reached an "accord" that was fully in effect in 1953, that permitted the Fed to pursue interest rate policy independently. The economy was booming and continued to boom.

The data in Tables 10.1 and 10.2 surely give the edge to the Keynesians. Fluctuations in aggregate demand for both investment and government spending clearly are the sources in fluctuations in real and nominal GNP. The money supply increased steadily in both economies but does not appear to be an independent source of the downturns. Changes in interest rates, in both directions, did have the hypothesized effects. Preponderance of the evidence to the Keynesians, but the Monetarists provide additional explanation. The fact that these years saw the development of increasingly complicated Keynesian models – and their commercialization – supports this conclusion.

11

The years of stagflation

Introduction

The next period we shall consider is the time of what is called "stagflation," when inflation was accompanied by high unemployment. This episode generated a massive rethinking of macroeconomics. The field was badly shaken. We follow our usual procedure of presenting the data, constructing a narrative of what happened, and then assessing the ability of the theories to match the narrative. The basic data for the United States are displayed in Table 11.1, and Table 11.3 contains the data for the United Kingdom. You are reminded to look at the data carefully before you read on.

The international monetary system

During the 1970s, the international monetary system was changed from the Bretton Woods system of fixed exchange rates with limited flexibility, to floating exchange rates. The system is described in Chapter 3. Keynes was a principal player in the creation of the system in 1944. As noted in Chapter 3, the system worked well as long as the major trading nations had low and similar rates of inflation.

The system began to break down in the late 1960s, when the United States experienced a rising rate of inflation relative to its trading partners. As shown in Table 11.1, net exports turned from positive to negative in the latter half of the 1960s, which required foreign monetary authorities to hold more and more bonds denominated in dollars. Foreign monetary authorities held dollars equal to more than three times the amount of gold in Fort Knox. It was clear that the United States could not keep its promise to sell gold. The exchange rate of the dollar was too high, and at the time, the level of domestic demand was too high. On August 15, 1971, President Richard Nixon ended the commitment of the United States to sell gold at $35 per ounce. Also, the nation imposed a 10 percent tariff on imports that would be removed when other major countries revalued their currencies relative to the dollar. They complied. The world formally shifted to permit floating

TABLE 11.1 U.S. Macroeconomic Data, 1970–1984

Year	Real GDP Change Pct	Real C Change Pct	Real I Change Pct	Real G Change Pct	Un-emp Pct	Infla-tion Pct	M1 Change Pct	Fed Funds Rate Pct	Crude Oil Price per Barrel	Net Ex-port ($bil)
1970	0.2	2.4	−6.1	−2.0	4.9	5.3	5.1	7.17	$1.50	1.2
1971	3.3	3.8	10.3	−1.8	5.9	5.1	6.5	4.67	$1.75	−3.0
1972	5.2	6.1	11.3	−0.5	5.6	4.3	9.2	4.44	$2.48	−8.0
1973	5.6	5.0	10.9	−0.3	4.9	5.4	5.5	8.74	$3.29	0.6
1974	−0.5	−0.8	−6.6	2.3	5.6	9.0	4.3	10.51	$11.58	−3.1
1975	−0.2	2.3	−16.2	2.2	8.5	9.3	4.7	5.82	$11.53	13.6
1976	5.4	5.6	19.1	0.5	7.7	5.5	6.7	5.05	$12.80	−2.3
1977	4.6	4.2	14.3	1.2	7.1	6.2	8.0	5.54	$13.92	−23.722
1978	5.6	4.4	11.6	2.9	6.1	7.0	8.0	7.94	$14.02	−26.1
1979	3.2	2.4	3.5	1.9	5.8	8.3	6.9	11.20	$31.61	−23.8
1980	−0.2	−0.3	−10.1	1.9	7.1	9.0	7.0	13.95	$36.83	−14.7
1981	2.6	1.5	8.8	1.0	7.6	9.4	6.9	16.39	$35.93	−14.7
1982	−1.9	1.4	−13.0	1.8	9.7	6.1	8.7	12.24	$32.97	−20.6
1983	4.6	5.7	9.3	3.8	9.6	3.9	9.8	9.09	$29.55	−51.4
1984	7.3	5.3	27.3	3.6	7.5	3.6	5.8	10.23	$27.56	−103

Source: Economic Report of the President and WTRG (crude oil prices)

exchange rates with an International Monetary Fund agreement in 1976, and there we are still. Gold became completely irrelevant as a part of the international monetary system. The nation members that adopted floating exchange rates now can concentrate on monetary policies aimed at stabilization of the domestic economy. The United States permits the dollar to float, as do the currencies of Japan, the United Kingdom, and a few others. The policies adopted by other countries vary widely, from "managed" floating, to a "crawling" peg, to being pegged to a major currency (such as the dollar). The European Union has had a single currency (the euro) since 1999, and its value floats as well.

The data and the narrative for the United States

What do see in Table 11.1? As we have seen in Chapters 8 and 10, the volatility of the change in real investment jumps out. At first, from 1970 to 1973, the growth rate of real GDP was picking up thanks to strong increases in investment spending. Government spending in real terms was falling as national defense spending was cut, as the United States exited from the Vietnam War. Unemployment and inflation were stable, both about 5 percent. The economy was at full employment, with a rate of inflation higher than one wishes to see. As noted previously, the Nixon administration devalued the dollar, but instead of lowering domestic demand, the economy was subjected to price controls from 1971 to 1974. It is generally agreed that these controls were not effective. Then something big happened.

The economy went into recession as real GDP declined in both 1974 and 1975. Real investment fell abruptly. Residential construction was especially volatile – down 19.6 percent in 1974 and 12.1 percent in 1975 (then up 22.1 percent in 1976 and 20.5 percent in 1977). Unemployment increased to 8.5 percent in 1975, and inflation jumped from 5.4 percent in 1973 to 9.0 percent in 1974 and 9.3 percent in 1975. What caused this sharp change? How could unemployment and inflation increase together? That is why these years are called a time of stagflation – economic stagnation coupled with inflation, a very bad macroeconomic outcome indeed. The rate of increase in the supply of money actually declined from 1973 to 1974, so we cannot blame inflation on the money supply. Besides, a reduction in the rate of growth of the money supply "should have" reduced inflation. One factor is the sharp increase in the federal funds rate – the short-term rate controlled by the Fed – from 4.44 percent in 1972 to 10.51 percent in 1974! Surely the drop in real investment was partly caused by the increase in interest rates.

Why did the Fed increase the interest rate? A large part of the answer comes from the price of oil. The price of oil is stated in terms of the U.S. dollar, so inflation in the United States means that the real price of oil was falling. The United States was (and is) a major importer of oil, and in 1974 the major exporters – the Organization of Petroleum Exporting Countries (OPEC) – increased the price from $3.29 to $11.58 per barrel, an increase of 3.5 times. In addition, the Arab members of OPEC imposed an embargo on oil sales to the United States that lasted from October 1973 to March 1974 because of U.S. support for Israel during the Yom Kippur War of 1973. The price increase and temporary embargo had two major impacts. First, the price of oil influenced the price of gasoline and many other commodities (and made gasoline purchasers wait in long lines). We see the impact in the inflation numbers. Second, the nation still had to import a lot of oil, and this created a large deficit in the balance of trade, as shown in Table 11.1. The Fed attempted to counter the trade deficit by raising interest rates in order to attract investment from abroad, but this also had the effect of cutting investment spending.

So here we have a negative shock to the supply side of the economy that came in the form of a sharp increase in the price and reduction in supply of a very basic commodity. It is fair to say that this episode motivated economists to devote more attention to shocks on the supply side and led to real business cycle theory. Inflation increased and real output fell, just as the theory indicates. How did the rest of the 1970s play out?

The economy settled down to a calmer mode during 1976 to 1979. Real GDP resumed its growth as real investment bounced back nicely, partly as a result of a cut in interest rates. Because of the recession, the Fed reversed itself and reduced the fed funds rate sharply back to less than 6.0 percent. The recovery also was partly fueled by an increase in the rate of growth of the money supply. The unemployment rate came down steadily to 5.8 percent in 1979. The price of oil drifted upward to $14.02 per barrel in 1978.

But then it happened again. OPEC lowered output and increased the price of oil to $31.61 per barrel for 1979. The increase in the oil price had to do partly with supply disruptions from the Iranian revolution that began in late 1978 and the Iran–Iraq War that began in 1980. The economy went into another recession in 1980. Residential construction fell by 20.9 percent in 1980. Inflation increased from 6.2 percent in 1977 to 9.4 percent in 1981, and unemployment hit 7.1 percent in 1980. The Fed had increased the fed funds rate in 1978 and 1979 to keep up with inflation. The increase in the rate of inflation from historically high rates for 1976 to 1979, to an unprecedented 9.4 percent in 1981, was very worrisome. There were months in which the economy had both unemployment and inflation in double digits. Were we destined to live with inflation and struggle to reduce unemployment in spite of the *Whip Inflation Now* buttons that were issued by the federal government?

The time from 1979 to 1982 is a period for which the basic data do not tell the full story. Paul Volcker was appointed Fed Chairman by President Jimmy Carter in August 1979. He perceived that inflationary expectations were running rampant, and he set out to wring inflation from the economy. He succeeded, as we can see from the reduction in the rate of inflation starting in 1982. By 1984, inflation was "only" 3.6 percent, the smallest inflation rate for the entire 1970–1984 period. So we did not have to live permanently with high inflation. How did he do it? And what were the side effects of what he did? Fed policy had been based on setting the federal funds rate, but Volcker decided to switch to controlling the money supply by controlling bank reserves using open market operations (i.e., selling government bonds). Interest rates would be free to move with supply and demand. We see in Table 10.1 that the growth of the money supply did slow down, from 8.0 percent in 1978 to 6.9 percent in 1979 (and 7.0 percent in 1980 and 6.9 percent in 1981). These increases are below the rates of inflation for those years, so the real supply of money was reduced. Note that the increase in the supply of money had been running at rates greater than the rates of inflation during 1976 to 1978.

The change in monetary policy produced a sharp increase in interest rates. The fed funds rate topped out at 16.39 percent in 1981; the new home mortgages rate hit 14.70 percent and the prime interest rate charged by banks for new loans hit 18.87 percent in the same year. The economy went into another recession in 1982. This time, real investment fell by 13.0 percent (with residential construction down by 18.1 percent after falling by 8.2 percent in 1981) and the unemployment rate hit 9.7 percent, the highest rate of unemployment since the end of the Great Depression. The rate of inflation fell from 9.4 percent in 1981 to 6.1 percent in 1982, and people began to expect that inflation would moderate. Interest rates started to come back to earth, and the economy resumed real GDP growth in 1983 of 4.6 percent as real investment came back. The comeback of the economy was assisted by the fact that the price of oil began to drop after it reached $36.83 per barrel in 1980. By 1984, the price had declined to $27.56 per barrel, but the comeback in the economy was a cause in the sharp increase in the balance of trade deficit. The price of oil collapsed to $14.43 in 1986.[1] Real GDP growth in 1984 was a very strong 7.3 percent as real investment growth was 27.3 percent, with residential construction up a remarkable 42.0 percent. Note one theme here: Residential construction was highly volatile during the entire period as interest rates fluctuated wildly.

Part of the story of the recessions and the recovery after 1982 involves the federal budget. Table 11.2 shows federal outlays and receipts and deficit. Recall from

TABLE 11.2 U.S. Federal Government Outlays and Receipts by Fiscal Year ($ Billions)

Year	Total Federal Outlays	National Defense Outlays	Total Federal Receipts	Individual Income Taxes	Corporate Income Taxes	Federal Deficit
1970	196	82	193	90	33	3
1971	210	79	187	86	27	23
1972	231	79	207	95	32	23
1973	246	77	231	103	36	15
1974	269	79	263	119	39	6
1975	332	86	279	122	41	53
1976*	468	109	379	171	50	89
1977	409	97	356	158	55	54
1978	459	104	400	181	60	59
1979	504	116	463	218	66	41
1980	591	134	517	244	65	74
1981	678	157	599	286	61	79
1982	746	185	618	298	49	128
1983	808	210	601	289	37	208
1984	852	227	666	298	57	185

Source: Economic Report of the President

* Includes transition quarter as federal fiscal year shifted from July 1 to June 30, to October 1 to September 30.

Chapter 6 that the Reagan administration adopted a version of supply–side economics that included cutting taxes, but in the "triumph of politics," Congress failed to cut spending. In Table 11.2, we see that the federal government was running a small deficit during 1970 to 1974, but spending increased in response to the recession in 1975 (and receipts were relatively flat). The deficit jumped from $6 billion to $53 billion. The calendar year 1976 was the year in which the federal government changed its fiscal year from July 1 to June 30 to the current fiscal year of October 1 to September 30, so the data for 1976 just sort of confuse matters. The deficit remained in the $40 to $50 billion range until 1980, when a sharp increase in outlays largely as a result of the recession was not matched by an equal increase in receipts, and the deficit increased to $74 billion.

President Reagan took office in 1981, and fiscal 1982 is the first fiscal year under his administration. By fiscal year 1982 the deficit had increased to $128 billion, largely as a result of an increase in outlays, some of which were related to the recession. However, 1983 was a recovery year. The effect of the Reagan tax cuts is seen clearly. Rather than increasing, as would have been expected in a recovery year, total receipts declined from $618 billion to $601 billion. Both individual and corporate income tax receipts declined. And spending increased; the increase in national defense outlays accounted for 40 percent of the increase. The deficit hit $208 billion. The deficit in fiscal year 1984 was not as large because the increase in outlays slowed down and receipts picked up, but the federal government was still running a very large deficit (for those days) of $185 billion. Cutting taxes and increasing government spending are straight out of the Keynesian playbook, are they not?

The data and narrative for the United Kingdom

The United Kingdom experienced stagflation as well. The story of the oil price shocks has already been recounted, so take these facts as given. However, Britain had its own oil supply in the North Sea, and therefore did not experience a huge increase in the trade deficit. Indeed, the U.K. balance on current account was positive throughout 1970 to 1984. The high oil price is reflected directly in the rate of inflation. Let us examine Table 11.3.

TABLE 11.3 U.K. Macroeconomic Data, 1970–1984

Year	Real GDP (£bil. 2013)	Real Cons- sump.	Real Invest- ment	Real Gov't Spend	Real Ex- port	Real Im- port	M1 (£mil.)	Empl. (mil.)	Un- emp. (pct)	Wh'sl Price*	Bank Rate (pct)	In- flate (pct)
1970	680	374	143	165	91	86	9947	24.7	2.44	10.47	7.21	7.1
1971	703	386	153	170	98	91	11474	24.5	4.14	11.41	5.92	9.0
1972	734	411	160	179	99	99	13063	24.6	4.34	12.00	6.08	5.2
1973	781	434	164	185	112	111	13922	25.0	3.65	12.90	10.10	7.5
1974	762	428	151	188	120	112	15447	25.0	3.65	15.78	11.90	22.3
1975	751	428	142	199	117	105	17543	24.9	4.50	19.40	10.75	22.9
1976	773	430	143	203	128	110	19353	24.8	5.40	22.60	11.81	16.5
1977	792	429	146	200	136	112	24067	24.8	5.59	26.89	8.17	19.0
1978	825	452	156	203	139	117	27996	24.9	5.51	29.30	9.25	9.0
1979	856	473	170	207	144	128	30545	25.2	5.38	32.77	14.13	11.8
1980	838	473	159	209	144	123	31894	25.1	6.81	38.00	16.17	16.0
1981	832	475	148	210	143	120	35601	24.4	9.65	42.06	13.13	10.7
1982	849	481	156	209	145	126	39799	24.0	10.72	45.65	11.83	8.5
1983	885	502	167	210	147	134	44290	23.8	11.47	48.62	9.79	6.5
1984	905	515	178	213	157	148	51367	24.3	11.77	51.51	9.75	5.9

Source: Thomas, R., and Dimsdale, N., Three Centuries of Macroeconomic Data, Version 2.3

* Wholesale price index scaled to 2010 prices.

We see that real GDP increased nicely (4.6 percent per annum) from 1970 to 1973. Then came the first oil shock. Real GDP declined by 1.9 percent per year from 1973 to 1975, and then started to increase. Private investment dropped sharply (down 6.7 percent per year) over these two years, and the unemployment rate moved up from 3.65 percent to 4.5 percent, and then increased some more in 1976 and 1977 to reach 5.59 percent. As we have seen for other time periods, sometimes the unemployment rate lags the other data. At the same time, the rate of inflation jumped from a rather high average of 7.2 percent per year during 1970–1973 to 22.3 percent in 1974. The rate of inflation remained very high until 1978. The average rate of inflation for 1974 to 1977 was 20.2 percent. There we have it. The rate of inflation shot up in 1974, real GDP declined, and unemployment increased with a lag of one year. That is not supposed to happen. The high rate of inflation persisted, and unemployment continued to go up. Recall that basic demand and supply analysis says that when supply declines (shifts to the left in the standard diagram), prices go up and output goes down. The evidence is that something happened on the supply side. That something was the supply of oil, which was a product domestically produced. But the same quantity was available, only at a much higher price. Also, note that the bank rate of interest moved roughly with the rate of inflation, as it is supposed to do. In fact, the oil price shock started on October 12, 1973. The bank interest rate apparently jumped immediately because inflation was expected.

The economy resumed robust growth in 1978 (up 4.2 percent over 1977), inflation cooled to 9.25 percent, and unemployment started downward. These promising trends did not last. The second oil price shock came in 1979. Real GDP fell in 1980, the unemployment rate increased to 6.81 percent and then continued to rise, and the rate of inflation moved up from 9.0 percent in 1978 to 11.8 percent in 1979 and 16.0 percent in 1980. It was happening again – supply shock followed by increased inflation, lower output, and increased unemployment.

So far, the U.K. economy and the U.S. economy were behaving similarly. The main difference is that a major source of oil for the United States was imports, while the United Kingdom had its own (much more expensive) oil. What about the years after the second oil shock? As we saw, the United States experienced a deep recession in 1982 as real GDP fell by 1.9 percent and the unemployment rate hit its highest level since the Great Depression at 9.7 percent. The United Kingdom was on the way to recovery in 1982 as real GDP increased by 2.0 percent, and continued to increase in 1983 and 1984. However, unemployment rates in both nations remained at very high levels. The United Kingdom had an unemployment rate of 11.8 percent in 1984. Interest rates declined in both countries in 1982 as inflation started to cool down. Real GDP in the United States increased in 1983 and 1984, as did real GDP in the United Kingdom. Real investment in both nations increased in 1983 and 1984. The highly publicized monetary policies in the United States designed to wring the inflationary expectations out of the economy were also followed in the United Kingdom under the Conservative government headed by Prime Minister Margaret Thatcher (who took office in 1979), and the records for the two nations remained roughly similar. The United Kingdom did not increase government expenditures as was done in the United States during 1983 and 1984. The United Kingdom relied on the increase in private investment to generate real growth.

The S&L Debacle in the United States

One important side effect of the inflation of the 1970s and the Volcker policies starting in 1979 has to do with the banks and savings and loan (S&L) industry in the United States. Do you recall the discussion in Chapter 1 of how a bank can go bankrupt? One scenario was called interest rate risk. During the 1960s the banks, and especially the S&Ls, issued long-term home mortgages (and other loans) at fixed rates of interest. Most of those loans were still being held by these financial institutions, so roughly speaking, they were living on incomes much of which was fixed in nominal terms. Then came the high interest rates of the 1970s, and the amazingly high interest rates under Volcker. Financial institutions could pay interest on time deposits and savings accounts, but those rates were regulated and were permitted only to increase slightly. A depositor had a big incentive to seek higher yields elsewhere, and so was born the money market mutual fund. These firms took in deposits (uninsured) and invested in government bonds and other instruments that had much higher yields than a depositor could earn at the local bank or S&L. Deposits migrated to the higher yields, and the higher interest rates meant that the loans on the books had dropped in market value. Bankruptcy ensued as banks and S&Ls ran out of money to pay off their depositors. I have wanted to ask Mr. Volcker whether he anticipated what is called the S&L debacle.

What happened next is, with benefit of hindsight, an absurd tale. The S&L industry was caught by the exit of deposits. Deposits were insured by the Federal Savings and Loan Insurance Corporation (FSLIC) up to $100,000, but deposits were leaving anyway to obtain higher yields. The interest rate on passbook savings at the S&Ls was regulated at 5.25 percent in 1979, but the rate on 3-month treasury bills was 10.72 percent (one of the assets that money market mutual funds held). The T-bill rate hit its highest at 16.30 percent in 1981. The regulatory agencies – the Fed for banks and the Federal Home Loan Bank Board (FHLBB) for the S&Ls – relaxed the regulations on rates for 6-month certificates of deposit, but this meant that the income from mortgages failed to cover costs. By 1982, 80 percent of the S&Ls were reporting losses.

A massive federal policy response followed. The FHLBB approved adjustable-rate mortgages in 1979, which meant that interest rates on new mortgages would adjust to changes in market interest rates. Congress passed two major laws – the Depository Institutions Deregulation and Monetary Control Act of 1980 and the Garn–St. Germain Depository Institutions Act of 1982. The provisions of these laws included the following:

- Adjustable-rate mortgages
- Expansion of the types of assets depository institutions could acquire, including credit cards, consumer loans (e.g., auto), and commercial real estate
- Payment of interest on checking accounts – Negotiated Order of Withdrawal (NOW) accounts
- Permission for the FHLBB to issue "net worth" certificates in return for promissory notes from the S&Ls, which counted as net worth
- Modification of accounting rules to increase net worth by deferring losses in asset values (so-called regulatory accounting principles)

Permission for the S&Ls to pay higher interest on deposits and to issue adjustable-rate mortgages are good ideas, but the rest of this list was a recipe for disaster. S&Ls began to invest in assets about which they knew little while being permitted to have fictional net worth. The idea was to deregulate the industry in the hopes that it could dig itself out a deep hole. Instead, much of the industry dug deeper.

The story has several twists and turns, but in 1987, 1,106 out of 3,147 S&Ls were unprofitable and 672 of the 1,106 were insolvent (negative net worth by standard accounting methods). The FSLIC went bankrupt. By 1988, 329 S&Ls had been liquidated or acquired by another firm. The problems had not been solved, so the Financial Institutions Reform, Recovery, and Enforcement Act (FIRREA) was passed in 1989. FIRREA abolished the FHLBB and the FSLIC, created tougher S&L regulation under the Office of Thrift Supervision in the Department of the Treasury, and moved deposit insurance to the Federal Deposit Insurance Corporation (FDIC), the agency that insures bank deposits. Lastly, FIRREA created the Resolution Trust Corporation (RTC), which was charged with the job of fixing the remaining S&L industry. In the end, the RTC resolved 747 S&Ls at a total cost to taxpayers of $124 billion – which now looks like chump change. This story has been related here because it should have been a warning.

Matching the theories to the narrative

The two oil price shocks of 1973 and 1979 are clearly identifiable negative shocks on the supply side of the economy. Keynesians, Monetarists, and Austrians had neglected the possibility of negative shocks to the supply side. The outcomes – decline in real output and price increases – match the implications of real business cycle theory. However, these two facts also match the implications of the Keynesian model of aggregate demand and supply from Chapter 3. Reductions in supply cut output and drive prices up. Do other facts from the episode match the other implications of the real business cycle theory? Recall that those other implications include rapid clearing of markets, absence of involuntary unemployment, and lack of need for federal stabilization policy. Rapid clearing of markets and lack of involuntary unemployment are the same idea when it comes to the labor market. Workers are presumed to adjust their supply of labor over time so that decline in labor demand in one year is matched by a decline in supply. But the unemployment rate increased in 1975 and again in 1980–1981 in both the United States and the United Kingdom.

Unemployed workers are those who are actively looking for work but cannot find a job. A sudden increase in their numbers certainly sounds involuntary. How do the real business cycle economists explain this? Lucas and Rapping (1969) did a study of the aggregate labor market that strongly influenced the subsequent development of real business cycle theory. Here is their explanation (1969, p. 748).

> As a corollary to the supply theory utilized in this paper, the survey-measured labor force (as used to compute unemployment rates) is viewed *not* as an effective market supply, part of which cannot find employment, but rather as the supply of labor that *would be forthcoming* at perceived normal wages and prices. Measured unemployment (more exactly, its nonfrictional component) is then viewed as

consisting of persons who regard the wage rates at which they could currently be employed as temporarily low, and who therefore choose to wait or search for improved conditions rather than to invest in moving or occupational change.

(emphases in original)

In short, the unemployed people are looking for the job that will pay the "normal" wage (for their occupation) rather than the lower wage that tends to be offered in a downturn. They search because they are hoping to get lucky, one supposes. Is this believable? First, are the wages really lower during a downturn? Second, the alternative view is that unemployed people are well aware of the wages that are being offered in the downturn and are looking because they want and need one of those jobs. The Lucas–Rapping story includes the fact that people drop out of the labor force during a downturn. These people quit looking for work, and many studies have confirmed this phenomenon. Do these people fit the real business cycle story too? Labor force dropouts are known as "discouraged workers," but discouraged by what? Is it the fact that they could find a job but at a lower wage than they think is fair for their skills? Or is it the idea that a lack of open jobs means that their chances of finding any kind of reasonable job are small? Or is it because they are taking time off and they will look for work later?

The idea that federal stabilization policy is useless runs up against the active monetary policy engineered by Paul Volcker and the big federal deficits of the Reagan administration. Real business cycle theory would say that a decline in the price of oil (positive supply shock) would bring the economy back to greater output and lower inflation. Monetary policy tightened in 1979 to 1981, the price of oil began to decline in 1981, and the federal government cut taxes and ran big deficits starting in 1983. A deep recession took place in 1982, but by 1983 real output was expanding and inflation had been whipped. The price of oil fell by 19.8 percent from 1980 to 1983 (and declined much more after that). But the declining price of oil is not consistent with the deep recession in 1982, unless we think that 1982 was a lagged effect of the oil price increase of 1979. Surely the tighter monetary policy is the main piece of the puzzle for 1982. The recovery in 1983 had all three factors providing a boost. The price of oil was declining, the federal government ran a very large deficit, and the rate of increase in the supply of money increased. In my view, the price of oil was not the main story during 1981 to 1983 and later. But the positive supply shock of the drop in oil prices and resulting output increase and abatement of inflation are consistent with the real business cycle theory.

What is the verdict? First of all, negative shocks to the supply side matter. We learned that the hard way. Second, the stable Phillips Curve was destroyed in the 1970s. Comparing one year to the next in Table 11.1, we see that unemployment and inflation moved in opposite directions in the United States six times (out of 14) – the usual Phillips Curve story. Unemployment and inflation moved in the same direction eight times, with both recording increases four times as the negative supply shocks had their impact. And unemployment and inflation declined together four times as apparently inflationary expectations subsided. In the United Kingdom, the unemployment rate and the wholesale price index both increased in eight years out of ten between 1975 and 1984. The explanation for the period requires a theory with both negative supply shocks and inflationary expectations that get built in and then wrung out.

Not exactly your grandfather's Keynesian theory (if he was a Keynesian). The Monetarists score points by emphasizing inflationary expectations, and the changes in the speed in the rate of the growth of the money supply had effects on the rate of inflation (both up and down). But the Monetarists had no theory of real supply shocks, only shocks to the supply of money. Fiscal policy was largely passive up until the Reagan tax cuts, but a good dose of Keynesian stimulus helped out in 1983 and 1984. But I think we cannot give the verdict to real business cycle theory because while it predicted that negative supply shocks cut output and raise prices, its implications for the labor market and the uselessness of stabilization policy are off base. Austrian and supply-side economics do not appear to be relevant in this period. For me, there is no clear winner among the real business cycle, Keynesian, and Monetarist theories. All three contribute to the story. No preponderance of the evidence. However, Temin and Vines (2014, pp. 93–94) give the verdict to the Keynesian theory that includes the aggregate supply and demand curves from Chapter 3.

Note

1   The collapse of the price of oil put enormous pressure on the economy of the Soviet Union, a major oil exporter. The lack of foreign exchange meant that the Soviets could not import the goods needed to modernize the economy. Service (2015) notes that the collapse of the oil price was a major factor in ending the Cold War.

12

Japan
Economic miracle to lost decade

Introduction

This chapter is a brief introduction to the postwar Japanese economy. The literature on the Japanese economy can fill a library, so perhaps the purpose of this chapter is to stimulate your interest in learning more about Japan. The basic outline of the period consists of:

- Control by the Allied powers through 1952
- Institution of a planned market economy
- Rapid economic growth in the 1950s and 1960s
- Oil price shocks in the 1970s
- Asset price bubble in the late 1980s
- Lost decade of the 1990s
- Continued slow economic growth thereafter

The Supreme Commander for the Allied Powers (SCAP) assumed power at the time of Japan's surrender on August 14, 1945. SCAP was headed by General Douglas MacArthur until 1951, and the Treaty of San Francisco ended the occupation in 1952. SCAP fostered the creation of a new democratic government and the end of Japan's militaristic nationalism. SCAP conducted public health and welfare programs that distributed food, improved sanitation, and revitalized Japan's health system. And MacArthur decided that Emperor Hirohito would not face war-crimes trials and need not abdicate.

During the years in which SCAP was in power, Japan devised its economic plan for recovery. The Ministry of International Trade and Industry (MITI) was created in 1949. MITI set up formal cooperation between industry and government. Major industries were permitted to form cartel-like units called keiretsu, which were then supported financially by the government. Each keiretsu was affiliated with a major bank, which in turn received funds from the Ministry of Finance via the Bank of Japan. Firms relied primarily on loans rather than sales of stock. The close relationship between a keiretsu and its bank ensured that companies could concentrate on the longer run rather than short-run profitability. MITI controlled all imports and focused on imported technology for the industries being promoted. Tariffs were used to protect industry and incentives for increasing exports were also part of the overall plan.

Japanese industry provided supplies for the United States and other allied military forces during the Korean War (1950 to 1953). But the real takeoff started in 1954. Initially, MITI concentrated on basic industries such as steel, coal, electric power, and shipbuilding. Steel became a major export industry for Japan. This author happens to know that Japanese steel could be delivered to Chicago at a price lower than that of nearby U.S. Steel. These industries supported other export industries, such as automobiles and electronic products such as television sets and VCRs (what's that?). Real GDP increased by an average of 9 percent per year in the 1960s to 1973. By the late 1960s, the Japanese economy was the second-largest economy in the world (second to the United States, of course). Japan is now the third-largest economy, behind the United States and China.

Japan was – as were many other nations – hurt by the oil price shocks of the 1970s. One solution was to switch to industries that rely on technology rather than energy. Production in other industries was switched away from energy to more environmentally conscious methods. Growth continued into the 1980s but at a slower pace. The decade of the 1990s is known as the "lost decade" because of the very low rate of growth.

Data and narrative

Macroeconomic data for Japan from 1970 to 2000 are displayed in Table 12.1. We see that the growth rate of real GDP from 1970 to 1980 was 4.36 percent. The population of Japan increased from 104.3 million in 1970 to 116.8 million in 1980 (12.0 percent), which as we shall see, was a large increase for them. These years include strong growth of 6.79 percent per year from 1970 to 1973, a small drop in real GDP in 1974, recovery in 1975, and growth of 4.29 percent per annum from 1975 to 1980. The unemployment rates in the early years of the 1970s were all below 1.5 percent, but the rate ticked up to over 2.0 percent in the latter half of the decade. Japan was affected by the oil price shocks in the 1970s. The decade was also marked by rapid growth in the money supply of 13 percent per year and rapid inflation, especially from 1973 to 1977. The rate of inflation in 1974 was an eye-popping 23.2 percent. The discount rate was set at 9.0 percent in 1974 (and 8.0 percent in 1975). All in all, one might conclude that the Japanese economy made it through the 1970s pretty well.

The economy of the 1980s displays a smoother growth in real GDP of 4.43 percent per annum. Population growth was 5.74 percent for the decade of 1980 to 1990, less than half of the growth in the 1970s. The rate of population growth continued to decline after 1990 and surely is a factor in Japan's economic difficulties. The unemployment rate continued to rise and reached 2.85 percent in 1986, then declined to 2.1 percent in 1990. The rate of inflation in the 1980s was much lower than in the 1970s and included virtually no inflation during 1986 to 1988. The supply of money increased an average of 5.2 percent per annum, instead of the double digits of the 1970s.

TABLE 12.1 Macroeconomic Data for Japan, 1970–2000

Year	Real GDP Trillion Yen (2011)	Real Investment Trillion Yen (2011)	Un-empl. (pct)	M1 Trillion Yen	GDP Deflator (pct)	Discount Rate, pct. (July)
1970	168.4	63.2	1.15	225	6.92	6.25
1971	176.8	63.7	1.22	275	6.40	5.25
1972	191.2	70.0	1.42	337	4.84	4.25
1973	206.5	78.3	1.27	431	11.61	6.00
1974	204.0	73.3	1.37	488	23.22	9.00
1975	210.3	69.5	1.89	547	11.73	8.00
1976	218.7	72.0	2.01	621	9.37	6.50
1977	228.3	74.2	2.02	664	8.16	5.00
1978	240.3	79.8	2.24	731	4.21	3.50
1979	253.5	84.9	2.08	810	3.30	5.25
1980	260.0	84.1	2.21	830	7.78	9.00
1981	271.6	85.8	2.35	858	4.91	6.25
1982	280.5	85.1	2.66	908	2.74	5.50
1983	290.5	81.9	2.71	941	1.90	5.50
1984	303.6	84.4	2.62	968	2.26	5.00
1985	319.4	91.8	2.76	1017	2.03	5.00
1986	330.1	96.1	2.85	1087	0.60	3.50
1987	345.7	102.3	2.53	1201	0.13	2.50
1988	369.1	117.6	2.27	1302	0.68	2.50
1989	387.1	127.7	2.11	1355	2.27	3.25
1990	406.0	137.0	2.10	1390	3.08	5.25
1991	419.9	140.7	2.10	1462	3.25	5.50
1992	423.4	135.6	2.50	1528	1.76	3.25
1993	421.3	131.1	2.15	1576	1.24	2.50
1994	425.4	128.2	3.89	1659	0.70	1.75
1995	437.1	134.2	3.15	1795	−0.13	1.00
1996	450.6	143.3	3.35	2049	0.14	0.50
1997	455.5	140.9	3.40	2219	1.75	0.50
1998	450.4	134.4	4.11	2409	0.66	0.50
1999	449.2	128.2	4.68	2662	−0.34	0.50
2000	461.7	131.9	4.72	2880	−0.68	0.50

Source: OECD Data

The 1980s were not the economic miracle of the 1950s and 1960s, but steady growth with low inflation spell a pretty good economy, do they not?

On the other hand, Japan was experiencing an asset price bubble of epic proportions in the late 1980s. Speculative fever was running rampant. From 1985 to 1990, commercial land in the six major metropolitan areas had increased in price by 303 percent. Residential land was up 180 percent, and industrial land had increased 162 percent over the same years. The Nikkei 225 stock index ran between 9,900 and 11,600 during 1984 and closed on December 29, 1989 at 38,900. It was said that the square mile of land under the Imperial Palace in central Tokyo was worth more than the whole state of California. Growth stocks had ratios of stock price to earnings of 60 or more – absurdly high.

How did the asset bubble start? One theory blames exchange rates. The U.S. dollar had appreciated by about 50 percent against the Japanese yen during the first half of the 1980s. Very high interest rates in the United States were one cause of this appreciation. The dollar had also appreciated against the European currencies. As you know, an appreciated currency makes imports to the United States cheaper and U.S. exports more expensive. U.S. exporters complained loudly and lobbied for protectionist policies. Instead, the Reagan administration began negotiations leading to the trade deal known as the Plaza Accord.

The Plaza Accord (signed at the Plaza Hotel in New York in 1985) was an agreement between the United States, Japan, and the major European nations to depreciate the U.S. dollar by about 50 percent. The central banks of these countries participated in the effort by selling dollars. The appreciation of the Japanese yen against the dollar reduced Japanese exports and created an incentive for expansionary monetary policies. From Table 12.1, we can see that the rate of growth of the money supply was 4.06 percent per year from 1980 to 1985, and then increased to 6.25 percent per year from 1985 to 1990. This increase in the supply of money is given some of the blame for the asset price bubble. However, speculative fever probably was the main cause of the bubble.

Now we come to the 1990s, the "lost decade." What do they mean by "lost?" First of all, the average growth rate for the 1990s was only 1.29 percent per year, and population grew from 123.5 million in 1990 to 126.8 million in 2000, only 2.67 percent for the decade (0.26 percent per year). We see in Table 12.1 that real GDP declined slightly (0.5 percent) in 1993 and barely changed from 1996 to 1999. The unemployment rate began the decade at 2.1 percent and in 2000 reached 4.72 percent. In an effort to get the economy moving, the discount rate was dropped from 5.50 percent in 1991 to 0.50 percent in 1996. We can see that private investment apparently did not respond to this policy move. The supply of money increased by 7.28 percent per year, but the rate of inflation declined and reached a negative number in 1995 of −0.13 percent. What Japan had lost was its ability to grow.

Assessment of theories

The oil supply shocks of the 1970s are seen in the Japanese case. Look at 1974. Inflation ballooned to 23.2 percent and real GDP declined. This is stagflation, just as in the United States and the United Kingdom in that year. The second oil supply shock of 1979 is less evident for Japan, although inflation did pop up from

3.3 percent in 1979 to 7.78 percent in 1980. The real business cycle theory scores a point. We can agree that perturbations on the supply side of the economy are important. We also see that rapid inflation was accompanied by rapid growth in the money supply. Score a point for the Monetarists. How about the Keynesians? As you know, Keynesians look to the volatility of private investment as a source of fluctuations, and we see that real private investment did indeed decline in 1974 and 1975 and did not exceed its former high level until 1978. However, the fluctuations in real investment do not come close to telling the whole story. An understanding of the 1970s for Japan requires parts of all three theories.

The 1980s were a time of relative peace and quiet in the macro economy of Japan. Real GDP grew steadily, real investment grew (except for a dip in 1982–1983), and inflation was low. There were no shocks on the supply side. The discount rate was reduced, and the supply of money grew by a rate that was slightly greater than the real growth rate of the economy (5.2 percent and 4.4 percent, respectively). One hopes that Milton Friedman was pleased. Japan seems to have been following Friedman's monetary policy rule. Score one for the Monetarists. The reasonably steady increase in real investment might lead Keynesians to say, "See, lack of fluctuations in investment mean a steady, growing economy."

As for the 1990s, the Keynesian economist Paul Krugman (2009) argues that Japan suffered from what is called the liquidity trap. As we know from Chapter 2, the liquidity trap is a Keynesian concept.

Increases in the supply of money will not reduce interest rates and influence real output, because interest rates are very low and holding money seems to be a good option. See Figure 12.1. It seems that at work is Tobin's theory of the demand for money as part of a risk-averse portfolio strategy. Fiscal policy – especially spending increases – must be used to bring the economy back. Recall that this case was discussed in Chapter 2. How did Japan manage to get into the predicament?

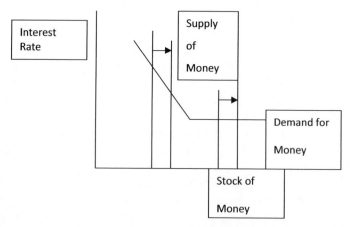

FIGURE 12.1 The Supply of and Demand for Money. The supply of money is fixed by the central bank. The demand for money declines with the interest rate because the interest rate is the cost of holding money, an asset which does not earn interest. At some very low rate, the interest rate no longer has any effect on the amount of money demanded. Increases in the supply of money will not lower interest rates and stimulate the economy. The horizontal demand function for money is the case of the liquidity trap, which some Keynesians such as Paul Krugman believe describes the situation faced by Japan in the lost decade

First, the asset bubble burst. As Hyman Minsky warned, a successful economy sometimes will lead people to expect that success will continue and they will bid up asset prices, which in turn will continue to rise because they continue to rise. Banks had become increasingly aggressive in making loans on real estate. Remember, asset bubbles happen sometimes, but not always. But when and under what conditions do bubbles occur? As we say, more research is needed. Second, Japan has an aging and stagnant population. Not enough energetic younger people are entering the labor force. And the unemployment rate data indicate that the economy was running below potential. Japan used fiscal policy – spending – in an effort to stimulate the economy, but concerns about the size of the government's deficit held back the spending.

Does the verdict go to Keynesian theory, augmented by Minsky's bubble story? Perhaps, but Hayashi and Prescott (2002) argue that the basic cause of slow growth was a lack of productivity growth, a negative supply shock. They point out that the financial system did not collapse and that financing for firms was still available. But what caused the lack of productivity growth? Could it have been negative "animal spirits"?

Conclusion

The Japanese miracle was organized by the government largely through MITI and the system for financing key industries. The growth rate cooled in the 1970s and 1980s but was still over 4 percent per year. Then an asset price bubble brought about a Keynesian liquidity trap situation with which monetary policy could not cope. Fiscal policy was exercised cautiously. During the 1990s, the economy experienced what can be called a growth recession – slow growth rate below the increase in the capacity of the economy. Would the "lost decade" turn into more lost decades? We shall see. . . .

13

The Great
Moderation

Introduction

The years from 1985 to a point early in the 21st century are known in the United States as the Great Moderation. As Bernanke (2013, p. 39) shows with two convincing graphs in his book that is recommended to you, the variability of GDP growth and inflation was much smaller during these years than during the years from 1950 to 1984. Alan Greenspan succeeded Paul Volcker as chairman of the Fed in 1987, and Bernanke thinks that stable monetary policy played an important role in the Great Moderation by maintaining the low inflation rate that had been achieved by 1983 and 1984. We shall judge for ourselves.

Did the United Kingdom experience the same low inflation and stable growth in real GDP during those years? The answer is no. The U.K. economy did not do very well until the late 1990s. We shall attempt to find out the reasons for the disappointing results.

The data and the narrative for the United States

The data in Table 13.1 depict a time of rather remarkable stability compared to the previous 15 years. The remainder of the 1980s after 1984 is marked by growing real GDP, declining unemployment, and inflation that picked up somewhat to 3.9 percent in 1989. Government spending increased in 1985 and 1986, largely because of increases in national defense spending under the Reagan administration, but further increases were modest until the next mild recession in 2001. The federal government deficit was about $150 billion per year for 1987 to 1989, down from $221 billion in 1986.

The economy had a mild recession in 1991, with residential construction down in real terms by over 8 percent in both 1990 and 1991 and unemployment up from 5.6 percent in 1990 to 6.8 percent in 1991 and 7.5 percent in 1992. The unemployment rate lags the other measures of macroeconomic activity. The unemployment rate was back down to 6.9 percent in 1993 and headed for much lower figures that include 4.0

TABLE 13.1 U.S. Macroeconomic Data, 1985–2003

Year	Real GDP Growth Pct	Real C Growth Pct	Real I Growth Pct	Residential Constr. Growth Pct	Real G Growth Pct	Unempl Pct	Inflation Pct	M1 Change Pct	Fed Funds Rate Pct
1985	4.2	5.3	−0.1	2.3	6.8	7.2	3.2	12.4	8.10
1986	3.5	4.2	0.2	12.4	5.4	7.0	2.0	16.9	6.80
1987	3.5	3.4	2.8	2.0	3.0	6.2	2.6	3.5	6.66
1988	4.2	4.2	2.5	−0.9	1.3	5.5	3.5	4.9	7.57
1989	3.7	2.9	4.0	−3.2	2.9	5.3	3.9	0.8	9.21
1990	1.9	2.1	−2.6	−8.5	3.2	5.6	3.7	4.0	8.10
1991	−0.1	0.2	−6.6	−8.9	1.2	6.8	3.3	8.8	5.69
1992	3.6	3.7	7.3	13.8	0.5	7.5	2.3	14.3	3.52
1993	2.7	3.5	8.0	8.2	−0.8	6.9	2.4	10.2	3.02
1994	4.0	3.9	11.9	9.0	0.1	6.1	2.1	1.9	4.21
1995	2.7	3.0	3.2	−3.4	0.5	5.6	2.1	−2.0	5.83
1996	3.8	3.5	8.8	8.2	1.0	5.4	1.8	−4.1	5.30
1997	4.5	3.8	11.4	2.4	1.9	4.9	1.7	−0.8	5.46
1998	4.5	5.3	9.5	8.6	2.1	4.5	1.1	2.1	5.35
1999	4.7	5.3	8.4	6.3	3.4	4.2	1.5	2.5	4.97
2000	4.1	5.1	6.5	0.7	1.9	4.0	2.3	−3.1	6.24
2001	1.0	2.6	−6.1	0.9	3.8	4.7	2.3	8.7	3.88
2002	1.8	2.6	−0.6	6.1	4.4	5.8	1.5	3.1	1.67
2003	2.8	3.1	4.1	9.1	2.2	6.0	2.0	7.1	1.13

Source: Economic Report of the President, 2020

percent in 2000. The inflation rate was quite stable compared to the prior 15 years as well; it was no higher than 3.9 percent and dropped to a very low 1.1 percent in 1998. As usual, real investment was the most volatile component of GDP, but there were no huge drops in the rate of investment that had characterized the previous decade or so. Residential construction was more volatile than total investment up through 1993 and was a major factor in the downturn in 1991, but actually was less volatile than total investment from 1994 to 2001.

After the shallow recession of 1991, the growth rate of GDP averaged 3.8 percent from 1992 to 2000. Another recession took place in 2001 (although the GDP actually decreased by only 0.1 percent in the annual data). Real investment growth was 8.3 percent per year and investment in residential construction was up 6.0 percent per year during 1992 to 2000. In other words, residential construction did not run hotter than investment as a whole in the 1990s. In fact, firms were investing in equipment, intellectual property, and nonresidential structures at a growth rate of 8.6 percent per year. The computer and information technology revolution was in effect, and the productivity data bear this out.

As we have seen, the 1990s ended on a high note. The so-called Y2K emergency (in which it was feared that all computers would go crazy because they would not be able to move dates forward from 1999 to 2000) did not occur. But not all was well. The stock market experienced a bubble in stock values associated with the Internet revolution. The tech-heavy NASDAQ stock index closed at its record high of 5048.62 on March 10, 2000 but declined by 10 percent on March 20. The losses continued until October 10, 2002, when the NASDAQ closed at 1108.49, a loss of 78 percent. The stock market losses precipitated a so-called mild recession in 2001 that lasted eight months. (Recall that a recession is defined as two successive quarters of negative growth in GDP.) Real GDP declined by 0.5 percent (annual rate) in the first quarter of 2001, increased by a weak 1.2 percent in the second quarter, and fell again by 1.4 percent in the third quarter. The recession of 2001 does not even show up as negative real growth in the annual data in Table 13.1. There was, however, a sizable decline in nonresidential fixed investment of 10.5 percent, and investment in inventories declined as well. Exports declined; net exports fell from negative $451 billion in 2000 to negative $548 billion in 2002 (and net exports continued to decline up through 2006). Many observers think that the entry of China into the World Trade Organization in 2001 was an important factor in the decline in U.S. exports and the jump in the trade deficit. The declines in investment and net exports were offset by increases in consumption and state and local government spending.

Now look at monetary policy, which beginning in 1987 was under the chairmanship of Alan Greenspan. The money supply increased by large amounts in 1985 and 1986 as the federal government continued to run deficits of over $200 billion per year. Under Greenspan, the money supply increased by an average of only 3.3 percent from 1987 to 1990, and the federal funds rate was raised from 6.66 percent in 1987 to 9.21 percent in 1989 and then lowered to 8.10 percent in 1990 after investment spending began to decline in real terms. The federal funds rate was cut sharply in 1991, 1992, and 1993 in response to the recession, and the money supply increased 11.1 percent during these years. Real GDP growth resumed in 1992, and the unemployment rate started declining in 1993. These years are regarded as an example of successful discretionary monetary policy. Federal fiscal policy helped by increasing expenditures and running large deficits of over $220 billion during 1990 to 1993 (with the largest deficit of $290 billion in 1992).

As noted earlier, the economy grew rapidly during the remainder of the 1990s and the unemployment rate reached 4.0 percent in 2000. The economy was buoyed by investment spending. Monetary policy focused on keeping inflation low by restraining the growth of the money supply and pushing the federal funds rate from the low 3.02 percent in 1993 up to over 5.3 percent from 1995 to 1999. Indeed, the supply of money did not grow at all from 1994 to 1999. These years enhanced the reputation of Greenspan and the Fed as practitioners of deft monetary policy. The strong growth in the economy produced increases in federal tax revenues that far exceeded the increases in government spending on goods and services. The federal government ran a surplus of $69 billion in total receipts over outlays in fiscal year 1998, and the surplus increased to $126 billion in 1999 and $236 billion in 2000. The mild recession of 2001 reduced revenues, but the government still ran a surplus of $128 billion in fiscal year 2001, the last fiscal year under President Bill Clinton. Bob Woodward, of Woodward and Bernstein fame from their investigations into the Watergate scandal, published a book in 2000 on Greenspan and the Fed titled *Maestro: Greenspan's Fed and the American Boom*. Greenspan also made news when he asserted that the stock market was influenced by "irrational exuberance" during the late 1990s.

In 2000, the federal funds rate was increased to 6.24 percent and the money supply fell by 3.1 percent. These changes probably contributed to the mild recession of 2001 that accompanied the crashing of the stock market bubble of the time. This recession had declines in investment spending (nonresidential in this case) and exports and an increase in unemployment. Recovery appeared to be weak, so the Fed cut the federal funds rate in 2001, 2002, and 2003 – down to 1.13 percent in 2003. The money supply increased by an average of 6.3 percent during these three years. The federal budget turned from surplus in 2001 to large deficits starting in 2002. The deficit was $378 billion in 2003 (and $413 billion in 2004) as tax rates were cut and expenditures increased under President George W. Bush. These and other responses to the recession of 2001 are discussed in greater detail in the Chapter 14.

Data and narrative for the United Kingdom

The U.K. experience in the second half of the 1980s differs from that of the United States. Data for the United Kingdom. are shown in Table 13.2. The United Kingdom, like the United States, came out of the second oil market shock with a high unemployment rate and high interest rates, but both persisted longer in the United Kingdom. The unemployment rate did decline from 11.77 percent in 1984 to 7.22 percent in 1989 as real GDP growth picked up to 4.10 percent per year during those years. Total employment increased from 24.3 million in 1984 to 26.7 million in 1989. Large increases in the supply of money (up 14.2 percent per year) seem to have given the economy a boost. Real government spending did not increase, so discretionary fiscal policy was not being deployed. It is well to recall that the U.K. government was being run by the Conservative Party and Prime Minister Margaret Thatcher during these years. The Conservative Party opposed the use of Keynesian fiscal policy. Ms. Thatcher remained PM until 1990, but the Conservative Party continued to run the government after she left office.

The United Kingdom was also hit by a recession in 1991. The United Kingdom and the United States had roughly similar outcomes during this recession. U.K. real GDP declined, and the unemployment rate increased and reached 10.37 percent in 1993. Total employment hit a bottom of 25.3 million in 1993, down 1.6 million compared to 1990. The apparent cause is a decline in real private investment of 7.6 percent in 1991, and this lower level of investment of about £215 to £220 billion continued up through 1995. Recovery from the recession was clear in 1994, and a solid increase in real exports can be given credit. The increase in exports of £44 billion from 1992 to 1994 is 61 percent of the increase in real GDP of £72 billion. Real consumption spending increased, but real government spending changed very

TABLE 13.2 U.K. Macroeconomic Data, 1985–2003

Year	Real GDP £bil. (2013)	Real Con-sump.	Real Invest-Ment	Real Gov't Spend	Real Export	Real Import	M1 (£mil.)	Empl. (mil.)	Un-empl. Pct.	Wh'sl Price*	Ave. Bank Rate Pct.
1985	943	542	181	216	167	151	61129	24.6	11.36	54.70	12.33
1986	972	574	179	215	174	162	75429	24.7	11.32	55.45	10.83
1987	1024	604	201	219	185	175	92780	25.2	19.43	57.34	9.63
1988	1084	649	232	219	187	197	105,968	26.1	8.57	59.45	10.29
1989	1111	674	243	221	196	262	124,257	26.7	7.22	62.29	13.92
1990	1112	681	237	227	207	213	132,876	26.9	7.10	66.18	14.75
1991	1107	678	219	233	217	204	137,986	26.2	8.82	69.74	11.54
1992	1111	684	215	236	227	218	142,918	25.5	9.95	71.91	9.42
1993	1139	705	217	234	248	225	152,065	25.3	10.37	74.76	5.92
1994	1183	728	220	237	271	239	156,882	25.5	9.50	76.63	5.48
1995	1213	743	219	240	291	252	175,694	25.8	8.62	79.71	6.69
1996	1244	772	229	242	314	276	188,667	26.1	8.10	81.83	5.96
1997	1283	810	216	241	324	299	210,881	26.5	6.97	82.63	6.58
1998	1324	841	244	249	331	326	227,894	26.8	6.26	82.68	7.21
1999	1367	881	250	258	361	348	247,986	27.2	5.98	83.13	5.33
2000	1418	924	259	267	363	380	274,679	27.5	5.46	84.32	5.98
2001	1457	957	256	278	366	392	304,711	27.7	5.10	84.07	5.08
2002	1492	992	263	290	386	408	332,839	27.9	5.19	83.96	4.00
2003	1543	1029	269	302	408	429	368,301	28.2	5.01	84.52	3.69

Source: Thomas, R., and Dimsdale, N., Three Centuries of Macroeconomic Data, Version 2.3

* Wholesale price index scaled to 2010 prices.

little during those two years. The average bank rate fell from 9.42 percent to 5.48 percent, and the supply of money increased by 6.4 percent.

Once the recovery from the 1991 recession had taken hold in 1994, the economy of the United Kingdom as measured by real GDP grew steadily by 2.95 percent per year from 1994 to 2003. The nation did not experience a recession in 2001. The unemployment rate declined steadily as well, reaching 5.01 percent in 2003, and total employment stood at 28.2 million in 2003, up from 25.5 million in 1994. Real investment increased in every year except 1997 but recovered quickly in 1998. Interest rates increased from 5.48 percent in 1994 to 7.21 percent in 1998, but then fell to 3.69 percent in 2003. The supply of money increased in every year from 1994 to 2003 at an average rate of 9.48 percent per year. In short, the U.K. economy did have a period that can be called a great moderation after recovery from the recession of 1991. It is reasonably clear that monetary policy, as reflected in the increasing supply of money, was a factor in producing the favorable outcome.

Changes in the financial sectors

The basic macroeconomic narrative of the previous sections fails to tell the story of financial sectors of the United States and the United Kingdom as they underwent massive changes in the 1980s and 1990s. We shall first consider the United Kingdom, and then will turn to the United States.

The structure of the U.K. financial system is a story of the emergence of large banks that provide a full range of financial services. As Davies et al. (2010) state, these large and interconnected banks became "too important to fail."

In the 1960s, the U.K. banking system consisted mainly of clearing banks that provided basic banking services and made conservative investments, as well as building societies that primarily concentrated on home loans. London became an international financial center in the subsequent decades as foreign banks entered the United Kingdom and British banks such as the Royal Bank of Scotland (RBS), Barclays, HSBC, and Lloyds Banking Group expanded in scale and scope. These very large banks, in addition to providing basic banking services, also offer securities underwriting and trading, foreign currency services including futures contracts, investment management, trading in derivatives, and various insurance services. Derivatives are securities with returns based on assets that are bundled together to create a new security. An example is the mortgage-backed security in which several thousands of individual loans are packaged into a security with several "tranches" – different securities that vary according to risk and return. More details about mortgage-backed securities are provided later in the discussion of the U.S. financial system. As Davies et al. (2010) noted, as of 2010, a majority of the earnings of these banks were of the noninterest variety (i.e., interest paid on loans to customers).

What factors account for the restructuring of banking in the United Kingdom? Davies et al. (2010) suggested four factors: economies of scale and scope, demand-side forces, regulatory changes, and being too important to fail.

Economies of scale refer to a lowering of unit costs from an expansion of existing product lines, while economies of scope are cost savings because some of the same costs can support more than one product – the unit cost of providing several services is lower than if those same services are offered separately. Economies of scale arise by the spreading of fixed costs, such as technology and corporate headquarters, over a larger output. Technical change is given credit for economies of scope. However, Davies et al. reviewed the empirical evidence and found that there is no compelling evidence of significant economies of scale or scope in banking.

The demand side of the market for financial services clearly played a role in the transformation of U.K. banking. Large companies prefer to have a variety of services provided by a single company. For example, U.K. firms are relying more heavily on bond and equity financing rather than bank loans. Thus, they need to be able to issue stock and have bonds underwritten. They also avail themselves of investment banking services. And they prefer a financial services firm with international presence.

Changes in regulatory policy in the United Kingdom have been designed to facilitate the transformation of banking. The Competition and Credit Control (CCC) provisions, adopted in 1971, permitted banks to widen the scope of their activities, ended collusion on deposit rates, and relaxed liquidity requirements. Prior to 1971, clearing banks had been required to hold reserves equal to 28% of deposits. After 1971, reserve requirements for all banks were set at 12.5 percent of certain liabilities. In 1979, restrictions on which banks could deal in foreign exchange were eliminated and controls on foreign exchange were ended. These two actions greatly expanded the flow of international capital. And in the 1980s, U.K. banks established branches in other countries, including the United States.

Then in 1986, the United Kingdom reformed what were thought to be uncompetitive practices in the London Stock Exchange. The changes are known as the "Big Bang." Rigid pricing of brokerage services was eliminated, and entry into the Stock Exchange was made easier. Fixed minimum commissions were ended, and brokers were permitted to trade on their own accounts. Foreign firms began to enter the London Stock Exchange. The relaxation of these restrictions, as described earlier, gave banks the opportunity to expand into new activities and therefore to conduct marketing campaigns emphasizing their new wide range of services.

These same years saw the introduction of international standards for bank regulation. The Basel Accord of 1988 introduced new standards for liquidity based on the ratings of various types of liabilities. Adherence to the new standards increased the fixed costs for banks, and therefore increased the incentive to grow larger to keep average fixed costs low.

As noted previously, the new gigantic banks became "too important to fail." In other words, firms perceived that the government had their backs. The failure of one of these banks would mean disruption in the functioning of the entire financial system, something the government could not let happen. In the language of microeconomics, banks would not "internalize" (recognize) the economic costs of possible failure. The implicit public subsidy means that market discipline would be weakened, and the banks would become more reliant on debt to finance their far-flung operations. Banks would take on increased risk to increase expected returns. And banks would increasingly rely on what is called wholesale funding, meaning large short-term loans provided by major institutions such as insurance companies and pension funds. Some of these loans were as short as a single day and would be renewed daily. Indeed, Davies et al. (2010) show that the median leverage ratio of U.K. banks increased from about 20 percent in 2000 to 47 percent in 2008.

The expansion of banks into derivative markets and securitization markets, plus reliance on wholesale funding, created the possibility that a negative shock to one bank could spread to other institutions and lead to a financial panic.

Now we shall take a look at the changes in the U.S. financial system. *The Financial Crisis Inquiry Report* (2011) provides a good background discussion of the changes in the United States, and is summarized here. This report identified four major changes in the financial system that set the stage for the financial crisis of 2008. These four are as follows.

Growth of shadow banking

There is no precise definition of shadow banking, but the basic idea is that lightly regulated (or unregulated) financial institutions perform many of the functions of traditional banks and may conduct many other operations as well. Early examples are the money market mutual funds (MMMF) that grew up in the wake of the high interest rates of the late 1970s and early 1980s. People withdrew their funds from traditional, regulated banks and savings and loan associations and invested in MMMFs to earn much higher returns. But MMMFs are lightly regulated, and the deposits are not insured. The most prominent shadow banks are the investment banks such as Goldman Sachs, Lehman Brothers, and Bear Stearns. These institutions funded themselves in part by the use of what are called repurchase agreements (repos). They borrowed money based on collateral that they promised to repurchase. Many of those repo agreements were of very short duration, such as one day. Typically, the lender would agree to roll over the repo and keep the loan in place. The investment bank would use the loan to invest in long-term financial assets such as mortgage-backed securities. But if the lender refused to roll over the repo, the investment bank could be insolvent in a matter of a few days (or hours).

Securitization and derivatives

This refers to the rapid growth in the market for securities based on assets of various kinds. The first such securities were the mortgage-backed securities created by Fannie Mae and Freddie Mac, the government-sponsored enterprises charged with facilitating lending for homeowners. Such a security starts with a big pile of individual home mortgages (say 1,000 of them) which are sold by the initiators of the loans (e.g., banks) to the creator of the security. The bank has removed the loan from its books and has money to make more loans. The security is created and pays a return to the investor from the payments made by the mortgage borrowers. Investment banks became big players in the creation of mortgage-backed securities and securities based on other types of assets, such as auto loans and credit card loans.

Securitization is not a bad idea by itself, because it permits a better matching of investors and investment vehicles. However, the downside is that the creators of the original assets, such as mortgages, have an incentive not to provide full information about the quality of the assets, and then the institution that acquires the mortgages has an incentive not to provide full information to the ultimate investor in the asset-backed security. This phenomenon is called moral hazard. A mortgage-backed security is an example of a derivative – a financial contract with a price derived from the value of some underlying asset, rate, index, or event. A major category of derivatives is called credit default swaps. The idea is that an owner of a mortgage-backed security, for example, could pay an annual fee to some financial firm, such as an investment bank, that would protect this owner against certain "events." Such events are an increase in the number of mortgage defaults or a decline in the rating of the security by the bond-rating firms. Credit default swaps were completely unregulated and traded over the counter (OTC), not on an organized exchange. Credit default swaps essentially are insurance policies, but regular insurance (life, accident, etc.) is regulated. The actual insurance company AIG became a big player in the unregulated credit default swap business. What could go wrong here?

Financial regulation and deregulation

A series of laws enacted in the United States in the 1990s permitted banks and other financial institutions to become much larger and offer a far more comprehensive menu of financial services. A 1994 law permitted bank holding companies to acquire banks in every state, preempting state laws limiting branch banking. A series of large mergers ensued, creating the mega-banks Bank of America, Citigroup, JPMorgan Chase, Wachovia, and Wells Fargo. The five largest investment banks that emerged were Goldman Sachs, Morgan Stanley, Merrill Lynch, Lehman Brothers, and Bear Stearns. Another major law, the Gramm–Leach–Bliley Act of 1999, eliminated the distinction between regular banks and investment banks that had been in place since 1933 (under the Glass–Steagall Act). The Act permitted bank holding companies to sell banking, investment, and insurance services. Investment banks could own savings and loan associations (with deposit insurance) without supervision by the Fed. (S&Ls were supervised by the Office of Thrift Supervision.)

Changes in mortgage lending

The securitization of mortgages was begun by Fannie Mae during the Great Depression, and only the government-sponsored enterprises created these securities prior to the 1980s. The private sector got into the business in that decade, and the securities became much more complex. A change in the income tax law was a complicating factor. According to the 1986 Tax Reform Act, interest on only home loans could be deducted, eliminating deduction of interest on other types of loans such as auto loans and personal loans. This change created the market for home-equity loans – loans based on the value of the home minus the outstanding balance on the existing mortgage. People started to borrow against their homes to pay for cars, college tuition, and other expenses. A company called The Money Store borrowed on short-term lines of credit, granted home-equity loans, and sold these loans in the secondary market. Some households borrowed more money against their home than it later was worth.

During the 1990s, lenders started to engage in what is called subprime mortgage lending, lending to households with weaker financial credentials. This market was characterized by numerous abusive practices such as high prepayment penalties, deception, high-pressure tactics, forged signatures, falsification of incomes and appraisals, and bait-and-switch tactics. The subprime lending market did not grow rapidly until after 2000, but it began in the 1990s. The Federal Reserve had the authority to regulate mortgages issued by member banks, but it failed to act. Other agencies oversaw the national banks and S&Ls, but they also failed to act. And private mortgage brokers, the originators of many of the subprime loans, were not regulated by anybody. Conservatives such as Wallison (2015) blame the growth of subprime mortgages on federal policy aimed at increasing lending to low- and moderate-income households. Starting in 1996, Fannie Mae and Freddie Mac were ordered to purchase more and more of these loans, which these agencies insured against default.

All of these changes added up to a financial system dominated by large firms (too big to fail?) subject to inconsistent (and nonexistent) regulation and shot through with moral hazard in the vast market for derivative securities. Why were all of these changes permitted to happen? Some people, such as Fed board member Edward Gramlich and Brooksley Born of the Commodity Futures Trading Commission (CFTC), did voice concerns. We may never have the full explanation. One factor was the widespread belief that financial markets are efficient. Risks are assessed accurately, and asset prices and returns reflect those risks. Investors make rational decisions. Anomalies in the markets are eliminated quickly. Investors know enough to avoid creating financial bubbles in which asset prices become divorced from underlying indicators of value. Needless to say. . . .

The Great Moderation and macroeconomic theories

Let us return to the more pleasant days of the later 1980s and the 1990s, when the U.S. and U.K. macro economies were reasonably stable and growing nicely. How do the theories stack up?

The economy was becoming higher tech. It was the heyday of discretionary monetary policy. In the United States,. Paul Volcker at the Fed had actually whipped inflation in the early 1980s and the federal budget under President Reagan had given the economy a nice Keynesian boost. Along with the folks in Silicon Valley, Maestro Greenspan and his minions were in charge. Keynesianism had returned to prominence in the United States. Or had it?

The discussion of monetary policy rules had broadened in the 1980s to include a wide variety of ideas that would involve the central bank responding to economic conditions in predictable fashion. John Taylor was a leader in this discussion, and he proposed his first "Taylor rule" in a 1993 article (1993). As noted in Chapter 4, the rule involves setting the target for the federal funds rate – the interest rate that banks charge each other on short-term loans used to meet reserve requirements set by the Fed. The Fed controls this rate directly by buying and selling government bonds, so the Taylor rule involves setting a policy instrument that is actually under control of the central bank. That rule is as follows:

$$i = 1 + 1.5p - 0.5y,$$

where i is the target federal funds rate, p is the rate of inflation over the previous four quarters, and y is the percent deviation of real GDP from a target. What does this equation say? For one thing, it says that if the rate of inflation is 2 percent and GDP is on target (y = 0), then the federal funds rate should be set at 4 percent, or 2 percent in real terms (after inflation). In short, 2 percent is a target for the rate of inflation and 4 percent is the accompanying federal funds rate. Does that sound familiar? It should, because that is the target rate for inflation espoused by the Fed.

Taylor (1993) showed that the hypothetical federal funds rate set according to the rule corresponded closely to the actual federal funds rate for 1987 to 1992. Subsequent research showed that the actual federal funds rate and the rate based on the Taylor rule were quite close from 1987 up through 2001 in the United States. Such was not the case in the United Kingdom. There, monetary policy produced large increases in the supply of money.

The Taylor rule and other similar rules are responses to the need for monetary policy to respond to short-term economic conditions and to the concern that unpredictable policy responses can interfere with the efficacy of private decisions and be just plain wrong. What are we to make of the fact that actual Fed discretionary policy pretty nearly followed the Taylor rule for more than a decade? Who wins the argument – the Keynesians, who argue for discretionary policy, or the Monetarists and others, who argue that monetary policy is a dangerous toy that children and bureaucrats are not to play with? Not entirely clear, is it? Later, Taylor (2009) wrote that the Fed made a big mistake during 2002–2005 by setting the federal funds rate too low. And former Fed chair Ben Bernanke disagreed vehemently with the Taylor rule advocates.

Does the period of the Great Moderation lend credence to either real business cycle theory or Austrian theory? Real business cycle theory looks for shocks on the supply side as a source of short-term fluctuations. The supply side of the economy was being expanded by the computer revolution, which was not a short-term shock. The mild recession of 1991 was the result of a drop in investment spending – primarily spending on construction that resulted from an increase in interest rates. The other mild recession of 2001 was set off by the crash in the stock market from the "irrational exuberance" of the tech boom. Neither of these comports with real business cycle theory. Indeed, they both sound Keynesian (with a Minsky-type bubble in the later one). Austrians look for an interest rate set by the central bank that causes too much real investment to take place. We now know that too much high-tech gear was installed (e.g., more fiber-optic cable than was needed for years). Was that caused by central bank policy? Hardly. It was the exuberance brought on by a new technology that promised great reward. Companies kept issuing stock, and buyers kept buying it at higher and higher prices until they did not. What about the fact that the economy quickly snapped back from the 1991 recession? We have already seen that the Fed acted aggressively by lowering interest rates and acting to increase the money supply – and that investment, especially residential construction, responded. Would the economy have improved quickly if the Fed had not acted? Both the real business cycle folks and the Austrians think that the economy can recover on its own. Mr. Greenspan was not going to chance it. And, as we shall see in Chapter 14, the economy was not snapping back from the 2001 recession in satisfactory fashion.

The period ends with the deeply conservative Greenspan in charge of the U.S. central bank, doing the job he was hired to do – conduct discretionary monetary policy in pursuit of high employment and low inflation – but the discretionary monetary policy was pretty close to a Monetarist rule. Both the Keynesians and the Monetarists score points. The United Kingdom did not use Keynesian fiscal policy and relied instead on discretionary monetary policy.

14

Financial crisis and deep recession

Introduction

We now come to the financial crisis and deep recession that began just a few years ago. You may have skipped ahead to this chapter. I would not blame you if you did. What caused the financial crisis? Was it "irrational exuberance" of the private sector or "monetary mischief" on the part of the U.S. Federal Reserve? Before we get our exercise jumping to conclusions, hitting the ceiling, and running amok, let's take another quick look at the alternative theories that purport to explain what happened.

A quick review of the troops reveals a startling lack of consensus, which we know is the usual state of affairs in macroeconomics. In rough chronological order:

Austrian business cycle theory (von Mises and Hayek) states that left to its own devices, a market economy will generate savings just equal to the proper amount of resources to allocate to real investment. The problems arise when the central bank causes the interest rate to fall below its "natural" rate. Monetary mischief distorts investment incentives – too much investment in houses and other things that will not be needed in the long run. The crash comes when people (or the monetary authorities) catch on to the distortion of asset values. The Austrians give themselves credit for predicting the Great Depression and the latest financial crisis.

John Maynard Keynes blamed the depression on a decline in aggregate demand, which was caused mainly by a collapse of private investment spending. Keynes recognized that investment can be influenced by the interest rate, but the primary determinant of investment is a psychological attitude about the future that he called "animal spirits." When investors are in a depressed state because of imponderable uncertainty about the future of the economy, Keynes argued, the national government needs to step in during a depression and raise aggregate demand. Monetary policy can work in more ordinary situations, but direct spending on goods and services (fiscal stimulus) is needed under more dire circumstances.

The late Hyman Minsky, a Keynesian who was ignored by most Keynesians in his lifetime, is now back in fashion. Minsky supplemented the Keynesian approach by arguing that during a boom period, the private sector will figure out ways and means of expanding credit and financial leverage that defeat attempts at regulation. Financial bubbles can exist. Then some event occurs that starts financial collapse and the process of deleveraging. Hedge investors (cash flow sufficient to cover all debt service) become speculative investors (cash flow only covers interest on debt), speculative investors become Ponzi investors (cash flow insufficient to cover interest payments), and Ponzi investors become zombies. Investment collapses, and Keynesian remedies are needed.

According to Wray (2016, p. 271), the adherents to Modern Monetary Theory agreed with Minsky's approach and think that they foresaw the crisis. Modern Keynesians also acknowledge that expectations of both inflation and Fed policies matter but are not necessarily "rational." They realize that policy mistakes have happened. They also recognize that supply shocks such as oil price jumps can happen – because they did.

Now let's turn our attention to the Monetarists and their descendants. Milton Friedman was the most prominent Monetarist, of course. His basic premise was that the money supply determines only the level of prices in the long run, but in the short run, fluctuations in the money supply influence the level of real output as well. Because this is true, the monetary authorities can (and do) cause real monetary mischief. Indeed, the headline from Friedman's *A Monetary History of the United States* (with Anna Schwartz) is that a garden-variety recession was turned into the Great Depression by a 33 percent drop in the supply of money. Consequently, Friedman argued that the monetary authorities should follow the simple rule of increasing the money supply by 3 to 5 percent per year (to accommodate real growth) and not engage in discretionary monetary policy. Anna Schwartz argued that the crisis of 2008 was caused largely by the U.S. Federal Reserve and its policy of rock-bottom interest rates following the recession of 2001, which was followed by the housing boom and subsequent crash.

Freidman's intellectual descendants include the rational expectations school (led by Robert Lucas and Kydland and Prescott), which made useful additions to the basic classical (conservative) approach. The rational expectations school points out that you can't fool all of the people all of the time. People form expectations about the economy in a rational manner – which includes the anticipation of changes in monetary and fiscal policy. For example, if people correctly anticipate that the monetary authorities will increase the supply of money, they will increase prices and wages so that monetary policy will have no impact on the real economy. There is no tradeoff between inflation and unemployment, unless you "fool" the people.

Kydland and Prescott gained fame by pointing out the "time inconsistency" problem. If policy makers say one thing (money supply will increase modestly), and then do something different (big increase in money supply), the private economy will have undertaken actions that turn out to be mistakes. Policy makers need to follow rules that make them predictable. The most famous rule is called the Taylor rule (after John Taylor), which stipulates that the federal funds rate should increase when inflation increases and should decrease when the economy is operating below capacity. Taylor has provided evidence that if the Federal Reserve had followed the Taylor rule during 2002–2004, the federal funds rate would not have been so low for so long, and housing starts would not have ballooned.

Lucas and Kydland and Prescott are also among the originators of the real business cycle school, which argues that variations in real output stem from shocks on the supply side – rather than shocks on the aggregate demand side that only affect prices. They have returned to the classical economists' view that the market economy will react efficiently to these shocks, and that public policy should not be used to attempt to mitigate their effects.

Now let's return to Minsky and his intellectual heirs. The late Charles Kindleberger's classic book *Manias, Panics, and Crashes: A History of Financial Crises* is based on Minsky's model. This book is an encyclopedic account of financial crises through history. Similarly, Robert Shiller has gained prominence from a series of books that argues that financial bubbles are the cause of financial crises. One of his latest is *The Subprime Solution*, in which he states that the housing market bubble began in 1997 (well before the Fed cut interest rates), and that the actions taken by the private sector can be explained by the existence of rising housing prices. Why not make loans to anyone when the price of the house will always go up? Who cares if the borrowers are not qualified? But housing suppliers responded and the bubble burst – as it always does.

The U. S. Financial Crisis Inquiry Commission (2011, p. xvi) stated:

> But our mission was to ask and answer this central question: *How did it come to pass that in 2008 our nation was forced to choose between two stark and painful alternatives –* either risk the total collapse of our financial system and economy or inject trillions of taxpayer dollars into the financial system and an array of companies, as millions of Americans still lost their jobs, their savings, and their homes?
>
> (emphasis in original)

The purpose of this chapter is to use our study of macroeconomics to provide at least some of the answer to that question. Queen Elizabeth is reported to have asked why none of the experts saw the financial crisis coming. Are we able to answer Her Majesty's question? We shall follow our usual steps and study the data for the United States, the United Kingdom, and Japan.

Macroeconomic data for the United States

We begin with a detailed examination of the United States because the financial crisis had its origins there. Basic U.S. macroeconomic data are shown in Table 14.1. The data begin in 1998 and run through 2018. These data do not show the financial crisis directly but do show its effects. Let us take a look.

We start with the mild recession of 2001 that resulted from the stock market crash and the drop in real investment. Note that residential construction increases fell to very low levels in 2000 and 2001 after the interest rate increases in 1999 and 2000, but the big drop in investment came in nonresidential structures and equipment. The nation had built too much commercial real estate such as office buildings and invested in too much equipment, including high-tech gear. The unemployment rate increased with its usual lag to 6.0 percent in 2003, and the ratio of employment to population fell from 64.4 percent in 2000 to 62.3 percent in 2003. The data show only a small decline in total non-agricultural employment, but a decline in manufacturing employment from 17.3 million in 2000 to 14.5 million in 2003 (16.2 percent) was worrisome. Real GDP growth resumed in 2003, and its growth averaged 3.2 percent

TABLE 14.1 U.S. Macroeconomic Data, 1998–2018

Year	GDP Real Grow Pct	Invest –ment Real Grow Pct	Resident Constr. Real Grow Pct	Govt Expen Real Grow Pct	Unempl Rate Pct	Empl Pop. Ratio	Total Non-Ag. Empl* (mil.)	Manuf Empl (mil.)	M1 ($bil.)	Fed Funds Rate Pct
1998	4.9	9.7	11.3	2.8	4.5	64.1	128.1	17.6	1095	5.35
1999	4.8	8.5	3.5	3.9	4.2	64.3	130.2	17.3	1122	4.97
2000	3.0	4.3	−1.5	0.4	4.0	64.4	134.4	17.3	1088	6.24
2001	0.2	−11.1	2.0	4.9	4.7	63.7	134.6	16.4	1182	3.88
2002	2.1	4.4	8.1	3.9	5.8	62.7	134.2	15.3	1220	1.67
2003	4.3	8.7	12.7	1.9	6.0	62.3	135.5	14.5	1306	1.13
2004	3.3	8.0	6.6	0.8	5.5	62.3	137.0	14.3	1376	1.35
2005	3.1	6.1	5.2	0.9	5.1	62.7	139.5	14.2	1374	3.22
2006	2.6	−1.5	−15.2	1.9	4.6	63.1	142.2	14.2	1367	4.97
2007	2.0	−1.8	−21.2	2.3	4.6	63.0	144.0	13.9	1373	5.02
2008	−2.8	−15.3	−24.7	2.5	5.8	62.2	143.2	13.4	1602	1.92
2009	0.2	−9.2	−11.5	3.0	9.3	59.3	137.8	11.8	1693	0.16
2010	2.6	12.1	−5.7	−1.3	9.6	58.5	136.9	11.5	1838	0.18
2011	1.5	10.4	5.3	−3.4	8.9	58.4	137.6	11.7	2164	0.10
2012	2.6	4.0	15.4	−2.1	8.1	58.6	140.3	11.9	2461	0.14
2013	2.9	9.3	7.1	−2.4	7.4	58.6	141.8	12.0	2664	0.11
2014	1.9	5.3	7.7	0.3	6.2	59.0	144.1	12.2	2940	0.09
2015	2.0	1.5	9.1	2.3	5.3	59.3	146.4	12.3	3094	0.13
2016	2.8	1.5	3.9	1.5	4.9	59.7	149.0	12.4	3340	0.39
2017	2.5	4.8	4.2	0.8	4.4	60.1	150.9	12.4	3607	1.00
2018	2.3	5.1	−4.4	1.5	3.9	60.4	153.3	12.7	3746	1.83

Source: Economic Report of the President, 2020

* Includes proprietors, self-employed persons, private household workers, and unpaid family workers.

from 2003 to 2006. Real investment picked up from 2003 to 2005, led by residential construction, but dropped to a low growth level in 2006 as residential construction fell by 15.2 percent. The unemployment rate declined from 6.0 percent in 2003 to 4.6 percent in 2006 and 2007. Total non-agricultural employment came back with an increase of 9.8 million jobs from 2002 to 2007. However, manufacturing employment continued to decline, albeit at a much slower pace.

Now look at what happened next. Residential construction collapsed in 2007, 2008, and 2009. Over the four years from 2006 to 2009, spending on residential construction fell by a cumulative 44.5 percent. Total real investment fell, but the initial cause of the drop in real investment was entirely to be found in residential construction. Housing starts had increased from 1.57 million in 2000 to 2.07 million in 2005, and then fell rapidly to 554,000 in 2009. The other forms of real investment actually increased by 7.3 percent in 2007 and declined by 7.0 percent in 2008. The drops in total investment in 2008 and 2009 add up to a decline of 16.5 percent (equal to $436 billion in real 2009 dollars). The decline in investment produced negative GDP growth in 2008 and essentially no growth in 2009 and brought the unemployment rate up to 9.3 percent in 2009 and 9.6 percent in 2010. There were some months in which the unemployment rate exceeded 10 percent. Total non-agricultural employment dropped by 7.1 million from 2007 to 2010, and manufacturing employment fell to 11.5 million, down by another 19.0 percent from 2006 to 2010. Fed chairman Ben Bernanke (2015, p. 363) writes:

> We know now that the U.S. economy shrank at a 2 percent annual rate in the third quarter of 2008, an astonishing 8.2 percent in the fourth quarter (the worst performance in fifty years), and at a 5.4 percent rate in the first quarter of 2009. It was easily the deepest recession since the Depression.

This is a picture of macroeconomic disaster.

Recovery from the disaster began in 2010 in the GDP data, and employment data show improvement beginning in 2011. However, the pace of recovery has been slow. GDP growth has been an average of 2.2 percent for the five years from 2010 to 2014, which is below the pace of recovery after the 2001 recession despite the fact that the recession of 2008–2009 was much deeper. Total non-agricultural employment returned to its 2007 level in 2014, but that was with a larger national population. The ratio of employment to population was 63 percent in 2007, 59 percent in 2014, and 60 percent in 2018.

What were the policy responses during these eventful years? First consider monetary policy. As noted earlier, the money supply decreased and the federal funds rate increased in 2000, which surely were part of the reason for the 2001 recession. The Fed changed its tune quickly. The money supply increased sharply (up 26.4 percent from 2000 to 2004), and the federal funds rate was brought down to 1.13 percent in 2003 and held roughly at that level until early 2005. Yes, the economy was recovering rather slowly from a mild recession (and stock market crash) and manufacturing employment was dropping, but Fed policy was driven by fears of deflation and seemed rather gripped by panic. The housing market responded to the easier credit and led real total investment into strongly positive growth territory during 2003–2005. As mentioned earlier, housing starts increased. As it turned out, too many houses were being built. But then the Fed people realized that they had overdone it and slammed on the brakes. The money supply did not increase from 2004 to 2007, and the federal funds rate was increased to 5.02 percent in 2007 from 1.35 percent in 2004. The chaos that began in 2008 brought a complete reversal of Fed policy. The federal funds rate was reduced basically to zero, and the money stock increased dramatically. The percentage increase in the money supply averaged 11.3 percent per year from 2008 to 2014.

TABLE 14.2 U.S. Federal Receipts and Expenditures, GDP, and Velocity of Money

Year	Rec'pt ($bil)	Expen-diture ($bil)	Surplus ($bil)	GDP ($bil)	Net Export ($bil)	Infla-tion Rate	Velocity of M1 Money	M2*	Velocity of M2 Money
1998	1722	1653	69	9,167	−166	1.1	8.37	4365	2.10
1999	1828	1702	126	9,713	−259	1.4	8.66	4627	2.10
2000	2025	1789	236	10,285	−373	2.3	9.45	4914	2.09
2001	1991	1863	128	10,622	−361	2.3	8.99	5422	1.96
2002	1853	2011	−158	10,978	−419	1.5	9.01	5760	1.91
2003	1782	2160	−374	11,511	−494	2.0	8.82	6054	1.90
2004	1880	2293	−413	12,275	−610	2.7	8.92	6405	1.92
2005	2154	2472	−318	13,094	−714	3.2	9.52	6668	1.96
2006	2407	2655	−248	13,856	−762	3.1	10.13	7057	1.96
2007	2588	2729	−161	14,478	−705	2.7	10.51	7458	1.94
2008	2524	2982	−459	14,719	−709	1.9	9.16	8181	1.80
2009	2105	3518	−1413	14,419	−384	0.8	8.49	8483	1.70
2010	2163	3457	−1294	14,964	−495	1.2	8.12	8789	1.70
2011	2304	3603	−1300	15,518	−549	3.0	7.16	9651	1.61
2012	2450	3537	−1087	16,163	−537	1.8	6.76	10,446	1.55
2013	2775	3455	−680	16,768	−461	1.5	6.32	11,015	1.52
2014	3022	3506	−485	17,421	−490	0.8	5.99	11,668	1.49
2015	3250	3692	−442	18,224	−499	0.7	5.89	12,330	1.48
2016	3268	3853	−585	18,656	−503	2.1	5.88	13,199	1.41
2017	3316	3982	−665	19,379	−550	2.1	5.37	13,836	1.40
2018	3330	4109	−779	20,552	−628	1.9	5.49	14,352	1.43

Source: Economic Report of the President, 2020

* M2 is M1 plus money market mutual fund balances and savings accounts.

Table 14.2 shows nominal GDP and the velocity of money (GDP divided by M1 from Table 14.1). We see that the velocity of money was running at roughly 9 to 10 until the great recession, but then fell sharply to about 6 or 7 during the slow recovery period because the interest rates were so low that people held a lot more money balances. More details of the Fed response to the great recession are provided later in this chapter. Table 14.2 also includes the inflation rate and the broader definition of the money supply, called M2. This measure includes M1 plus money market mutual fund balances and savings accounts, and it tends to correlate more closely with nominal GDP than does M1. Look at the consistent velocity figures for 2001 to 2007. But we see that the velocity of M2 also plunged, from 1.94 to 1.50 and lower during the crisis and aftermath. Huge increases in M2 did not translate into large increases in nominal GDP or inflation.

Now consider fiscal policy. Table 14.1 shows that total government expenditure in real terms grew relatively rapidly in 2001 and 2002 (at 4.9 percent and 3.9 percent), and then increased at a more moderate pace of 1.6 percent per year from 2003 to 2007. A more detailed look at these expenditures reveals that federal spending increased, including spending on national defense, and was responsible for the increases in 2001 and 2002. Government expenditures picked up the growth pace starting in 2008 and 2009. The increase of 3.2 percent in 2009 was the result of the economic stimulus package enacted early in that year at the beginning of the Obama administration. Federal non-defense spending increased 6.2 percent in 2009 but spending by state and local governments increased only 1.0 percent in that year. The growth in government spending in real terms stopped in 2010 and turned negative in the subsequent years. Federal spending in real terms has declined by an average of 2.3 percent in the four years of 2010 to 2013.

Table 14.2 provides a closer look at the federal budget, this time in nominal (not corrected for inflation) terms. The federal government had increasing budget surpluses in 1998–2000 as receipts grew with the economy (and expenditures, which include transfer payments that are not government purchases of goods and services, increased relatively modestly). The impact of the 2001 recession is seen; receipts fell, expenditures increased modestly, and the surplus was reduced. This was the final year of a Clinton administration budget. The following three years (2002–2004) show a decline in receipts as a result of tax cuts along with sizable increases in expenditures, including spending on national defense. The surpluses were turned into deficits, reaching $413 billion in 2004. With tax cuts and spending increases, these early years of the George W. Bush administration are actually an example of a sizable Keynesian stimulus. The sizes of the deficits declined substantially from 2005 to 2007 as growth in receipts outpaced spending increases. These were years of economic growth. Then the nation is hit by the big recession. The deficit in 2008 returns to over $400 billion in 2008, and then balloons to $1.4 trillion in 2009, the year of a huge drop in receipts and large increase in spending largely from the economic stimulus package. Federal spending in nominal terms has remained relatively constant since 2009, and the (albeit) slow economic recovery has brought receipts back enough to produce a smaller deficit of $485 billion in 2014. Increases in spending starting in 2016 and a decline in receipts in 2017 and 2018 have increased the deficit to $779 billion in 2018. The corporate income tax rate was reduced at the end of 2017.

The macroeconomic policy tools were in use during these years, but how well were they used? The mild recession of 2001, with its weak job growth caused mainly by declines in manufacturing, was followed by strong stimuli from both monetary and fiscal policy – large cut in the federal funds rate, sizable increase in the money supply, tax cuts, and government spending increases that turned federal surpluses into large deficits. It is not clear that there was much, if any, coordination between the Fed and President Bush and Congress, but this looks like all hands on deck. The economy responded. Real GDP growth picked up and the unemployment rate fell to 4.6 percent. Not only that, but inflation was pretty well under control, at an average of 2.7 percent for the years 2003 to 2007. However, as Table 14.2 shows, the nation was running a large deficit in the balance of trade that increased sharply during this time. On the whole, a success story? Not so fast. This little recitation leaves out some very important facts.

Financial crisis

You will recall the major changes in the financial system introduced in Chapter 13. These changes produced a housing market that lost its collective mind. Here is a mercifully brief (I hope) list of what took place in the United States.

■ Housing prices had an unprecedented rise that became a bubble, a situation in which prices are unhinged from underlying indicators of value. Economists do not agree on the start date for the bubble. Shiller (2009) thinks the start date was in 1997, while Zandi (2009) puts the date later, in 2003. The Case–Shiller home price index shows that prices increased in real terms by 90 percent from 1997 to 2006. There is no dispute about the consequences of the bubble.

■ Interest rates for home buyers declined from 7.52 percent in 2000 to 5.80 percent in 2003 for standard 30-year mortgages, and the first-year rate on adjustable-rate mortgages hit 3.4 percent in 2004. The use of adjustable-rate mortgages increased rapidly. One popular option was the 2–28 loan (low interest rate for two years, followed by a sizable rate adjustment). The Financial Crisis Inquiry Commission (2011, p. 85) stated that:

Low rates cut the cost of homeownership: interest rates for the typical 30-year fixed-rate mortgage traditionally moved with the overnight fed funds rate, and from 2000 to 2003, the relationship held. By 2003, creditworthy home buyers could get fixed-rate mortgages for 5.2%, 3 percentage points lower than 3 years earlier. The savings were immediate and large.

■ Home lending was extended to the subprime market to buyers who would not have qualified previously, and this market expanded rapidly. In addition, lending standards to other buyers became lax. Some buyers were not required to document their incomes, a violation of long-standing industry practice.

■ Homeowners took out second mortgages in order to "cash out" the increase in market value of their home so that the money could be spent. This cash boosted aggregate demand. These actions meant that homeowners had little equity left. A small decline in housing prices would make the outstanding loans larger than the value of the house.

■ Use of mortgage-backed securities boomed. The basic idea is to bundle large numbers of mortgages together to reduce risk and to remove the loans from the balance sheets of the lending banks. It turned out that risk was not reduced. Fannie Mae and Freddie Mac, the major government-sponsored enterprises, entered the subprime market and created securities that included mortgages of this type. These agencies guarantee the securities.

- Bond rating agencies, which are private firms paid by the issuers of the securities, gave unrealistically high ratings to the mortgage-backed securities. Investors relied heavily on these ratings because risks posed by the securities are difficult to understand.

- Some major insurance companies, such as AIG, provided insurance in huge amounts to investors in mortgage-backed securities and other types of derivative securities and held grossly insufficient reserves.

- Government failed to regulate many of the risky practices. Commercial banks are regulated by the Fed, but investment banks – the institutions that created a large volume of mortgage-backed securities – are not.

- The home building industry boomed in response to the high and rising prices and lax lending standards. But, according to Zandi (2009, p. 143), the number of vacant homes increased from 1.25 million in 2004 to 2.1 million in 2007.

- Many actors in the market – from homeowners to banks, to investors to Fannie Mae and Freddie Mac – increased leverage (borrowing) dramatically. Some of that borrowing by investment banks and others was on a very short-term basis (e.g., overnight).

What could go wrong? Just about everything.

The popping of the house price bubble began in 2006 and picked up speed in 2007. The Case–Shiller home price index fell by 33 percent from 2006 to 2009. This price drop created millions of "underwater" homeowners – owners of homes worth less than the outstanding balance on the mortgage loan(s), in many cases much less for those who had purchased the home during the bubble years. Why is being underwater a big problem? Why would we even ask? Go back to Table 14.1 and note the big drop in employment and increase in unemployment. People who lose their jobs cannot make their mortgage payments, and besides, the house is worth less than the loan amount. According to Zandi (2009, p. 168), defaults on mortgages (missed or late payments in violation of the mortgage contract) increased from an annual rate of 775,000 at the end of 2005 to 1.5 million in the summer of 2007. By the end of 2008, the annual rate had jumped to 3.0 million. Private mortgage lending basically ceased, and the values of mortgage-backed securities plunged because their values are based on the payments that the borrowers make. During the crisis and aftermath, most of the mortgages were purchased by Fannie Mae and Freddie Mac and bundled into securities. These firms were taken over by the U.S. Department of the Treasury in August 2008. Many of those securities were purchased by the Fed. In effect, the federal government sustained the mortgage market.

Bear Stearns, the smallest of the five largest investment banks and a major player in the mortgage-backed securities market, was essentially worthless in March 2008. It was purchased by JPMorgan Chase with an assist from the Fed (in which the Fed agreed to absorb losses on Bear Stearns securities). As noted, in August the U.S. Treasury took control of Fannie Mae and Freddie Mac (the government-sponsored purchasers of mortgages), and Lehman Brothers (another big five investment bank) went bankrupt in September. The bankruptcy of Lehman was the final alarm bell. It was clear that the entire financial system might collapse in the sense that no one would lend to anyone because the financial health (i.e., ability to pay interest and principal) of just about everyone was in doubt. Fed Chairman Bernanke is one person who was critically aware that the condition of the financial system as the downturn unfolded would determine the ultimate severity of the recession. His research (1983) on the Great Depression had shown as much.

What caused the housing price bubble and crash? Clearly, the craziness in the mortgage market fueled the bubble. Beyond that, researchers disagree. Indeed, one prominent economist thinks that the bubble caused the craziness in the mortgage market. The additional main contending causes are as follows.

- The interest rate policy of the Fed that cut the federal funds rate a lot and then increased it again – a lot
- Lax regulation that "permitted" the mortgage market craziness
- Federal deficits
- Reductions in mortgage interest rates, with the rate on adjustable-rate mortgages of particular import
- Net capital flows from abroad that came about because of large deficits in the balance of trade
- Interactions between housing prices and home foreclosures (house sold by lender, borrower evicted). This dynamic operated when prices started to fall, leading to foreclosures, leading to more price declines, and so on

Here is a sampling of opinion from leading economists. As noted previously, Anna Schwartz (2009) of Friedman and Schwartz (1963) put the blame squarely on Fed interest rate policy, as one would expect. She also blamed Congress and Fannie Mae and Freddie Mac for promoting home ownership for low- and moderate-income borrowers, financial "innovations," and the rating agencies. But Fed interest rate policy topped her list. Also as expected, the Austrians such as Woods (2009) blamed the Fed interest rate policy for pushing rates too low and stimulating investment that was a misallocation of resources. Indeed, Thornton (2009) pointed out that some Austrians predicted trouble in 2003–2005.

John Taylor (2009) agreed that Fed interest rate policy is to blame, and his research showed that if the Taylor rule had been followed, the federal funds rate would not have been cut to 1 percent. For example, the Taylor rule rate would have been 4 percent in the first quarter of 2004, rather than the actual 1 percent. His study showed that the result of following the Taylor rule would have been much smaller housing price increases and far fewer housing starts.

Hyman Minsky was not around to say, "I told you so," but Nobel Prize winner Robert Shiller was and is. Shiller's view (2009) is that the housing bubble began in 1997, well before the Fed starting cutting interest rates and roughly at the time when the federal capital gains tax on the home effectively was eliminated. He views the housing boom as a "social contagion." There is more. Shiller argues that many of the other alleged causes of the housing bubble (including loose lending standards, inaccurate bond ratings, and failure of regulators to stop risky lending) were *caused* by the housing price bubble. Housing prices would always go up, so don't worry, be happy. He does acknowledge that the interest rate cuts might have accelerated the boom, but first the bubble fueled the mortgage market craziness.

Paul Krugman, another winner of the Nobel Prize, sees it rather differently. He stated (2009a, p. 148) that: "We know why home prices started rising: interest rates were very low in the early years of this decade." But then the rising home prices caused "a complete abandonment of traditional principles" regarding mortgage lending practices. Loose credit standards fed the housing bubble, and rising home prices fed back into loose credit standards. Mark Zandi, who dates the start of the bubble in 2003, (2009, p. 9) called the lowering of the federal funds rate the "fuse" that started it all.

Barth (2009) emphasized the role of the interest rate on one-year adjustable-rate mortgages, which fell by a larger amount than the rate on standard 30-year mortgages and promoted lending to subprime borrowers. Adjustable-rate loans were used because riskier borrowers should be charged higher rates that were beyond what they could afford. As Gorton (2010, p. 68) stated:

> So the challenge was (and remains) to find a way to lend to such borrowers. The basic idea of the subprime loan recognizes that the dominant form of wealth of low-income households is potentially their home equity. If borrowers can lend to these households for a short time period, 2 or 3 years, at a high but affordable interest rate, and equity is built up in their homes, then the mortgage can be refinanced with a lower loan-to-value ratio, reflecting the embedded price appreciation.

The interest rate increase built into the mortgage was large enough to force the borrower to refinance after 2 or 3 years. Lenders are safe only if house prices rise. Prices did not rise.

Fed officials such as Greenspan (2007), Bernanke (2013), and Blinder (2013) deny that the federal funds rate policy is culpable, but empirical evidence by McDonald and Stokes (2013, 2015) indicates otherwise. They found that the federal funds rate is one cause of movement in house prices. McDonald and Stokes (2015) also tested for the impact of net capital flows from abroad and found that this variable was not a cause of the housing price bubble, given that other causes are included in the model.

Macroeconomic data for the United Kingdom

Data for the United Kingdom for 1997 to 2014 are displayed in Table 14.3. This table follows the same format as is used for earlier time periods. We see that the U.K. economy was doing well from 1997 to 2007. Real GDP advanced by 2.89 percent per year for those ten years, and the unemployment rate declined steadily from 6.97 percent in 1997 to 4.75 percent in 2004 (with an uptick to 5.33 percent in 2007). Inflation averaged 0.94 percent per year over the ten years. The money supply increased by 9.48 percent per year; the velocity of money was declining from 6.08 to 3.15.

TABLE 14.3 U.K. Macroeconomic Data, 1997–2014

Year	Real GDP £bil. (2013)	Real Con-sump.	Real Invest-ment	Real Gov't Spend	Real Export	Real Import	Empl. (mil.)	Un-empl. Pct.	M1 (£mil.)	Wh'sl. Price*	Ave. Bank Rate Pct.
1997	1283	810	216	241	324	299	26.5	6.97	210,881	82.63	6.58
1998	1324	841	244	249	331	326	26.8	6.26	227,894	82.68	7.21
1999	1367	881	250	258	361	348	27.2	5.98	247,986	83.13	5.33
2000	1418	924	259	267	363	380	27.5	5.46	274,679	84.32	5.98
2001	1457	957	256	278	366	392	27.7	5.10	304,711	84.07	5.08
2002	1492	992	263	290	386	408	27.9	5.19	332,839	83.96	4.00
2003	1543	1029	269	302	408	429	28.2	5.01	368,301	84.52	3.69
2004	1582	1063	277	313	430	460	28.5	4.75	412,436	85.35	4.40
2005	1630	1096	287	320	472	480	28.8	4.83	465,647	87.01	4.65
2006	1670	1113	296	327	490	516	29.1	5.42	510,370	88.77	4.65
2007	1713	1145	313	331	495	535	29.4	5.33	544,207	90.81	5.52
2008	1702	1138	293	338	452	525	29.6	5.69	534,070	96.94	4.63
2009	1629	1101	248	342	479	477	29.2	7.61	574,448	97.40	0.63
2010	1660	1107	260	342	507	516	29.2	7.87	580,110	100.02	0.50
2011	1685	1102	266	343	510	520	29.4	8.11	578,402	104.77	0.50
2012	1707	1121	272	349	516	536	29.7	7.97	617,937	106.96	0.50
2013	1740	1138	280	350	524	555	30.0	7.61	683,436	108.38	0.50
2014	1793	1163	299	358	550	570	30.8	6.18	733,695	108.36	0.50

Source: Thomas, R., and Dimsdale, N., Three Centuries of Macroeconomic Data, Version 2.3

* Wholesale price index scaled to 2010 prices.

The first sign that something was wrong with the U.K. financial system came in 2007, when a bank called Northern Rock failed. A run on this bank took place because deposits were insured only up to a limit. Northern Rock was an active originator of mortgage loans, which it sold to other investors. The bank used wholesale funding that was available for short terms and maintained a very high leverage ratio at 60–80 to 1. The wholesale lenders began to doubt the viability of the bank's business model, failed to roll over the short-term loans, and brought Northern Rock bankruptcy very suddenly in the fall of 2007. The Bank of England made lender-of-last-resort (LOLR) loans to Northern Rock and saved the institution.

Let us see what happened to the U.K. macro economy. Table 14.3 shows that real GDP fell by 4.9 percent from 2007 to 2009, and the unemployment rate increased to 8.11 percent in 2011. Recall that the unemployment rate often is a lagging indicator. Real investment declined by £65 billion, which accounts for 77 percent of the decline in real GDP.

The Bank of England responded in a big way in October 2008 with a bank rescue package of £500 billion (about $850 billion in U.S. dollars). The U.K. stock market had declined sharply, and there was deep concern about the stability of the major U.K. banks. The rescue package included the purchase of bank equity by the government, as well as loans and loan guarantees. The supply of money increased from 2009 to 2014 by 4.9 percent per year. However, Table 14.3 shows that fiscal policy was not used to purchase goods and services to stimulate the economy. The recovery was not as robust as had been hoped; real GDP increased by 1.92 percent per year after 2009. Real GDP did not regain its 2007 level until early 2013. The unemployment rate fell from 8.11 percent in 2012 to 6.18 percent in 2014, and it continued to fall to its 2007 level in 2015 at 5.38 percent.

Macroeconomic data for Japan

As we know from Chapter 12, Japan suffered through its "lost decade" in the 1990s. Not only that, but the subsequent decade brought slow growth as well. The real GDP increased from 1990 to 2000 only by 1.29 percent per year, and population growth was only 2.67 percent for the entire decade. The unemployment rate drifted steadily upward from 2.10 percent in 1990 to 4.72 percent in 2000. As shown in Table 14.4, the nation experienced small amounts of deflation in 1999 and 2000. The discount rate charged by the Bank of Japan was lowered to 0.50 percent in 1996 and remained at that level, and real investment fluctuated but did not really increase. The next chapter of the story is that the 2000s are called a second lost decade. How did the first decade of the new century unfold?

First of all, population growth in Japan was only 1.03 percent from 2000 to 2010 (0.10 percent per year). The subsequent eight years, from 2010 to 2018, brought a decline in population from 128.1 million to 126.5 million (a loss of 1.25 percent). Overall population growth in Japan was just 2.43 percent from 1990 to 2018 (0.09 percent per year) – 28 years of barely any population growth. This is not the way to generate economic growth, is it?

The years 2000 to 2007 brought real GDP growth of just 1.27 percent. The Bank of Japan lowered the discount rate again to 0.10 percent in 2002, but the volume of real investment during these years was actually less than the amounts seen in the 20 years from 1990 to 2000. The supply of money increased from 2000 to 2006 by 8.62 percent per year, but the result was mainly a decrease in the velocity of money. Japan experienced deflation in five of the seven years from 2000 to 2007. Japan was on track to have another lost decade. Then came the financial crisis.

Real GDP fell by 6.46 percent in the two years from 2007 to 2009. Real investment declined from 126.7 trillion yen to 102.8 trillion yen (down 18.9 percent over two years). The decline in real investment accounts for 73 percent of the decline in real GDP. The unemployment rate had declined to 3.84 percent in 2007 but retreated to 5.07 percent in 2009. Wholesale prices declined in 2009 and 2010.

A real attempt to raise Japan out of its lost decades began in 2013 with the election of Shinzō Abe as Prime Minister. While I recoil at the attachment of a

TABLE 14.4 Japan Macroeconomic Data, 1997–2018

Year	Real GDP Trillion Yen (2011)	Real Investment	Unempl. (pct.)	M1 Trillion Yen	July Disc. Rate	GDP Deflator (pct)
1997	455	141	3.40	2219	0.50	1.75
1998	450	134	4.11	2409	0.50	0.66
1999	449	128	4.68	2662	0.50	−0.34
2000	462	132	4.72	2880	0.50	−0.68
2001	463	130	5.03	3125	0.25	−0.74
2002	464	121	5.37	3984	0.10	−0.92
2003	471	122	5.26	4305	0.10	−0.26
2004	482	124	4.72	4484	0.10	−0.01
2005	490	127	4.42	4693	0.10	−0.28
2006	497	127	4.14	4832	0.40	0.25
2007	505	127	3.84	4828	0.75	0.06
2008	499	123	3.99	4804	0.75	1.38
2009	472	103	5.07	4829	0.30	−1.35
2010	492	106	5.05	4924	0.30	−0.72
2011	491	101	4.58	5158	0.30	−0.27
2012	499	113	4.35	5345	0.30	−0.05
2013	509	116	4.02	5602	0.30	0.35
2014	511	120	3.59	5865	0.30	2.76
2015	517	124	3.37	6165	0.30	0.79
2016	520	123	3.12	6598	0.30	−0.12
2017	531	127	2.08	7119	0.30	0.47
2018	533	126	2.44	7556	0.30	0.98

Source: OECD Data

politician's name to the word economics (e.g., Reaganomics), I think that the term Abenomics actually has meaning. The program consists of coordinated monetary policy, fiscal policy, and economic growth programs to stimulate private investment. Inflation is targeted at 2 percent per annum, appreciation of the yen is moderated, negative real interest rates are envisioned, assets are purchased by the Bank of Japan (quantitative easing), and public investments are expanded. Haruhiko Kuroda was appointed Governor of the Bank of Japan with the mandate to target inflation at 2 percent by aggressive quantitative easing. Out of deference to Mr. Abe, the data for Japan are extended to 2018.

The policy package lowered the value of the yen by 25 percent against the U.S. dollar, and increased the stock market index by 22 percent. The unemployment rate fell to 3.59 percent in 2014 and continued to fall to 2.08 percent in 2017. Real investment did increase by 8.8 percent in 2018 over its 2013 level. The supply of money increased from 2013 to 2018 by 5.98 percent per year. However, the rate of economic growth was only 1.05 percent from 2014 to 2018. Mr. Abe served as Prime Minister until 2020.

Data versus theories

So which macroeconomic theory gives us the best explanation? Chapter 1 of this book says that the various theories have been in the pot for decades, and the latest crisis has brought the macroeconomic pot to a boil. Let us do our work. This section lays out some ideas, but by now you know enough to make up your own mind – at least tentatively, until more data arrive, of course.

Because monetary policy has played such a prominent role throughout the period, let us begin with Monetarism. Basically, they have a strong case for the United States when it comes to the precrisis years, but their story falls apart badly after that. A federal funds rate cut and a money supply increase, followed by a complete reversal of policy – that is a recipe for trouble. However, the Monetarists also tend to be people who believe in the efficiency of the financial markets when ruled by self-interest. Anna Schwartz (2009) did recognize that craziness in the mortgage market, i.e., financial "innovation," made things worse, but as noted, Fed policy is on top of her list.

Why did the Fed reduce the U.S. interest rate to 1.13 percent in 2003? Temin and Vines (2014, p. 101) provide an interesting analysis of this decision. As noted in Chapter 1, China (among others) has followed a strategy of export-led development by keeping its exchange rate low and exports high. China was admitted to the World Trade Organization in 2001, and thus was able to expand exports. The United States was running a large deficit in the balance of trade, in part because China was purchasing U.S. bonds to keep its exchange rate low. Table 14.2 shows that net exports (the deficit in the balance of trade) doubled from $396 billion in 2000 to $802 billion in 2006. But China's export-led strategy and the rapid loss of manufacturing jobs in the United States forced the Fed to reduce interest rates in order to stimulate the production of non-traded goods, such as housing, to bring the economy back from the 2001 recession. The tax cut and federal spending increase adopted under the George W. Bush administration added to aggregate demand. The price of housing responded to these factors, and the financial sector overdid it, as outlined earlier. McDonald and Stokes (2015) provide empirical evidence that both the federal funds rate and the federal deficit were factors in causing the housing market bubble.

The United Kingdom did not have inconsistent monetary policy prior to the financial crisis. It did have a shaky financial system similar to that of the United States. The decline in real investment in 2009 basically accounts for the decline in real GDP and the increase in unemployment. It would appear that real investment projects were not pursued because of the increase in uncertainty emanating from the financial system.

What about Japan? The Japanese had problems of their own with slow growth over decades. As we saw in Table 14.4, the financial crisis caused a drop in real investment. The Bank of Japan had held the discount rate at 0.10 percent since 2002 but then increased it to 0.75 percent in 2007. Was that enough to cause investment to decline? Was it a "garden variety" monetary policy mistake? The move to increase the discount rate certainly came at the wrong time. The supply of money declined in 2008, then returned to its 2007 level in 2009 and continued to increase. The discount rate was reduced promptly to 0.30 percent in 2009 and remained there going forward.

Let us give the U.S. case more consideration. As shown in Table 14.1, the federal funds rate was reduced drastically from 5.02 percent in 2007 to 1.92 percent in 2008 and 0.16 percent in 2009. So far, we have been using the federal funds rate (or the discount rate on loans to banks from the Fed for earlier periods) to measure the

TABLE 14.5 U.S. Interest Rates (Figures in Percentages)

Year	Federal Funds Rate	Baa Corporate Bond Rate	Bank Prime Rate	30-year Mortgage Rate
1999	4.97	7.87	8.00	7.04
2000	6.24	8.36	9.23	7.52
2001	3.88	8.95	6.91	7.00
2002	1.67	7.80	4.67	6.43
2003	1.13	6.77	4.12	5.80
2004	1.35	6.39	4.34	5.77
2005	3.22	6.06	6.19	5.94
2006	4.97	6.48	7.96	6.83
2007	5.02	6.48	8.05	6.41
2008	1.92	7.45	5.09	6.05
2009	0.16	7.30	3.25	5.14
2010	0.18	6.04	3.25	4.80
2011	0.10	5.66	3.25	4.56
2012	0.14	4.94	3.25	3.69
2013	0.11	5.10	3.25	4.00
2014	0.09	4.85	3.25	4.22

Source: *Economic Report of the President*, 2015, Table B-17

interest rate in the economy. But there are several interest rates that are important, and they do not always move together. Several different interest rates are reported in the *Economic Report of the President*; some of them are shown in Table 14.5. Consider the data from 2000 to 2014. What is known as the Prime Rate, the interest rate charged by banks to its best customers, moves in lockstep with the federal funds rate at a level higher by 3 percent. Interest rates on U.S. Treasury bonds (not shown) moved with the federal funds rate as well. The interest rate on standard 30-year home mortgages usually moved with the federal funds rate and declined from 6.41 percent in 2007 to 5.14 percent in 2009, as the Fed was slashing the federal funds rate. After 2009, mortgage rates moved down for three years and then increased in 2013 and 2014, as the federal funds rate did not change.

Now look at the rate on mid-level corporate bonds (rating of Baa). This bond rate usually moved with the federal funds rate from 2000 to 2007 (six out of eight years), but then something rather drastic occurred. In 2008, the Baa corporate bond rate increased by 0.97 percent (from 6.48 percent in 2007 to 7.45 percent) as the federal funds rate was cut by 3.10 percent (from 5.02 percent to 1.92 percent). In fact, more detailed monthly data show that the Baa rate hit 9.0 percent at the end of 2008 (up from 6.8 percent at the beginning of the year). The yearly data in Table 14.5 show that 2008 was followed by a very small change in the Baa rate in 2009 as the federal funds rate was cut by another 1.76 percent. The Baa rate declined from its plateau during 2010 to 2012 to 4.94 percent, but during the height of the financial crisis this important interest rate was totally uncoupled from the federal funds rate. The Fed had no control over the rate at which average corporations could borrow in the bond market during a crucial time.

Why did the Fed lose control over at least one important interest rate during this time? The answer surely has to do with the financial crisis. Recall that bonds based on mortgages were losing value rapidly because mortgages were defaulting. Evidently the "bond market" (whoever that is) thought that there was much greater risk associated with other bonds not of the highest quality. What is known as the risk premium suddenly increased.

Now consider the data for the recovery period. Under Chairman Bernanke's leadership, the Fed bought up trillions of dollars of assets – longer-term Treasury bonds and mortgage-backed securities. Infelicitously, this is called quantitative easing. The Fed balance sheet increased from about $900 billion in assets in 2008 to almost $2.9 trillion in 2012. As you recall (presumably), when the Fed buys assets, it credits the member banks with more reserves. Most of that increase in reserves became excess reserves (reserves in excess of the required level). Blinder (2013, p. 247) shows that excess reserves increased from zero in 2008 to $1.6 trillion in 2011. The story is that banks stopped lending. But the fact is that the money supply increased pretty rapidly beginning in 2008, in part because some of the assets purchased by the Fed were from sellers (other than banks) that received checks drawn on the Fed, i.e., money. The money supply had increased by 34 percent from 2007 to 2010 and increased by another 34 percent in just two years from 2010 to 2012. Clearly, lending picked up after 2010. By 2014, the money supply had more than doubled over its 2007 level (up 114 percent), while GDP in nominal terms had increased by just 20.3 percent.

Recall that the velocity of money in Table 14.2 plummeted. People and firms had money in their bank accounts that was not being used. Both the Monetarists and the Keynesians would be quick to say that the low interest rates are the reason. The opportunity cost of holding money is at historic lows. People and firms are waiting for better investments to come around. In the meantime, they are not spending their cash at the usual rate. Firms are sitting on their profits. But the economy is in (albeit rather slow) recovery mode, which according to Friedman and Schwartz (1963), means that the velocity of money should be increasing, not plummeting. Furthermore, the huge increase in the money supply is not translating into inflation. The Fed says that its inflation target is 2 percent, and we did reach that target in 2016. It surely is true that inflation is (nearly) always and everywhere a monetary phenomenon, but evidently big increases in the money supply are not always and everywhere inflationary.

Consider the Keynesians. First, investment was the volatile component of aggregate demand. If we tack on Minsky's financial instability story to the Keynesians, then we have a pretty good explanation for the precrisis bubble and collapse in the United States and elsewhere. We need not review all of the financial shenanigans here that Minsky would have suggested are consistent with his hypothesis and that lead to unstable investment spending. A "Minsky moment" happened in the United States. But what about the deep recession and the failure of active fiscal and monetary policy to snap the economy back quickly? When the alarm bell that was the Lehman bankruptcy went off, the federal government quickly passed in October 2008 the Troubled Asset Relief Program (TARP) that was used to shore up financial institutions such as Citicorp and the insurance giant AIG (and General Motors and Chrysler), so as to prevent the collapse of the entire financial system. TARP was followed up with the new President Obama's economic stimulus package in March 2009. That package included $790 billion in spending and tax cuts; $289 billion in tax relief, $144 billion for state and local government relief, and $357 billion in federal spending programs that included infrastructure, energy programs, and federal social programs. Recall that the decline in investment spending from 2007 to 2009 was $766 billion in real terms. The Keynesians argue that these actions were not enough and included too much in tax cuts. Tax cuts do not help much if the money is used to pay off debts. And some of the federal spending programs were spread over a couple of years. We have seen that government purchase of goods and services did increase by 3.0 percent in 2009. But overall government purchases did not increase in real terms in 2010 and have declined in real terms ever since. The cause of this decline largely rests with the federal government, which has reduced its nominal spending (not corrected for inflation) on goods in 2012 through 2014. Even though the federal government ran huge deficits, the Keynesians argue that fiscal policy has been insufficiently active.

These points can be made with a Keynesian diagram from Chapter 3. Figure 14.1 shows the standard IS–LM diagram. Suppose that Figure 14.1 depicts the relationships between real output and the average interest rates in the economy that affect real investment. We have seen that investment spending fell drastically during 2007–2009, which means that the IS curve shifted to the left as shown. The Fed reduced the federal funds rate almost to zero, and other interest rates such as the mortgage rate declined. But the rate on riskier bonds increased, so the average interest rate that affects real investment may not have declined (and may have increased). The Fed was not able to influence all interest rates by lowering the federal funds rate. The shift of the IS curve to the left tends to lower interest rates,

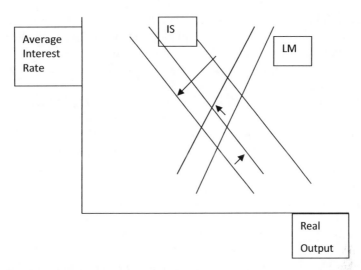

FIGURE 14.1 Aggregate Supply and Aggregate Demand. During 2007–2009, aggregate demand fell (IS curved shifted to the left). The average of all interest rates is the interest rate shown. The decline in aggregate demand was accompanied by a large increase in the perceived risk of bonds, which offset the effect of the large reduction of the federal funds rate and may have shifted the LM curve to the left. The stimulus of program of 2009 shifted the IS curve to the right but was insufficient to bring the economy back to full-employment output

but the increase in perceived risk may have shifted the LM curve to the left as well. The result is a double impact on real output from the decline in aggregate demand and the increase in the interest rate. The outcome motivated the Fed to engage in a program of purchasing bonds called quantitative easing. Figure 14.1 also includes a shift of the IS curve to the right to depict the economic stimulus of 2009. The figure shows that the stimulus was not large enough to bring the economy back to full-employment output.

What about monetary policy in response to the crisis? Here is where Keynes steps to the fore. The Great Depression was characterized by the liquidity trap, the situation in which increasing the money supply (i.e., increasing liquidity) has no impact on output. This is exactly what Keynes was talking about, say the Keynesians such as Krugman (2009a) in *The Return of Depression Economics and the Crisis of 2008*. Even if you can get the banks to lend money, the increase in the money supply will not lower interest rates because rates already are very low, and more money sitting in banks does nothing to create the optimism about the future needed to stimulate real investment. Keynes did not use the term "liquidity trap," but he did state (1936, pp. 246–247) that the state of the economy is governed by

> three fundamental psychological factors, namely, the psychological propensity to consume, the psychological attitude to liquidity and the psychological expectation of future yield from capital assets. . . .

As you know already, under depression conditions, the Keynesian remedy is active and sustained fiscal stimulus by the government. We have hypothesized that Japan had been in a liquidity trap since 1990, and the financial crisis only added to the problem. The Keynesians say that the fiscal stimulus in the United States was not enough and stopped too soon. Fiscal stimulus was not used in the United Kingdom or in Japan during the period immediately after the financial crisis hit. What do you think? Do you think Keynes and the liquidity trap story are on target for all three nations?

What about the Austrians? As noted previously, they blame the housing price bubble and boom in housing investment on Fed low interest rate policy during 2001 to 2004. The Monetarists agree. And the Austrians argue that the misallocation of resources towards investment resulted in the inevitable collapse. Not only that, but Austrian theory says that the longer interest rates are kept too low, the worse will be the collapse and the longer it will take to recover. Their story seems to hang together up to this point. Indeed, the Austrian story gains added credence if you believe that the interest rate cut was the "fuse" that set off the housing price explosion that unhinged housing prices from underlying indicators of value such as the ratio of rent to value. But remember that Robert Shiller thinks that the housing price bubble began years before the interest rate cuts. Memo to the Fed – do not cut rates in the middle of an asset price bubble. What about cutting the federal funds rate to zero in 2008–2009 in response to the crisis? The Austrians think, as the Millennials say, OMG. This policy action will prevent the economy from snapping back to normal by permitting markets work their deleveraging and bankrupting will. They issue warnings that another great collapse is coming. But there is one problem for that part of their story. Real investment spending has increased in the United States since 2010, but that came after large declines in the previous two years. Very low rates in the United Kingdom have stimulated some investment spending, but not by enough to see investment recover to its 2007 level as of 2014. In Japan, the very low interest rates have not increased real investment by very much since the mid-1990s. It is fair to say that firms and households have been pretty cautious about making real investments. Where are the misallocations of resources? Maybe they are coming . . . when?

The real business cycle folks have not been pushing their theory. Their dog did hunt in the 1970s but does not hunt so well this time. It is possible to argue that the financial crisis was a shock to the supply side of the economy – in this case, the supply of financial services. In fact, as cited by Skidelsky (2009, p. 47), Robert Lucas has argued that an unforeseeable shock, the bankruptcy of Lehman Brothers, caused a collapse of the money supply. He approved of the Fed's response to inject a huge increase of bank reserves into the system in late 2008 in the form of loans via the discount window. He stated (2008):

> It entails no new government enterprises, no government equity positions in private enterprises, no price fixing or other controls on the operation of individual businesses, and no government role in the allocation of capital across different activities. These seem to me important virtues.

Skidelsky (2009, p. 47) pointed out:

> This concession to reality involves Lucas in theoretical breakdown. For according to New Classical theory, market economies don't need stimulating. They always respond efficiently to shocks.

The more extreme supply-siders, such as Arthur Laffer, are not quiet. As usual, they argue that we need to cut taxes and reduce regulations to get businesses going again. During 2015, Laffer has been dispensing his advice to several Republican candidates for President. They sound like Ronald Reagan, but remember that the Reagan economy was stimulated by the Keynesian recipe of tax cuts and spending increases that yielded large deficits (by the standards of that time).

So basically, I have given the nod to the Keynesians as long as Minsky is included. That is not to say that the Monetarists are off base for the period up to 2008. A high degree of volatility in monetary policy is not a good thing. The Austrians have a good point about interest rate cuts by the monetary authorities done in an effort to stimulate the economy. At the very least, the cut in the early 2000s added fuel to the fire in the United States. But I think we have seen that cutting interest rates to manage aggregate demand is not always a bad idea. A combination of the Minsky financial instability hypothesis (i.e., in this case, mortgage market and other forms of financial insanity) coupled with policy mistakes by the Fed that Monetarists warned about can provide an explanation for the United States. In the United Kingdom, the shaky financial system coupled with negative "animal spirits" seems to provide an explanation. And Japan continued with its lost decades, but the Bank of Japan seems to have committed a monetary policy mistake that made things worse. What do you think about my conclusion? The failure of the economy to recover quickly presents a puzzle that the Keynesians think they can solve, but they have not been given a real chance to do it.

A popular book (for a book about economics) by Reinhart and Rogoff (2009) studied financial crises over the centuries and found that recoveries from banking crises, as opposed to other kinds of financial crises, are slow. The ironic title of their book is *This Time Is Different*. They found that the run-up to the crisis had the standard indicators: asset price inflation; increasing financial leverage; large, sustained trade deficits; and slower-than-typical economic growth. Knowing these indicators perhaps can help in avoiding the next crisis. What happens in the aftermath of a banking crisis? Again, the United States was typical in that the asset price decline (i.e., housing and stock prices) was deep and lasted a long time, large declines in output and employment occurred, and government debt increased dramatically. What can be done to shorten the aftermath and alleviate the suffering once the crisis happens? Reinhart and Rogoff do state that monetary authorities have more flexible tools and policies than in the past (as subsequently shown by the Fed's actions), but they (2009, p. 238) end with, "On the other hand, we do not wish to push too far the conceit that we are smarter than our predecessors." In short, the crisis of 2008 is pretty typical of banking crises. Reinhart and Rogoff think there is not much that could have been done to speed up recovery, in part (2009, p. 223)

> because in analyzing extreme shocks such as those affecting the U.S. economy and the world economy at the time of this writing, standard macroeconomic models calibrated to statistically "normal" growth periods may be of little use.

For my part, I find that statement too pessimistic if they mean any form of "standard" macroeconomic theory. There are different macroeconomic theories, and I am not prepared to discard all of them, even in an extreme financial shock.

15

Economics of the European Union

Introduction

This chapter is a brief examination of the economics of the European Union. After World War II, Europeans were determined to create political and economic structures so as to prevent another war, such as those in 1914–1918 and 1939–1945 – two catastrophic wars that took place in a span of just 31 years. The United States provided assistance with the Marshall Plan, as discussed in Chapter 9, and the North Atlantic Treaty Organization (NATO) was founded as a military alliance between the major western European nations and the United States and Canada. The "European Project" was greatly influenced by the refusal of the Soviet Union to participate even in the Marshall Plan. The Soviets had their own ideas for the future of Europe under Soviet influence. On the one hand, Soviet policy prevented the eastern European nations from cooperating with the western Europeans, but on the other hand, the Soviet threat brought France, Western Germany, and others together in NATO and helped to foster further steps toward cooperation.

The first step toward economic integration was the Coal and Steel Community agreement of 1952, which integrated these French and German heavy industries. The next step was the European Common Market in 1959. This major agreement ended tariffs between the members and also set uniform tariffs between the members and other nations. In other words, U.S. exporters faced the same tariff in France, West Germany, and the other members. Member nations agreed not to compete with each other on tariff policy. Other policies include standardization of regulations (even traffic signs) and elimination of barriers preventing the movement of people across borders. And the name of the organization was changed to the European Union (EU). It is worth noting that the nations of the EU maintained their own currencies and conducted their own economic policies not covered by the EU agreements.

The EU was a great success. The people of Western Europe were enjoying unprecedented prosperity, and NATO was providing security. The idea of a uniform currency was under discussion, but evidently the time was not right for this step. The EU did experiment with an exchange rate mechanism that attempted to fix the exchange rates of the members to the German mark. This experiment broke down because nations found that sticking to a regime of fixed exchange rates with major trading partners in Europe was unworkable. An analysis of the problem of fixed exchange rates is provided next. Over time, the size of the permissible variations in exchange rates made the agreement largely meaningless. Then came the collapse of the Soviet Union in 1991 and the freeing of the Eastern European nations to decide their own fates. One major question was whether Germany should be reunited. The resolution of the German question and the creation of a common European currency, the euro, apparently are connected. Joseph Stiglitz (2016, p. 6) states:

> In the case of the euro, Helmut Kohl, the German chancellor, reportedly agreed to its creation in return for French president François Mitterrand's acceptance of the reunification of Germany.

Review of the macroeconomics of balance of payments, exchange rates, and interest rates

Before we go on to consider the euro, the common European currency, it is helpful to review and extend the analysis of the balance of payments and exchange rates from Chapter 1. Recall the rule that money going out equals money coming in; the balance of payments always balances and consists of:

	Money Flow
Current Account	
Exports of Goods and Services	+
Imports of Goods and Services	−
Financial/Capital Account	
Foreign Investment in the Home Country	+
Home Country Investment in Foreign Countries	−

The supply-and-demand diagram for the home country currency is displayed in Figure 15.1. Also remember that the flows of investment in the financial/capital account are sensitive to interest rates. An increase in interest rates in the home country will increase foreign investment, so long as interest rates in other countries do not change.

Consider the case in which the demand for the home country's exports declines (demand for home country currency shifts to the left as in Figure 15.1). Given the supply curve, the decline in demand will lower the value of home currency. Foreigners wish to buy fewer units of the home currency. The decline in the value of the home currency means that home country exports are cheaper because foreign currency can now buy more units of home country currency. Home country GDP does decline because of the decline in exports, but the decline in the value of the home country currency, as shown in Figure 15.1, partly offsets the decline in the demand for its exports.

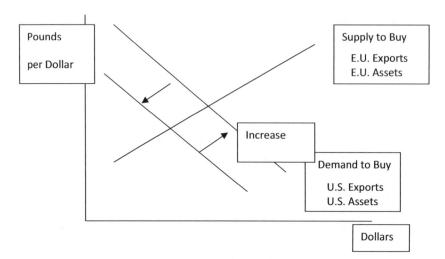

FIGURE 15.1 The Market for U.S. Dollars in Foreign Exchange. The demand for U.S. exports declines, shifting the demand for dollars to the left as shown. U.S. GDP declines. The value of the dollar in foreign exchange falls. An increase in interest rate in the U.S. will shift the demand for dollars to the right because foreigners will increase their demand for U.S. assets. The increase in interest rates causes a further decline in U.S. GDP

Now suppose that the home country wishes to prevent the value of its currency from declining in the face of a drop in the demand for exports. What can be done? The simple answer is that an increase in interest rates in the home country can restore the demand for home country currency by making investment in home country assets more attractive for foreigners. The central bank can engineer an increase in interest rates, of course. You know all about that. But there is a serious downside to increasing interest rates; domestic investment and possibly consumer spending on durable goods will be reduced. In other words, the drop in exports has reduced home country GDP, and the policy used to offset the resulting decline in the value of home country currency makes the decline in GDP even larger. In this case, interest rate policy to maintain the exchange rate is an "automatic destabilizer," as opposed to an automatic stabilizer.

The lesson here is that if a country wishes to maintain a constant exchange rate, it must have the ability to set interest rates. Or, if a country wishes to set interest rates to maintain full employment, then the exchange rate must be free to "float." I think these lessons are what we need to know to examine the economic problems in the euro zone.

The euro system

The treaty designed to move Europe to a single currency was signed shortly after the collapse of the Soviet Union and the agreement to permit the reunification of Germany. The conditions under which a common currency can be successful for a group of independent nations were set out decades earlier by Robert Mundell (1961). Mundell used the term "optimum currency area" to denote a region in which the common currency would work best. What are the characteristics of such a region?

Mundell imagined a region with uniform industrial composition across the components of the region; highly mobile labor and capital within the region because the same jobs and industries exist in all components of the region; no labor or capital mobility into or out of the region; and inflexible wages and prices in the downward direction in the short run. This last assumption means that a decline in aggregate demand will generate unemployment. Also, a common currency implies that there is a single central bank. Call the components of the region A and B. Assume A and B are enjoying full employment. Now suppose that the demand for output produced in B declines and unemployment in B increases. What happens? The assumption of highly mobile labor and capital will mean that unemployed resources migrate to A and unemployment declines in B and increases in A. Now suppose that the monetary authorities act to stimulate the economy by increasing the supply of money. As we know, in the short run, both prices and real output increase. Unemployment declines in both A and B, and the price level increases.

The scenario in the previous paragraph assumed that labor and capital mobility occurs before the monetary authority acts to increase the supply of money. Now suppose that the monetary authority acts first. Aggregate demand rises in A. As B has unemployment, both output and prices increase there. The price difference between A and B will stimulate migration of labor and capital to A. Full employment will be restored in both A and B, but with fewer jobs in B and higher prices all around. As Mundell (1961, p. 659) put it,

> Full employment thus imparts an inflationary bias . . . to a currency area with a common currency.

The conditions for a common currency system to work well seem to be highly restrictive; the region for a common currency might be very small. Mundell pointed out that having a large number of small currency areas is costly because of problems of money–changing and setting values. Money is a convenience, but a very large number of different currencies is inconvenient. So the question becomes one of benefits and costs of adopting a common currency system.

In the end, Mundell (1961) opts for a system of common currencies within regions in which the benefits of the system outweigh the costs, coupled with a system of flexible exchange rates across regions. In other words, have regions large enough to have the convenience of a common currency but not so large that the components of the region have economies of different composition. Indeed, he concludes that a system of flexible exchange rates requires a world made up of regions as he defined.

The euro

The adoption of the European common currency, the euro, began with the Maastricht Treaty of 1992. The euro was established in 1999 when Austria, Belgium, Finland, France, Germany, Ireland, Italy, Luxembourg, the Netherlands, Portugal, and Spain joined. Greece joined in 2001, followed by Slovenia in 2007,

Cyprus and Malta in 2008, Slovakia in 2009, Estonia in 2011, Latvia in 2014, and Lithuania in 2015. Are all of the countries that adopted the euro sufficiently similar in economic structure to be parts of a Mundell region? The European Central Bank (ECB) was established in 1998, with headquarters in Belgium. The ECB sets interest rates for the euro area.

The United Kingdom did not adopt the Euro. London had become one of the world's premier financial centers, and the Bank of England, at 324 years of age, is the second-oldest central bank on the planet (second to the Swedish central bank, the Riksbank, by 26 years). One might hypothesize that it did not make sense for the United Kingdom to adopt the euro and be subject to policies made by the European Central Bank. Also, at the time of publication for this book, the United Kingdom is in the process of leaving the EU (i.e., the "Brexit").

Adoption of the euro means that all member nations have the same nominal exchange rate with each other – namely 1.0. Recall that the real exchange rate can be written as the nominal exchange rate (1.0) times the price level in the home country divided by the price level in the other country. In equation form:

$$\text{Real exchange rate} = 1.0(P_h/P_f).$$

Here P_h is the price level in the home country and P_f is the price level in the other country. A home country with a high price level will have a difficult time selling its export products. The equation tells us that one method for devaluing the home country currency in real terms is to lower its price level. How can this be done? The answer is to have a recession and hope that prices (and wages) are flexible in the downward direction. Not good.

The treaty stipulates that countries can join if they satisfy convergence criteria intended to make the members into components of a Mundell region. Those requirements include a limit on government deficit of 3 percent of GDP and total government debt of less that 60 percent of GDP. It was thought that these criteria would be sufficient to avoid a situation in which one nation is having a recession while others are not. Also, the criteria were supposed to prevent the case in which one nation would have a large trade deficit while others would have a trade surplus. What could go wrong? Plenty, it turned out.

Consider what happens if one country (such as Spain) has a large trade deficit and another country (such as Germany) has a large trade surplus. Spain must attract financing (borrow money) to finance its trade deficit. Spain cannot devalue its currency, of course, and cannot increase its interest rate. The normal tools for addressing a trade deficit are not available. The ECB can, and does, make loans to countries, but Spain's government debt is limited to 60 percent of GDP. What else can be done? Spain can suffer unemployment, wages and prices can decline, and Spain's export goods can become cheaper, and imports can decline because of lower wages and higher unemployment. The trade deficit can be solved by very painful adjustment.

Here is another scenario. Suppose one country suffers a deep recession. Can it use standard macroeconomic policies? No, because interest rates are set by the ECB, and fiscal policy is limited by the 3 percent government deficit rule. And currency devaluation is off the table, too. So the country suffers. Will the ECB and other member countries make loans to the country in recession? Yes, they will, maybe.

It turned out that the different member countries had different built-in rates of inflation. With the inability to devalue the currency, nations with higher rates of inflation developed trade deficits that produced the scenarios described earlier.

The financial crisis of 2008 caused great difficulties for the eurozone. While the euro initially was considered to be a success at reducing transaction costs and stimulating trade within Europe, some problems cropped up early on. First, consider Finland. Finland has played by all the rules but started to run into trouble when its exports failed to grow after 2000. The structure of the Finnish economy is different from that of other member nations. Two of Finland's main exports at the time were the flip phone by Nokia and paper products. Nokia was 4 percent of the Finland economy when the nation joined the eurozone in 1999, but the iPhone from Apple made the flip phone yesterday's high-tech gadget. The value of Finland's exports remained flat for five years, from 2000 to 2004. The normal policy response for a small nation heavily dependent on exports is to devalue the currency. Indeed, with flexible exchange rates devaluation would occur automatically. This option was not available, of course, nor was monetary policy in the form of a cut in interest rates. Fiscal policy could be used to stimulate the economy, but the Maastricht Treaty imposes limits on a nation's ability to run government deficits. Declines in wages would bring the price of exports down, and wages did decline. However, as you know, Keynes argued forcefully that wage cuts are painful and unnecessary so long as basic macroeconomic policies are followed. Yes, but. . . .

If the case of Finland is a cautionary tale, then the case of Greece is a story of ongoing disaster. Greece was admitted to the eurozone in 2001. The nation had spent the 1990s attempting to get its fiscal status in order to meet the criteria for membership, but admission in fact was based on falsified data. Greece had hoped that admission would stimulate the economy enough that the admission criteria (3 percent government deficit and national debt no more than 60 percent of GDP) actually would be achieved. Admission to the eurozone did result in lower interest rates, which permitted both firms and the government to borrow more, and the Greek economy grew rapidly from 2001 to 2008. But Greece had a large trade deficit and long-standing fiscal problems that were not solved. Government expenditures were not greater than was typical for European nations, but revenues fell short. The government of Greece lacked revenue because of massive tax evasion. Another major problem was that the level of productivity in Greece was lower than in Germany (and other nations as well), so that Greek exports were not competitive. So here were two structural features making Greece different from other members of the eurozone. In short, Greece was not part of the Mundell region that the eurozone hoped to be. The problems Greece faced were magnified by the financial crisis of 2008.

Four nations and the euro

Examine the data in Table 15.1. This table shows the real GDP, unemployment rates, and trade balances for France, Germany, Spain, and Greece from 2000 to 2018. It is helpful to know the relative sizes of these four nations. The population of Germany in 2010 was 81.8 million. In that same year, France's population was

TABLE 15.1 Real GDP (Billion Euros), Unemployment Rate (Percentage) and Trade Balance (Percent of GDP) for France, Germany, Spain, and Greece: 2000–2018

Year	France GDP Unempl.	France Trade Balance	Germany GDP Unemp.	Germany Trade Balance	Spain GDP Unemp.	Spain Trade Bal.	Greece GDP Unemp.	Greece Trade Bal.
2000	1478 9.6	1.11	2109 8.0	−1.76	658 11.9	−4.31	141 11.2	n.a.
2001	1530 8.7	1.57	2173 7.9	−0.37	701 10.6	−4.38	152 10.7	n.a.
2002	1588 8.6	1.15	2198 8.7	1.88	750 11.4	−3.73	163 10.3	−6.83
2003	1631 8.5	0.83	2212 9.8	1.41	802 11.5	−3.88	179 9.7	−8.45
2004	1704 8.8	0.54	2263 10.5	4.54	859 11.0	−5.47	194 10.6	−7.71
2005	1765 8.9	0.11	2288 11.3	4.68	927 9.1	−7.25	199 10.0	−8.87
2006	1848 8.8	0.25	2385 10.2	5.76	1064 8.5	−8.84	218 9.0	−11.49
2007	1941 8.0	−0.10	2500 8.5	6.25	1076 8.2	−9.42	233 8.4	−15.19
2008	1952 7.4	−0.70	2546 7.4	5.69	1110 11.3	−8.98	242 7.8	−15.11
2009	1936 9.1	−0.55	2446 7.6	5.84	1069 17.9	−4.09	238 9.6	−12.35
2010	1985 9.3	−0.63	2564 7.0	5.76	1073 19.9	−3.66	224 12.7	−10.02
2011	2058 9.2	−0.86	2694 5.8	6.22	1063 21.4	−2.72	203 17.9	−8.61
2012	2088 9.8	−0.97	2745 5.4	7.13	1031 24.8	0.10	188 24.5	−1.48
2013	2117 10.3	−0.51	2811 5.2	6.54	1020 26.1	2.04	180 27.5	−1.43
2014	2150 10.3	−0.96	2927 5.0	7.19	1032 24.4	1.70	177 26.5	−0.74
2015	2198 10.4	−0.37	3026 4.6	8.61	1078 22.1	2.03	176 25.0	−0.81
2016	2234 10.8	−0.49	3135 4.1	8.57	1114 19.6	3.17	174 23.6	−1.73
2017	2297 9.4	−0.77	3260 3.8	7.78	1162 17.2	2.77	177 21.5	−1.89
2018	2361 9.0	−0.56	3356 3.4	7.37	1204 15.3	1.91	180 19.3	−2.83

Source: OECD Data

64.5 million, Spain's was 46.5 million, and Greece's was only 11.1 million. Recall that the euro was adopted by France, Germany, and Spain in 1999, and Greece joined in 2001. The financial crisis began in earnest in the United States in 2008. Real GDP in France increased by 3.48 percent per year from 2000 to 2008, and Germany grew at a slower pace of 2.35 percent per year over these same eight years. Now look at Spain and Greece. Membership in the eurozone coincides with rapid real GDP growth for both nations; 6.73 percent per year for Spain and 6.75 percent per year for Greece. Unemployment rates in Europe are much greater than are normally seen in the United States or the United Kingdom. From 2000 to 2007, unemployment rates fluctuate and are then lower in France, Spain, and Greece in 2007 than in 2000. Unemployment in Germany started at 8.0 percent, hit a high point of 11.3 percent in 2005, and then fell to 8.5 percent in 2007. Real GDP declined in all four countries in 2009 (but only by 0.8 percent in France). Unemployment rates increased sharply in 2009 in France, Spain, and Greece, but did not in Germany.

Real GDP growth in France after the recovery year of 2010 had slowed to 2.17 percent per year, in contrast to the 3.48 percent in the first eight years of the decade. The unemployment rate in France has held at over 9.0 percent or greater up through 2018. Real GDP in Spain continued to decline up through 2013, and then recovered at a rate of 3.32 percent from 2013 to 2018. Unemployment in Spain hit a high of 26.1 percent in 2013 and then declined.

Spain has shown signs of recovery after 2011, the year in which Mario Draghi took over the European Central Bank and vowed to save the euro by making loans to countries in need. Greece was in dire straits. Table 15.1 shows that the real GDP of Greece declined every year from 2008 to 2016, a total decline of 28 percent (−4.12 percent per year). The unemployment rate reached 27.5 percent in 2013. The signs of recovery after 2013 exist, but they are weak.

On the other hand, real GDP in Germany grew at an annual rate of 3.36 percent from 2010 to 2018, and unemployment in Germany continued to fall throughout the decade and reached 3.4 percent in 2018. What was going on?

Now look at the data on trade balances (value of exports minus value of imports) in Table 15.1. The data show the trade surplus (positive numbers) or trade deficits (negative numbers) as a percentage of GDP for France, Germany, Spain, and Greece. The year 2000 is the first full year of the euro; recall that Greece joined in 2001. Both Greece and Spain began their time with the euro with sizable trade deficits, while France had a trade surplus and Germany had a small trade deficit that was erased by 2002. The clear messages from Table 15.1 are that Germany built a large trade surplus that persists, and Greece and Spain had trade deficits that increased up through 2008. France had trade balances very close to zero up through 2008. Clearly, Greece and Spain had large trade deficits that needed to be financed somehow. The normal methods for addressing a trade deficit, devaluation and increases in interest rates, were not available. So the "solution" is lower wages and higher unemployment, the latter as shown in Table 15.1. Greece and Spain "solved" the trade deficit by suffering unemployment, which did reduce imports. The trade deficits for Greece and Spain did indeed decline sharply, and even became trade surpluses for Spain starting in 2012. The large trade surpluses for Germany permitted the unemployment rate to fall to a very low number in 2018 of 3.4 percent. The case of France is a bit puzzling. The unemployment rate remained high, over 9 percent until 2018, but the trade balance has been in consistent deficit since 2007. However, these deficits are not large.

As noted previously, when Mario Draghi became President of the European Central Bank in 2011, he vowed to make loans to the nations with large trade deficits. He declared in 2012 that the ECB "is ready to do whatever it takes to preserve the euro." The program of loans to banks and purchases of government bonds has enabled the euro system to persist but does not eliminate the structural issues of the eurozone. Draghi favors more a more extensive set of EU institutions that would require nations to give up more of their individual authority.

The data presented in Table 15.1 show that the nations in the eurozone with large trade deficits had to suffer high rates of unemployment to lower the deficit. The trade deficit became especially large for Greece during the financial crisis of 2008, and Greece and Spain both experienced unemployment rates in excess of 25 percent, which is Great Depression territory. Germany, with the strongest economy in the region, had large trade surpluses and low rates of unemployment. France fell somewhere in the middle of these two extremes.

Joseph Stiglitz (2016) has written a book titled *The Euro: How a Common Currency Threatens the Future of Europe*. What is the answer to the problems created by the adoption of a common currency by a large group of disparate countries that fail to satisfy the conditions for a Mundell region?

Can a common currency work for Europe?

The eurozone system was built with automatic destabilizers. What can be done to make the system work? Paul Krugman (2020a, p. 177) calls the euro "the road to hell . . . paved with good intentions." So I guess he would opt for ending the experiment. A more modest proposal has been voiced by Stigliz (2016), of moving to more than one common currency zone in Europe. In particular, Germany and perhaps other nations of northern Europe would form one currency area, while nations of southern Europe such as Greece, Italy, and Spain would form another. The southern group then could set its own interest rate and devalue its currency against the northern group currency. Or maybe three common currency areas would make sense. But can the existing euro be made to work?

Stiglitz (2016) suggests an extensive set of changes as follows:

- Form a banking union with a common deposit insurance fund and regulatory system
- Create a Eurobond that is mutual indebtedness, with the borrower nation required to spend the funds to make its economy more productive (e.g., education, infrastructure)
- Create a system of automatic stabilizers
- Have a true convergence policy that would, for example, put pressure on countries with trade surpluses to reduce them
- Use macroeconomic policy to promote stability and growth for the entire eurozone
- Harmonize tax systems

■ Recognize that markets are not perfect – reform the financial system, force corporate governance to focus less on short-term returns, facilitate bankruptcy, and have a carbon tax to encourage investments that help the environment

More recently, Stiglitz (2020) has led a large group of European experts in proposing new rules for the European economy. This lengthy report covers all aspects of the economy from monetary policy to poverty programs, regulations to promote competition, and more. Most of the suggestions from Stiglitz's list are included. Europeans are doing some hard thinking about their European Project, and we'll just have to see what happens.

16

COVID-19 and the economic collapse of 2020

This chapter provides a brief look at the macroeconomic impacts of the COVID-19 pandemic in the United States, the United Kingdom, Japan, and Germany. By March of 2020 it had become obvious that because of the COVID-19 outbreak, it was necessary to restrict human activities to reduce transmission of the disease. A great deal of economic activity was shut down by order of state and local officials and by voluntary actions.

The four nations included in this chapter differ greatly in the number of COVID-19 cases and deaths. See Table 16.1, which shows that the United States by far had the greatest number of cases, cases per population (47,422 per million), and deaths as of December 10, 2020. The United Kingdom has a much smaller population than the United States but had fewer cases per million population. However, the United Kingdom had far more deaths per case compared to the United States (3.54 percent versus 1.89 percent). Germany had 15,275 cases per million population and 1.65 percent deaths per case. In sharp contrast, Japan had only 165,000 cases and 1,329 cases per million population. The death rate in Japan was 1.45 percent per case. In summary, the United States, the United Kingdom, and Germany were all hit pretty hard by the pandemic, with cases per million population especially high in the United States and the death rate per case greatest in the United Kingdom. But Japan had only a small case load and the lowest death rate per case among the four nations. What about the economic impacts?

TABLE 16.1 COVID-19 Cases as of December 10, 2020

Nation	COVID-19 Cases (million)	Cases Per Million Population	Deaths (1,000s)
United States	15.28	47,422	288.5
United Kingdom	1.77	26,768	62.6
Japan	0.66	1,329	2.4
Germany	1.24	15,275	20.4

Source: Johns Hopkins University

Tables 16.2 through 16.9 display economic data for the United States, the United Kingdom, Japan, and Germany. Tables 16.2 through 16.4 display data for the United States for GDP, unemployment rate, employment, and labor force participation. Table 16.3 shows unemployment rate and employment data for

TABLE 16.2 U.S. Real GDP, Quarterly at Seasonally Adjusted Annual Rate ($ Billions)

	Q4 2019	Q1 2020	Q2 2020	Q3 2020	Q4 2020
GDP	19,254	19,011	17,302 (−8.99%)	18,596 (+7.48%)	18,780 (+0.99%) (−2.46%) annual
Consumption	13,354	13,118	11,860 (−9.59%)	12,925 (+8.98%)	13,005 (+0.62%)
Investment	3413	3334	2850 (−14.52%)	3330 (+16.84%)	3523 (+5.80%
Gov't Spending	3337	3348	3369 (+0.63%)	3327 (−2.25%)	3317 (−0.30%)
Exports	2558	2495	1927 (−22.77%)	2166 (+12.40%)	2277 +(5.12%)
Imports	3142	3283	2702 (−17.70%)	3185 (+17.88%)	3398 (+6.69%)

Source: U.S. Bureau of Economic Analysis

TABLE 16.3 U.S. Unemployment Rate and Change in Non-farm Employment by Month

Month	Unem Rate 2018	19	20	08	09	10	Empl Ch'ng 1,000s 2018	19	20	08	09	10
Jan.	4.1	4.0	3.6	5.0	7.8	9.8	121	269	214	11	−784	2
Feb.	4.1	3.8	3.5	4.9	8.3	9.8	406	1	251	−79	−743	−92
March	4.0	3.8	4.4	5.1	8.7	9.9	176	147	−1373	−49	−800	181
April	4.0	3.6	14.7	5.0	9.0	9.9	137	210	−20787	−240	−695	231
May	3.8	3.6	13.3	5.4	9.4	9.6	278	85	2725	−177	−342	540
June	4.0	3.7	11.1	5.6	9.5	9.4	219	182	4781	−171	−467	−139
July	3.8	3.7	10.2	5.8	9.5	9.4	136	194	1761	−196	−340	−84
Aug.	3.8	3.7	8.4	6.1	9.6	9.5	244	207	1493	−278	−183	−5
Sept.	3.7	3.5	7.9	6.1	9.8	9.5	80	208	672	−460	−241	−65
Oct.	3.8	3.6	6.9	6.5	10.0	9.4	201	185	638	−481	−199	268
Nov.	3.7	3.5	6.7	6.8	9.9	9.8	134	261	245	−727	12	125
Dec.	3.9	3.5	6.7	7.3	9.9	9.3	182	184	−140	−706	−269	72

Source: U.S. Bureau of Labor Statistics

2018–2020 and for 2008–2010, so that the time patterns for the two periods can be compared. Note that the data for 2020 show a sharp increase in unemployment and decline in employment, while the data for the financial crisis of 2008 show more gradual, but disastrous nonetheless, changes. Data for the United Kingdom are contained in Tables 16.5 (GDP) and 16.6 (unemployment rate). GDP data for Japan are displayed in Table 16.7, and labor market data are provided in Table 16.8. Table 16.9 has GDP and labor market data for Germany.

TABLE 16.4 U.S. Labor Force Participation in 2020

Month	Labor Force Participation (%)
Jan.	63.4
Feb.	63.4
March	62.7
April	60.2
May	60.8
June	61.5
July	61.4
Aug.	61.7
Sept.	61.4
Oct.	61.7
Nov.	61.5
Dec.	61.5

Source: U.S. Bureau of Labor Statistics

TABLE 16.5 U.K. GDP

Quarter	GDP £bil.	Percentage Change
2019 Q1	541.2	
2019 Q2	541.1	0.0%
2019 Q3	542.9	0.3%
2019 Q4	543.7	0.1%
2020 Q1	530.0	−2.5%
2020 Q2	425.0	−19.8%
2020 Q3	490.9	15.5%

Source: Office of National Statistics

TABLE 16.6 U.K. Unemployment Rate, 2019–2020

Period	Unemploy-ment Rate
Nov. – Jan.	3.9%
Dec. – Feb.	4.0%
Jan. – March	4.0%
Feb. – April	4.0%
March – May	4.1%
April – June	4.1%
May – July	4.3%
June – Aug.	4.5%
July – Sept.	4.8%
Aug. – Oct.	4.9%

Source: Office of National Statistics

TABLE 16.7 Japan GDP

Quarter	Real GDP, Trillion Yen	Percentage Change	GDP Deflator
2019 Q1	135.3		101.6
2019 Q2	131.6	0.9%	104.7
2019 Q3	134/0	1.7%	101.7
2019 Q4	135.0	−0.7%	105.3
2020 Q1	132.9	−1.8%	102.5
2020 Q2	118.2	−10.2%	106.2
2020 Q3	126.2	−5.8%	102.8

Source: Japanese Cabinet Office

TABLE 16.8 Japan Labor Force, Employment, and Unemployment

Month	Labor Force (mil.)	Employed (mil.)	Unemployed (mil.)	Unemploy-ment Rate
Oct. 2019	6951	67.87	1.65	2.4%
Nov. 2019	6913	67.62	1.51	2.2%
Dec. 2019	6883	67.37	1.45	2.2%

(Continued)

TABLE 16.8 (Continued)

Month	Labor Force (mil.)	Employed (mil.)	Unemployed (mil.)	Unemployment Rate
Jan. 2020	6846	66.87	1.59	2.4%
Feb. 2020	6850	66.91	1.59	2.4%
March 2020	6876	67.00	1.76	2.5%
April 2020	6817	66.28	1.89	2.6%
May 2020	6854	66.56	1.98	2.9%
June 2020	6865	66.70	1.95	2.8%
July 2020	6852	66.55	1.97	2.9%
Aug. 2020	6882	66.76	2.06	3.0%
Sept. 2020	6899	66.89	2.10	3.0%
Oct. 2020	6872	66.58	2.14	3.1%
Nov. 2020	6856	66.42	1.98	2.9%

Source: Ministry of Internal Affairs and Communication

TABLE 16.9 German GDP and Labor Market Data

Quarter	Real GDP (Base 2015)	Percentage Change	GDP Euro, bil.	Labor Force (mil.)	Employment (mil.)	Unempl. Rate
2019 Q1	106.36		845.8	46.3	44.8	3.1%
2019 Q2	105.36	−0.3%	846.9	46.4	45.1	2.9%
2019 Q3	107.74	1.2%	870.1	46.5	45.2	2.9%
2019 Q4	107.79	0.2%	886.1	46.8	45.4	2.9%
2020 Q1	104.56	−1.7%	851.8	46.5	45.0	3.3%
2020 Q2	93.47	−11.3%	768.8	46.5	44.6	4.2%
2020 Q3	103.52	8.5%	843.0	46.6	44.6	4.3%

Source: Statistisches Bundesamt

Go through the tables and compare the GDP data. You see that all four nations experienced small declines in real GDP in the first quarter of 2020. Only the month of March appears to have been affected by the pandemic. But then all four nations experienced very large declines in GDP in the second quarter of 2020. These declines are:

United States   −9.0% decline in real GDP

United Kingdom   −19.8% decline in GDP

| Japan | −10.2% decline in real GDP |
| Germany | −11.3% decline in real GDP |

The data for the United Kingdom are nominal GDP figures, but the nation experienced very little inflation during this time. The consumer price index increased by only 0.55 percent from February 2020 to October 2020. Thus, it appears that the decline in real GDP suffered by these major nations in the pandemic was quite large regardless of whether the COVID-19 case load was high, medium, or low. From these data, it appears to be an international slowdown in economic activity.

Now look at the GDP data for the third quarter of 2020. All four of the nations had sizable recoveries in real GDP. The United States rebounded by 7.5 percent, the United Kingdom gained back 15.5 percent, Japan was up 6.8 percent, and Germany regained 8.5 percent. All four nations undertook policy actions, including large spending programs as well as expansive monetary policies, to help their economies recover from the second quarter. These policies are at least partially, and perhaps mainly, responsible for the bouncebacks. The aid package in the United States was $2.2 trillion, about 10 percent of GDP. The aid commitment in Japan was 108 trillion yen (20 percent of GDP), and the package in Germany was 750 billion euros (about 20 percent of GDP). The United Kingdom enacted a series of aid measures worth a total of £78 billion, plus more funds depending upon the number of households and firms that participate, which would total at least 15 percent of GDP.

Now examine the data on employment and unemployment. Here, experiences differ. In the United States, the unemployment rate increased from 3.5 percent in February 2020 to 4.4 percent in March, and then shot up to 14.7 percent in April. The unemployment rate has declined steadily since April and reached 6.7 percent in November and December. Between March and April, U.S. employment declined by 22.2 million jobs. Total employment in February was 152.2 million, so total employment had dropped by 14.6 percent. The gains in employment since April total 12.2 million, so as of December the United States was down 10.0 million jobs from February. Note the decline in December of 140,000 jobs. One result of this lack of jobs has meant that labor force participation has declined – from 63.4 percent in February to 61.5 percent in November and December. A decline in labor force participation of 1.9 percent means that the labor force declined by about 3.1 million persons.

In contrast to the United States, the other three nations did not experience large increases in the unemployment rate. The U.K. unemployment rate went from 4.0 percent in January–March to 5.0 percent in September–November. In Japan, the number of unemployed workers increased from 159,000 in February to 214,000 in October (an increase of 35 percent), but the unemployment rate registered an increase of only 2.4 percent to 3.1 percent. Total employment declined by 630,000 from February to April but has since regained the February employment level of 66.9 million in September. Employment declined to 66.4 million in November but went back up to 66.7 million in December. The labor force also declined during this period, so the unemployment rate for November and December declined to 2.9 percent. The German unemployment rate was 2.9 percent in the fourth quarter of 2019, increased to 3.3 percent in the first quarter of 2020, and then "jumped" to 4.2 percent in the second quarter. Total employment in Germany fell from

45.4 million in the fourth quarter of 2019 to 44.6 million in the second quarter of 2020, or about 800,000 jobs. The United States lost 20.8 million jobs in April alone. Somehow these other three nations were able to avoid huge increases in the unemployment rate even as GDP fell by amounts that were as large, or larger, than the decline in the United States.

What have we learned from this brief excursion into macroeconomic data during 2020, the year of the pandemic? First, real GDP took a big hit in the second quarter of the year in the United States, the United Kingdom, Japan, and Germany. And then much, but not all, of the decline in real GDP was regained in the third quarter. But the U.S. labor market behaved quite differently compared to the other three nations. The job losses in the United States were massive; 22.2 million jobs were lost in March and April, and many of those jobs (10.0 million) had not returned by December. The other three nations experienced increases in the unemployment rate but by and large avoided huge declines in employment levels. So the big question for me (and maybe for you, too): Why? One reason might be the relatively larger aid packages used by the other three nations. More research is needed. . . .

The pandemic of 2020 in effect created a new category of economic downturn – a government-ordered shutdown of much of the economy. Government officials ordered that the supply side of the economy should contract. Furthermore, people reduced their activities because of the risk of contracting the disease and because of an increase in unemployment. So we seem to have both supply and demand shocks at the same time. Furthermore, the supply and demand shocks interact. A large decline in demand will cause some businesses to close, which adds to the decline in supply, which will mean a further decline in demand because access to goods and

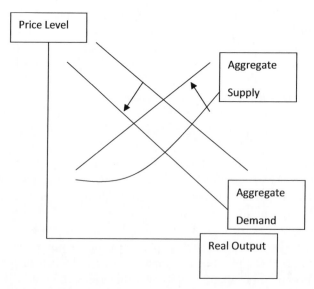

FIGURE 16.1 Aggregate Supply and Demand. The pandemic caused a negative supply shock ordered by government officials. Businesses were ordered to reduce capacity, and many closed altogether. At the same time, aggregate demand declined because people wished to avoid the risk to their health and because many people were unemployed. The result was a large decline in real GDP in the second quarter of 2020

services is reduced. Or an exogenous reduction in supply causes demand to fall because of reduced access, which causes further declines in supply.

How does the story of macroeconomics during a pandemic relate to the macroeconomic theories we have been considering? Look at Figure 16.1. Clearly, we have a negative supply shock, so the aggregate supply-and-demand model of Chapter 3 is relevant. We can shift the aggregate supply curve to the left, and then shift the aggregate demand curve to the left as well, because some workers were unemployed and because people sought to avoid the risk to their health. The shift in supply tends to increase prices, but the shift in demand acts to lower prices. The overall effect on the price level is uncertain.

The recovery in the third quarter of 2020 can be depicted by a rightward shift in supply as restrictions on economic activity were lifted partially, and the increase in demand is also a rightward shift in the aggregate demand curve. However, only in Japan did the recovery approach a return to the output level of the first quarter. In short, the new Keynesian model of aggregate supply and demand can serve as a pretty good explanation for the macroeconomics of the pandemic. What do you think?

17

Conclusion

What approaches do people in authority use?

Introduction

While macroeconomic outcomes affect our lives, for most of us macroeconomic theory is a spectator sport. While we do vote, we are not in the game of making policy or making a living in the macroeconomic forecasting business. Some people are in this very serious game with actual responsibilities, so how do they decide what to do? Which macroeconomic theory speaks to them, and what does it say? This chapter is an unscientific survey of such people that includes some of those who have put their views in readily accessible writing. The book ends with a brief summary and some conclusions.

Six prominent public officials

We begin with the maestro, Alan Greenspan, the U.S. Fed chair from 1987 to 2006. The period of his chairmanship is called the Great Moderation, and the data presented in Chapter 13 suggest that for most of that period, discretionary monetary policy was handled deftly. What macroeconomic theory spoke to the Chairman? Since leaving the Fed, he has written a book in which he states clearly (2014, pp. 6–7):

> By the 1980s, with inflation under control – thanks in part, to the Federal Reserve's restraint of money supply growth – a rejuvenated but somewhat chastised Keynesianism, with a stagflation fix to reflect the importance of inflation expectations, reemerged. Such models worked reasonably well for the next two decades, largely as a consequence of an absence of any serious structural breakdown in markets. The model constructed by the Federal Reserve staff, combining elements of Keynesianism, monetarism, and other more recent contributions to economic theory, seemed particularly impressive and was particularly helpful to the Fed's Board of Governors over the years of my tenure.

So Greenspan was relying on Keynes, supplemented by inflation expectations, and on Monetarist thinking. So far, so good (2014, p. 7):

> But leading up to the almost universally unanticipated crisis of September 2008, macromodeling unequivocally failed when it was needed most, much to the chagrin of the economics profession. The Federal Reserve Board's highly sophisticated forecasting system did not foresee a recession until the crisis hit.

Greenspan argues that macroeconomics needs a theory that includes a far more elaborate treatment of the financial sector. He states (2014, p. 16) that September 2008 "has forced us to find ways to incorporate into our macromodels those animal spirits that dominate finance." Those animal spirits, about which Keynes wrote, are not purely random but can be modeled – at least in part. Greenspan's book is an effort to begin to identify the nonrandom animal spirits. His list includes fear, euphoria, risk aversion, competitive drive, inbred herding, inertia, and home bias. He proposes that motivations such as these should be modeled and incorporated into conventional macroeconomic theory, which he sees as a combination of Keynesian and Monetarist elements. The idea would be to find variables that represent these factors, and then test both what causes changes in those variables and how those variables affect macroeconomic variables. This is a big research agenda. Macroeconomic models need to be fixed (most everyone agrees), and once that is accomplished, we can go back to conducting wise discretionary monetary policy.

It is interesting that Greenspan (2014) does not cite Minsky or Kindleberger on the financial instability hypothesis that stability breeds instability. It is also fair to say that Minsky's efforts to build a formal theory that can be incorporated into Keynesian models did not meet with much success. He did produce a theory of investment (1975, Chapter 5), but the model is obscure and I do not recommend that you attempt to read it now (maybe much later).

It is fair to say that Greenspan skates over the Fed policy to lower the federal funds rate drastically during 2002–2005. He looked at the data for 2002–2005 and concluded that long-term rates started to fall six months before the Fed began to lower the federal funds rate in 2001, and long-term rates continued to fall after the Fed began to raise rates in 2004. Greenspan stated (2010, p. 237):

> But the fixed-rate mortgage clearly delinked from the federal funds rate in the early part of this century. The correlation between them fell to an insignificant 0.10 during 2002–2005, the period when the bubble was most intense, and as a consequence, the funds rate exhibited little, if any, influence on home prices.

As we have seen, Anna Schwartz and John Taylor disagree strongly with Greenspan. They see Fed policy as a classic mistake that Monetarists warn against. Subsequent research by McDonald and Stokes (2015) over a longer time period showed that the interest rate on the standard 30-year mortgage was driven partly by the federal funds rate, but that this mortgage rate was not a cause of the housing price bubble. Instead, the short-term rates, the federal funds rate, and the rate on adjustable-rate mortgages were among the causes of the housing price bubble.

Sir Mervyn King is another very prominent central banker. He served as Governor of the Bank of England from 2003 to 2013, and has written a penetrating book titled *The End of Alchemy* (2016). The alchemy has two parts. First, there is fiat money – used because everyone else uses it. What if we lose confidence that others will accept our bucks backed by nothing? Second, there is the role of banks (and other financial institutions) to take in deposits, which are safe, and turn them into risky loans. This is the transformation of risk into certainty (or is it the other way around?). So we have deposit insurance to make our deposits safe and central banks as "lenders of last resort," but that only provides an incentive for banks to take on even riskier loans. How are we to end the alchemy?

Sir Mervyn's answer is to replace central banks with a pawn broker for all seasons (PFAS). What does that mean? The idea is to require collateral equal to the value of a loan. Central banks should continue making loans against a wider range of collateral than had been used prior to the financial crisis, and therefore create money. When there is a sudden demand for more liquidity, the central bank should step up and provide emergency money against illiquid and risky assets. A central bank can do this. The idea is that banks will always have access to sufficient cash to meet demands by depositors and other short-term lenders. This system will force banks to think hard about what collateral they are willing to pledge. Banks will have collateral "pre-positioned" and will therefore know how much cash they can access from the central bank.

King (2016, pp. 272–273) provides an example of how the PFAS scheme would work. Suppose a bank has liabilities of $100 million and assets consisting of $10 million of reserves at the central bank, $40 million in reasonably liquid assets, and $50 million in illiquid loans to businesses. The central bank examines the bank's assets and imposes a 10% "haircut" on the liquid assets and 50% on the illiquid assets. All of this means that the bank has effective liquid assets of $71 million ($10 + $36 + $25). The bank is required to have $71 million in deposits and short-term debt. So the bank would have to alter the composition of its assets.

Where does Sir Mervyn stand on macroeconomic theories? He does think the liquidity trap is real, but he is quite clear (2016, p. 306):

> To sum up, neither Keynesian nor neoclassical theories provide an adequate explanation of booms and depressions.

He rejects Minsky's story because it involves a boom before every bust and it requires people to be irrational. He prefers to think of people trying to be rational under conditions of Keynesian radical uncertainty. Misperceptions and mistakes happen. "Animal spirits" do not occur independently of economic circumstance. Rather, those bad animal spirits result from rational people trying to cope. So there is much to do to develop models of rational people coping. Here he seems to agree with Greenspan's research agenda.

The United Kingdom has implemented several policies designed to make the financial system safer. A few of the provisions include:

- Increases in capital requirements for large banks
- More intrusive bank supervision
- Financial Stability Board designed to monitor risks in the entire system and promulgate new rules such as central clearing of derivative securities

- Increase in deposit insurance limit
- Effective bank resolution system with no cost to taxpayers

You will note the similarity to the Dodd–Frank system adopted by the United States in 2010, described later.

Timothy Geithner is a central figure in the financial crisis and aftermath. He served as President of the Federal Reserve Bank of New York from 2004 to 2009, and then became Secretary of the Treasury under President Obama in 2009. He served in that capacity until 2013. He has written a book (2014) that is well worth reading. He is not a PhD economist, but he gained important experience as a staff member at the Treasury Department dealing with financial crises of various nations around the world, including the Asian crisis of the late 1990s. During that time, he read Kindleberger's *Manias, Panics, and Crashes*, and found that the book is consistent with what he had observed. Recall that Kindleberger cited Hyman Minsky as an important influence on his thinking. In 2007, Geithner got around to reading Minsky's theory that stability can breed instability.

Geithner describes (2014, p. 80) his first speech as president of the New York Fed as follows:

> In my very first speech at the New York Fed in March 2004, I tried to push back against the complacency, telling a room full of bankers that the wonders of the new financial world would not necessarily prevent catastrophic failures of major institutions, and should not inspire delusions of safety on Wall Street. I even cited my favorite theorist on financial irrationality, the leading promoter of the idea that periodic financial crises are practically inevitable. "These improvements are unlikely to have brought an end to what Charles Kindleberger called manias and panics," I said. "It is important that those of you who run financial institutions build in a sufficient cushion against adversity."

Message transmitted, but evidently not well received. During early 2007, the New York Fed conducted studies on what might happen if housing prices fell sharply (as housing prices had already begun to decline in 2006). Geithner (2014, p. 113) summarizes the results of those efforts:

> We didn't foresee that falling housing prices alone would trigger widespread mortgage defaults that could cause significant problems in the banking system, because we didn't examine the possibility that the initial fears associated with subprime mortgages and the general fall in house prices could trigger a classic financial panic, followed by a crash in household wealth and a collapse of the broader economy. This was the arc of crisis described in Kindleberger's book; manias, followed by panics, ending in crashes. And this was the death spiral I had seen so often at Treasury during the emerging-market crisis of the 1990s.

Geithner is influenced by Kindleberger, so why did he not foresee what could happen? He says that the system was more vulnerable than he realized because he did not know that non-banks were very highly leveraged using short-term loans. So here is a key guy who was as well informed as possible at the time who did not understand the situation well enough. He came to understand, but too late.

As Treasury Secretary, Geithner agreed with the rest of President Obama's advisors that Keynesian-type stimulus was needed. Initially, he thought that the stimulus should be temporary, because he thought the markets needed that assurance. Some of the other advisors, such as Lawrence Summers, agreed with him, but others thought that the stimulus should be larger and longer. The President agreed with Geithner and Summers. The stimulus of $792 billion in spending increases and tax cuts was passed in March 2009. Geithner came to change his mind. The crisis was worse than they had realized; unemployment increased more than the President's economists had predicted. Along with other advisors, he argued for more stimulus. Geithner thinks that the stimulus package was effective at preventing an even worse macroeconomic and financial decline.

Geithner is a Keynesian/Minskyite.

Secretary Geithner played a major role in the formulation of the reform of the financial system, the Wall Street Reform and Consumer Protection Act of 2010 (known as Dodd–Frank after its Senate and House of Representatives sponsors). Dodd–Frank represents a major overhaul in the regulation of the financial system. The basic idea is to reduce the ability of the financial system to generate Minsky-like financial instability. Major provisions are as follows.

- Creation of the Bureau of Consumer Financial Protection to regulate financial products, including preventing the issuing of toxic mortgages
- Creation of an Orderly Liquidation Authority that permits the FDIC to prevent a destructive bankruptcy of a major financial institution, funded by assessments on the major financial institutions
- Other provisions to promote the safety and soundness of financial institutions, including regulation of the market for credit-default swaps, expanded authority of the Fed to supervise risk management of financial firms, specific rules such as requiring mortgage lenders to hold a percentage of loans they issue, and limits on the ability of banks to trade risky assets (the Volcker Rule)

The details of Dodd–Frank and its pros and cons are beyond the scope of this book, but financial reform is an important part of the story. Blinder (2013) provides a detailed account of the road to Dodd–Frank. Will Dodd–Frank work? Only time will tell.

Ben Bernanke succeeded Alan Greenspan as Fed Chair in 2006 and served until 2014. He is a strong advocate for discretionary monetary policy and has written a very good (and short) book (2013) that is recommended reading for you, as well as a long memoir (2015) of his time as Fed chairman. Bernanke is a prominent scholar of the Great Depression, and his research showed that the depleted condition of the financial system as events unfolded was an important determinant of the severity of the depression. Recall that he blamed the Fed for making huge mistakes in the early 1930s, and he vowed that it will not happen again. He acknowledges that he and his Fed colleagues did not understand the extent to which the financial system was vulnerable to a drop in housing prices. One reason is that the stock market bubble and crash of 2001 did not lead to a huge disaster. His books describe the extraordinary steps taken by the Fed to be the lender of last resort to the financial system that he (and many others) believes saved the financial system from complete collapse.

Bernanke is a strong critic of monetary policy rules in general and the Taylor rule in particular. First of all, he believes a policy rule is not to be followed slavishly but rather is a guide to making policy. As for the specific Taylor rule, Bernanke argued that the rule should include a forecast of inflation, not the rate of inflation from the previous time period. Monetary policy operates with a lag, so setting policy should be forward looking. His paper on the subject (2010) showed that if the Fed's forecast of the inflation rate is used instead of the past rate of inflation, the actual federal funds rate and the rate under the Bernanke version of the Taylor rule would be closer together. For example, the actual federal funds rate during 2003 was 1 percent, the Taylor rule rate was 3 to 3.5 percent, and the Bernanke version was about 2 percent. At the beginning of 2006, the actual rate was 5.25 percent, the Bernanke version was about 4.9 percent, and the Taylor rule was 5.25 percent. By the way, both the Taylor and Bernanke rules yield a federal funds rate of just above zero as of 2009, about equal to the actual rate.

Bernanke writes (2013, pp. 52–54) about the causes of the housing price bubble. He agrees that one purpose of setting a low federal funds rate early in the 2000s was to stimulate the demand for housing and thus strengthen the economy. But he doubts that the federal funds rate played an important role in the housing price bubble. First, he notes that housing price bubbles occurred in other countries, such as the United Kingdom, that had tighter monetary policies. He contends that the surge in housing prices was much larger than could be explained by the reduction in interest rates, and foreign investors flooded the United States with capital because they were looking for safe investments in the wake of the Asian financial crisis. Lastly, he cites Robert Shiller to the effect that the housing price bubble began in the late 1990s, well before the cut in the federal funds rate. His views are backed up by highly technical research conducted by Fed researchers. Another Fed official who absolves the Fed's interest rate policy. I am waiting for a Fed official to take the opposite view. It may be a long wait.

As for macroeconomic theories, Bernanke is a new Keynesian. This is basic Keynes supplemented by expectations of inflation, possible shocks to the supply side, and formal models that explain why wages and prices are not very flexible in the short run. His explicit statement (2015, pp. 29–30) is:

> Over time, I have become convinced that New Keynesian ideas, leavened with insights from other schools of thought, including elements of the New Classical approach, provide the best framework for practical policymaking.

He also acknowledges Shiller's analysis of asset price bubbles as social contagions that can be born out of a reasonably stable economy. As a researcher, he did not find the work of Minsky compelling. Early in his career (1983, p. 259), he cited Minsky and Kindleberger as they argued that the financial system is inherently unstable, "but in doing so have had to depart from the assumption of rational economic behavior." He went on to say (1983, p. 259):

> I do not deny the importance of irrationality in economic life; however, it seems that the best research strategy is to push the rationality postulate as far as it will go.

Bernanke was strongly influenced by Friedman and Schwartz (1963) and their seminal work on the monetary history of the United States, which showed that the collapse of the money supply was an important cause of the Great Depression. But was there more? This statement from his memoir is a hint about the research agenda he has pursued ever since:

> Freidman and Schwartz's perspective was eye-opening, but I wondered whether the collapse of the money supply and the ensuing deflation, as severe as it was, could by itself explain the depth and length of the Depression.

He took up the challenge he had made of himself, and argued (1983) persuasively that the failure of 9,700 banks during 1931–1932 disrupted the financial system and made it extremely difficult to obtain credit. It is not just a decline in the supply of money but also the condition of the financial system that matters. So he states (2015, pp. 35–36):

> My reading and research impressed on me some enduring lessons of the Depression for central bankers and other policymakers. First, in periods of recession, deflation, or both, monetary policy should be forcefully deployed to restore full employment and normal levels of inflation. Second, policymakers must act decisively to preserve financial stability and normal flows of credit.

This is a pretty good summary of the approach to monetary policy that he followed as Fed chairman. Not only did he lead the Fed in reducing the federal funds rate a figure close to zero, but he also engineered the Fed purchase of trillions of dollars of longer-term securities from a variety of financial institutions and convinced the Fed to adopt an inflation target of 2 percent per year. The inflation target is designed to signal to the private economy how the Fed will act in the future. Both deflation and a high rate of inflation will be prevented.

Bernanke thinks that discretionary monetary policy should be conducted to the best of the Fed's ability, and he argued repeatedly that fiscal policy should have provided more stimulus after 2009. The Fed could not do the entire job alone. He called U.S. fiscal policy (2015, p. 568) "a headwind during most of the recovery." For example, referring to the federal budget deal of 2013:

> The nonpartisan Congressional Budget Office would later estimate that fiscal measures in 2013 would lop off 1.5 percentage points off economic growth in 2013 – growth that we could ill afford to lose.

Janet Yellen succeeded Bernanke as Chair of the Federal Reserve in 2014. She studied with leading Keynesian James Tobin at Yale (and is a PhD 1971 classmate of mine). She is a Keynesian who has made important theoretical contributions along "new" Keynesian lines. Those models are intended to explain, among other things, why wages are not very flexible over a short-to-medium time period and therefore why discretionary fiscal policy and monetary policy are needed. She has a long history of service at the Fed that includes President of the San Francisco Fed and Vice Chair of the Federal Reserve System. In her service as Chair, she has grappled with the issue of when to start raising the federal funds rate. When is the economy strong enough that it can get off the rock-bottom interest rate regime? Under her leadership, the Fed ended its policy of quantitative easing – the policy of purchasing a variety of financial assets. The next step would be to bring the federal funds rate up to a "normal" level as the economy returns (one hopes) to full employment and satisfactory growth with low inflation.

The Fed adopted an explicit goal for inflation of 2 percent in 2012, and Chairwoman Yellen repeatedly had restated this goal. Recall that 2 percent inflation is the rate that is consistent with the Taylor rule if GDP is at its goal and the federal funds rate is 4 percent (2 percent after inflation). The Fed believes that this inflation goal is consistent with a stable and growing economy. The idea is to avoid volatile inflationary expectations that occurred in the past and led to economic instability.

Chairwoman Yellen outlined her views in a detailed paper (2015) delivered to an audience at the University of Massachusetts. Her conclusions are as follows:

> following the dual mandate established by Congress, the Federal Reserve is committed to the achievement of maximum employment and price stability. To this end, we have maintained a highly accommodative monetary policy since the financial crisis; that policy has fostered a marked improvement in labor market conditions and helped check undesirable deflationary pressures. However, we have not yet fully attained our objectives under the dual mandate: Some slack remains in labor markets, and the effects of this slack and the influence of lower energy prices and past dollar appreciation have been significant factors keeping inflation below our goal. But I expect that inflation will return to 2 percent over the next few years as the temporary factors that are currently weighing on inflation wane, provided that economic growth continues to be strong enough to complete the return to maximum employment and long-inflation expectations remain well anchored. Most Federal Open Market Committee participants, including myself, currently anticipate that achieving these conditions will likely entail an initial increase in the federal funds rate later this year (i.e., 2015), followed by a gradual pace of tightening thereafter. But if the economy surprises us, our judgments about appropriate monetary policy will change.

In other words, my job is to conduct discretionary monetary policy in pursuit of the dual mandate. I will not state a monetary policy rule, other than to move the federal funds rate up as the rate of inflation begins to approach 2 percent. Yellen does not state that the federal funds rate will be 4 percent (i.e., the Taylor rule rate at 2 percent inflation and target GDP). She is a New Keynesian who sees an economy that is no longer in a Keynesian (depression) situation under her watch. Her job is to conduct monetary policy cautiously while paying close attention to data. Indeed, the speech was given shortly after the Fed decided not to raise the federal funds rate in September 2015. She was replaced after one term as chair of the Fed in 2018 by Jerome Powell, who was appointed by President Donald Trump.

Haruhiko Kuroda is another prominent central banker. He was appointed Governor of the Bank of Japan by Prime Minister Abe in 2013 and continues in that role. He fully supported the Prime Minister's program of stimulative monetary policy, fiscal policy, and economic growth strategies. Upon his appointment, he stated that there was plenty of room for the Bank of Japan to purchase assets well beyond the traditional menu of government bonds, including corporate bonds and stocks. Mr. Kuroda favors an "all hands on deck" policy of monetary and fiscal policy – very Keynesian. As you know, the Fed in the United States had been following a policy of quantitative easing well before Mr. Kuroda took over at the Bank of Japan.

A couple of very good forecasters

We have done a short survey of some policy makers who have put themselves on record. Now we turn to an even shorter survey of PhD professional economic forecasters who make their living by producing accurate, or at least convincing, forecasts. These two guys have been at it for a long time, so that tells you something. Do bad forecasters last in the business? No comment, other than to point out that weather forecasters seem to hang around.

Our first example is Mark Zandi, who is chief economist for Moody's Economy. com. He is a frequent guest on television shows and was an economic advisor to John McCain's presidential campaign in 2008. One wonders what sort of advice he gave to the Republican candidate. He earned his PhD in economics at the University of Pennsylvania, where he studied under Nobel laureate macro economist Lawrence Klein. Zandi has written a good book on the crisis titled *Financial Shock* (2009) that I have used in class in the past. This book is now dated, but it gives a good blow-by-blow description of the lead-up to 2008 and early postcrisis events. The book also indicates where he worships in the macroeconomic theory pantheon (i.e., the temple of all of the gods).

Zandi made a strong statement (2009, p. 254):

> The most fundamental lesson of the Great Depression for today's crisis is that government must be extraordinarily aggressive. In normal times, government must be strong but little seen; in times of crisis, it must be overwhelming and everywhere. Policymakers working fast and taking big steps will make mistakes, even mistakes that can make matters worse. But with consumers, businesses, bankers, and investors panicked and pulling back, only government has the resources and the will to fill the resulting void.

He argues that the Fed must shore up the financial system – buy Treasury securities of all kinds, find a way to buy municipal bonds (now prohibited), lend cheap money to non-banks, and guarantee losses. Except for buying municipal bonds, the Fed actually did all of these and more. On the fiscal policy side, he was clear as well (2009, p. 256):

> The $800 billion stimulus that began working its way into the economy in Spring 2009 might also not provide the economic pop needed. Although it's big, it's not enough. The money will be spread out over more than two years, and the economy's problems have only gotten worse since its passage.

He also argued for aggressive steps to stop the housing foreclosures that included loan modifications.

These statements put him squarely in the discretionary macroeconomic policy camp when it comes to dealing with a crisis, which is identified with Keynesianism.

He does not discuss monetary policy rules, but it is clear that he thinks rules do not apply in a crisis. Indeed, he is not afraid that mistakes will be made.

Zandi weighed in on the economic impact of the stimulus package of 2009 in a study coauthored with Alan Blinder, Princeton University professor of economics and former Fed board member. They used Zandi's New Keynesian-style model (described later) to estimate the impact of the stimulus on unemployment and found that the unemployment rate would have been 1.7 percent greater without the stimulus. This estimate is very close to the 1.8 percent figure issued in early 2009 by Christina Romer, chair of the President's Council of Economic Advisors. The problem with the Romer study was that it claimed that the unemployment rate would not go above 8 percent. Unemployment was already at 7.8 percent in January 2009, but Romer and her staff did not know it. This misstep by the President's economists was widely criticized and was used as evidence that the stimulus package failed. The actual unemployment rate reached 10 percent, but without the stimulus it would have been almost 12 percent, according to the Blinder–Zandi study. These matters, including the political fallout, are discussed by Blinder (2013, pp. 230–234).

Zandi, as chief economist for the economic research firm Moody's Analytics, is in charge of Moody's large-scale macroeconomic model of the U.S. economy. Zandi and Hoyt (2015) provide a detailed description of that model, which consists of more than 1,800 equations. The model is designed to produce cyclical short-term forecasts, long-term forecasts for up to 30 years, and construction of alternative scenarios. Zandi and Hoyt (2015, p. 1) describe the underlying theory behind the model as follows.

> The macroeconomics profession continues to enjoy spirited methodological debates, but over the last few decades, heated arguments over the most appropriate way to model the economy have evolved towards a consensus view best described as "Keynesian in the short run, and classical in the long run."

I hope that you have been enjoying the spirited debate too. Aggregate economic activity in the model depends upon the interaction between aggregate demand and aggregate supply. In the short run, fluctuations in aggregate demand determine real GDP. Prices and wages adjust slowly (as described in Chapter 3). In the long run, changes in aggregate supply determine the potential GDP of the economy, which depends upon growth in labor, capital, and changes in technology (as discussed in Chapter 6).

The model consists of equations for these variables:

- Consumption in real terms, broken down into several categories
- Gross private domestic investment in real terms, broken down into several categories
- International trade in real terms, broken down into several categories for exports and imports
- Government spending in nominal terms, broken down into categories for both federal and state and local spending, with federal spending exogenous (except for transfer payments)

- Government receipts in nominal terms (i.e., tax payments) for federal and state and local governments
- Aggregate supply (potential GDP) based on growth of inputs, productivity improvements, and the full employment level for labor, where full employment is the non-accelerating inflation rate of unemployment (NAIRU) based on the Phillips Curve supplemented by expectations of inflation
- Inflation as a function of the gap between aggregate demand and potential GDP and input prices, including wages and energy costs, broken down into 60 components for producer prices
- Interest rates, including the federal funds rate (based on an equation similar to the Taylor rule from Chapter 4 – but with more variables – that describes Fed policy), the ten-year Treasury bond rate, corporate bond rate, municipal bond rate, and others
- Demands for financial assets, including different measures of money and various measures of reserves held by the banking system
- Personal income broken down by industry and type of income (wages, interest, and so on)
- Corporate profits, and the S&P 500 stock market index
- Labor market; employment broken down by industry, and the labor force
- Housing, including equations for housing permits, starts, existing home sales, house prices, mortgage lending, and mortgage delinquency and foreclosure rates

This tedious recitation of the components of the model have been included to illustrate the basic Keynesian structure of the model, supplemented by several features supplied by critics of the original Keynesian model. Monetary policy is determined inside the model according to a version of the Taylor rule for the federal funds rate, and the Phillips Curve is supplemented by expectations of inflation (as discussed in Chapter 4). Indeed, potential GDP is estimated as a function of supply factors. The recitation of the model also indicates how Moody's Analytics as a successful business has a product that can be marketed to many users in government and private industry.

Our next example is Maury Harris, a very experienced forecaster who has just published an excellent book (2015) on how to make and use forecasts. He earned his PhD in economics from Columbia University, and was an economist at the New York Fed, forecaster at the Bank of International Settlements, chief economist at PaineWebber, and chief economist at UBS investment bank. His undergraduate degree is from the University of Texas at Austin, where I was his first economics instructor. He has been in the business of economic forecasting for 40 years. In his view, successful forecasting combines science and art (i.e., some intuitive judgment). Our purpose here is not to train you to be a forecaster, although you may now be motivated to learn more about economic forecasting. Rather, our inquiry is to find out what Harris thinks about the different macroeconomic theories. He is well aware of these theories and uses an eclectic approach rather than a large-scale model.

Harris discusses four "gurus" of economics (2015, Chapter 4) who are, in order: Hyman Minsky, supply-siders, Monetarists, and Keynesians. Yes, he discusses

Minsky first, maybe because Minsky made a favorable comment on a paper Harris presented one time. Harris does recognize that Minsky was a Keynesian but chooses to discuss him separately. You already know Minsky's hypothesis, so what does Harris think about it? Harris advises that the successful forecaster must be paying attention to possible financial instability by watching for increases in financial leverage, institutional changes in the financial system, and changes in investor (i.e., lender) psychology. For example, a survey is conducted by the Fed of senior loan officers regarding lending standards. Harris's use of this survey was commended by Minsky as a good method to detect a credit crunch. Harris recognizes that stability does not always lead to instability. Just sometimes. The trick, of course, is to know when.

Harris reviews the evidence regarding the supply-side argument that tax cuts and reductions in business regulations stimulate the economy. So far, the evidence does not support the supply-siders, but probably more research is needed. In the meantime, supply-side arguments have political force. That influence affects government policy, so the smart forecaster will keep an eye on whether the supply-siders will succeed in winning adoption of another part of their agenda. Harris does not discuss the real business cycle theory, just the supply-siders. Also, he does not mention the Austrians. Evidently, he does not find compelling the idea of rapid market adjustments to changes in supply and demand that bring the economy to full employment.

Harris includes a detailed discussion of Monetarism and concludes that one should not dismiss Monetarist arguments regarding the impact of the money supply on the economy. He notes the huge increase in the Fed's balance sheet and the accompanying huge increase in excess bank reserves. He is well aware of the large drop in the velocity of money after 2008. The potential for a further large increase in the money supply is there, so bank lending standards bear watching.

Harris buys into a lot of Keynes (in addition to Minsky). The Keynesian framework is used to assemble a forecast of GDP, and accurate estimates of the Keynesian multiplier are useful to forecasters. Investment depends upon Keynesian "animal spirits." But Harris warns that Keynesian forecasting models have limitations. (See the comments by Alan Greenspan noted earlier.)

How does all of this play out for Harris in the practice of forecasting? We will consider a couple of examples. Business investment is an important variable to forecast (very Keynesian). Harris has found that gauges of business confidence, while they can be politically biased, are leading indicators of business spending on capital goods and inventories. Surveys regarding expected sales and adequacy of current inventories do anticipate spending on inventories. Capital spending responds to capacity utilization measures but is not very sensitive to interest rates. In short, animal spirits can be quantified to a meaningful extent, perhaps as Greenspan and King hope.

Inflation is another important variable to forecast. Are accurate forecasts based on the money supply, the Phillips Curve, both, or neither? First of all, energy and food prices can vary substantially in the short run because of supply factors. The forecaster must pay attention to such things. Harris recognizes the potential importance of the money supply and that its impact on prices depends upon whether the economy is at full employment. He warned again of the large amount of excess bank reserves as of 2014. (Go back to the earlier discussion of Minsky.) But then he finds that most economic forecasters now use the Phillips Curve with an adjustment for expected inflation. In other words, inflation for the next time period depends upon the rate of unemployment and the expected rate of inflation. In particular, inflation can be sensitive to changes in unemployment when the economy is at or near the non-accelerating inflation rate of unemployment (NAIRU). What is the NAIRU? The United States got to 3.5 percent unemployment in February 2020 with low inflation. When is inflation about to break out? There are no signs of it yet. So inflation forecasting makes use of supply-side information, money supply data, inflation expectations surveys, and the Phillips Curve concept. In short, Harris finds that there is value to be found for forecasters in all four of his gurus of economics.

Conclusion

This is the end of the book. We have been through a lot together, from working our way through the different macroeconomic theories to attempting to sort out what happened during macroeconomic episodes from the Great Depression to the pandemic of 2020. What have we learned? What will you remember years from now?

Start with what you will remember. I hope that you will remember that you had to look at data, tried to concoct a narrative of what was happening, and then were asked to consider how well alternative theories comport with that narrative. You were confronting theories with data (or the other way around), trying to make sense of things and not just compiling facts. That is what economics is about, and it is messy. And maybe you will remember the tentative conclusions that you reached. But mostly I hope you will remember the method to this madness. The method applies to many things, of course. People in the business world are doing this sort of thing all of the time.

As for more specific findings, I think we have learned that we cannot do without both the Keynesian and Monetarist theories as amended by experience, including the shocks on the supply side in the 1970s. Investment spending is volatile, but that was known before Keynes wrote. Keynesian theory puts volatile investment into a theory to explain recessions and depressions. It did turn out that, contrary to Milton Friedman's assertion, the propensity to consume is more stable (but more complex than Keynes assumed) than the demand for money, however measured. The Monetarist critique that Keynesian models had not built in expectations was correct. The notion of animal spirits was correct, but Keynes did not provide a way to incorporate it into a theory. Hyman Minsky looks like a prophet now, but not every period of stability leads to instability. The trick is to figure out when it does and why, and then to fix the architecture that aids and abets the tendency to instability. There were red flags all over the place in the first half of the 2000s, but the people who could do something about it failed. Dodd–Frank in the United States and the changes in the U.K. financial system address this problem, but we do not yet know whether the fix is on target. That time, the U.S. Fed pulled out all of the stops to prevent complete financial collapse and to support the economy in its recovery – but the fiscal stimulus provided by the federal government was more timid than the Keynesians wanted.

As a point of personal privilege, let me refer back to a quote from James Tobin in Chapter 3. It is well to remember that Keynes developed his theory in response to the Great Depression. Does it apply all of the time? Leading Keynesian Tobin, as quoted by Snowdon and Vane (2005, pp. 150–151), stated:

> Sometimes the economy is in the classical situation where markets are clearing (demand equals supply) and the economy's ability to produce output is supply-constrained. . . . At other times the economy is in a Keynesian situation in which the constraint on actual output is *demand* – aggregate spending.
>
> (emphasis in original)

The Keynesian situation calls for aggressive efforts by the national government to increase aggregate demand. How did Tobin's view stack up against the evidence? Pretty well, as we have seen. How does an economy get itself into trouble – into the Keynesian situation? Two have taken place already in your lifetime. Why does investment spending tank? This is a critical question. The five schools of thought provided answers. Monetarists said a big decline in the money supply is the main cause of a crash, and also warned against big increases in the money supply creating inflation that also creates crises. Austrians (sort of) agreed by arguing that pushing interest rates "too low" brought on crises. Minsky built on the Keynesian idea of animal spirits and explained how a stable economy can lead to increasing financial leverage, asset bubbles, and instability. Kindleberger backed up the idea with a trip through the history of financial panics, and Shiller used Alan Greenspan's term "irrational exuberance." Modern Monetary Theory adherents agree with Minsky. The real business cycle people worked out the implications of shocks on the supply side of the economy. The savvy forecaster Maury Harris takes note of all of these points and incorporates them into a framework that includes Keynes/Minsky and Monetarism, while watching for negative supply factors. He discounts the Austrians and the real business cycle theories by not mentioning them, most likely because (as many have pointed out) both theories rely on the assumption of rapid market clearing.

The other critical question is, "How do we recover from a big downturn?" The pandemic year presented a big problem after the economic activity dropped suddenly. The nations examined – the United States, the United Kingdom, Japan, and Germany – all used discretionary fiscal policy and monetary policy. Governments do not rely only on market forces to right the ship.

But what I say is in print, not carved in stone. And even something carved in stone is not forever. The name of the university at which I taught for 38 years was changed from the University of Illinois at Chicago Circle (UICC) to the University of Illinois at Chicago (UIC). Several displays that were carved in stone had to be covered over.

References

Anderson, Leonall, and Carlson, Keith, 1970, A Monetarist model for economic stabilization, *Federal Reserve Bank of St. Louis Review*, Vol. 52, pp. 7–25.

Atack, Jeremy, and Passell, Peter, 1994, *A New Economic View of American History*, 2nd ed., New York: Norton.

Barth, J., 2009, *The Rise and Fall of the U.S. Mortgage and Credit Markets*, Hoboken, NJ: Wiley.

Baum, L. F., 1900, *The Wonderful World of Oz*, Chicago: George M. Hill Co.

Baumol, William, 1999, Say's Law, *Journal of Economic Perspectives*, Vol. 13, pp. 195–204.

Bernanke, Ben, 1983, Non-monetary effects of the financial crisis in the propagation of the Great Depression, *American Economic Review*, Vol. 73, pp. 257–276.

Bernanke, Ben, 2000, *Essays on the Great Depression*, Princeton, NJ: Princeton University Press.

Bernanke, Ben, 2002, *On Milton Friedman's Ninetieth Birthday*, Washington, DC: Federal Reserve Board.

Bernanke, Ben, 2010, Monetary policy and the housing bubble, *paper presented at the annual meeting of the American Economic Association, Atlanta, GA*, January 3.

Bernanke, Ben, 2013, *The Federal Reserve and the Financial Crisis*, Princeton, NJ: Princeton University Press.

Bernanke, Ben, 2015, *The Courage to Act: A Memoir of a Crisis and its Aftermath*, New York: Norton.

Blinder, Alan, 2013, *After the Music Stopped: The Financial Crisis, the Response, and the Work Ahead*, New York: Penguin Press.

Caldwell, B., 1995, *Contra Keynes and Cambridge*, Indianapolis: Liberty Fund.

Christ, Carl, 1966, *Econometric Models and Methods*, New York: Wiley (for the Cowles Foundation for Research in Economics at Yale University).

Cochrane, John, 2009, How did Paul Krugman get it so wrong? *University of Chicago, Booth School of Business*, http://faculty.chicagobooth.edu/john.cochrane/research/papers/#news.

Darby, Michael, 1976, Three-and-a-half million U.S. employees have been mislaid: Or, an explanation of unemployment, 1934–1941, *Journal of Political Economy*, Vol. 84, pp. 1–16.

Davies, R., Richardson, P., Katinaite, V., and Manning, M., 2010, Evolution of the UK banking system, *Bank of England, Quarterly Bulletin*, 4th Quarter, pp. 321–330.

Denison, E., 1985, *Trends in American Economic Growth*, Washington, DC: The Brookings Institution.

Eichengreen, Barry, 1992, *Gold Fetters: The Gold Standard and the Great Depression, 1919–1939*, New York: Oxford University Press.

Fellner, William, 1948, Employment theory and business cycles, in H. Ellis, ed., *A Survey of Contemporary Economics*, Vol. 1, Homewood, IL: Richard D. Irwin, Inc., pp. 49–98.

Financial Crisis Inquiry Commission, 2011, *The Financial Crisis Inquiry Report*, New York: Public Affairs (Perseus Books).

Fleming, J. M., 1962, Domestic financial policies under fixed and floating exchange rates, *IMF Staff Papers*, November.

Friedman, Milton, 1948, A monetary and fiscal framework for economic stability, *American Economic Review*, Vol. 38, pp. 245–264.

Friedman, Milton, 1953, The case for flexible exchange rates, in M. Friedman, ed., *Essays in Positive Economics*, Chicago: University of Chicago Press, pp. 157–203.

Friedman, Milton, 1956, The quantity theory of money: A restatement, in M. Friedman, ed., *Studies in the Quantity Theory of Money*, Chicago: University of Chicago Press, pp. 3–21.

Friedman, Milton, 1959, The demand for money: Some theoretical and empirical results, *Journal of Political Economy*, Vol. 67, pp. 327–352.

Friedman, Milton, 1962, *Capitalism and Freedom*, Chicago: University of Chicago Press.

Friedman, Milton, 1968, The role of monetary policy, *American Economic Review*, Vol. 58, pp. 1–17.

Friedman, Milton, 1974, Schools at Chicago, *Archives of the Communication Department of the University of Chicago*.

Friedman, Milton, 1993, The 'plucking model' of business fluctuations revisited, *Economic Inquiry*, Vol. 31, pp. 171–177.

Friedman, Milton, and Schwartz, Anna, 1963, *A Monetary History of the United States, 1867–1960*, Princeton, NJ: Princeton University Press for the National Bureau of Economic Research.

Galbraith, J., 1954, *The Great Crash*, Boston: Houghton, Mifflin Co.

Garrison, Roger, 2005, The Austrian school, in B. Snowden and H. Vane, eds., *Modern Macroeconomics*, Cheltenhem, UK: Edward Elgar, pp. 474–516.

Geithner, Timothy, 2014, *Stress Test*, New York: Broadway Books.

Giordano, C., Piga, G., and Trovato, G., 2013, Italy's industrial great depression: Fascist price and wage policies, *Macroeconomic Dynamics*, pp. 1–32.

Gorton, Gary, 2010, *Slapped by the Invisible Hand*, New York: Oxford University Press.

Greenspan, Alan, 2007, *The Age of Turbulence*, New York: Penguin Press.

Greenspan, Alan, 2010, The crisis, *Brookings Papers on Economic Activity*, pp. 201–262.

Greenspan, Alan, 2014, *The Map and the Territory*, 2nd ed., New York: Penguin.

Hansen, Alvin, 1953, *A Guide to Keynes*, New York: McGraw Hill.

Harris, Maury, 2015, *Inside the Crystal Ball*, Hoboken, NJ: Wiley.

Hautcoeur, P., 1997, The Great Depression in France (1929–1938), in D. Glasner, ed., *Business Cycles and Great Depression: An Encyclopedia*, New York: Garland, pp. 39–42.

Hayashi, F., and Prescott, E., 2002, The 1990s in Japan: A lost decade, *Review of Economic Dynamics*, Vol. 5, pp. 206–235.

Hayek, Friedrich, 1931, *Prices and Production*, London: Routledge & Sons.

Hayek, Friedrich, 1944, *The Road to Serfdom*, Chicago: University of Chicago Press.

Hayek, Friedrich, 1984, The fate of the gold standard, in Roy McCloughry, ed., *Money, Capital and Fluctuations, Early Essays of Friedrich A. von Hayek*, London: Routledge, pp. 118–135.

Hicks, J. R., 1937, Mr. Keynes and the classics: A suggested interpretation, *Econometrica*, Vol. 5, pp. 147–159.

Hoover, Herbert, 1932, *Address at Madison Square Garden in New York City in October 1932*.

Keynes, J. M., 1919, *The Economic Consequences of Peace*, London: Macmillan.

Keynes, J. M., 1924, *A Tract on Monetary Reform*, London: Macmillan.

Keynes, J. M., 1936, *The General Theory of Employment, Interest, and Money*, London: Macmillan.

Keynes, J. M., 1937, The general theory of employment, *Quarterly Journal of Economics*, Vol. 51, pp. 209–233.

Keynes, J. M., 1940, *How to Pay for the War*, London: Macmillan.

Kindleberger, Charles, 1989, *Manias, Panics, and Crashes: A History of Financial Crises*, 2nd ed., London: Macmillan.

King, M., *The End of Alchemy*, 2016, New York: W. W. Norton & Co.

Klamer, A., 1983, *Conversations with Economists*, Totowa, NJ: Rowman & Allenheld.

Knight, Frank, 1937, Unemployment and Mr. Keynes's revolution in economic theory, *Canadian Journal of Economic and Political Science*, Vol. 3, pp. 100–123, February.

Krugman, Paul, 1990, *The Age of Diminished Expectations*, Cambridge, MA: MIT Press.

Krugman, Paul, 2009a, *The Return of Depression Economics and the Crisis of 2008*, New York: Norton.

Krugman, Paul, 2009b, How did economists get it so wrong? *New York Times Magazine*, September 2, 2009, MM36.

Krugman, Paul, 2020a, *Arguing with Zombies*, New York: W.W. Norton.

Krugman, Paul, 2020b, What's wrong with functional finance? in P. Krugman, ed., *Arguing with Zombies*, New York: W.W. Norton, pp. 152–154.

Kydland, Finn, and Prescott, Edward, 1977, Rules rather than discretion: The inconsistency of optimal plans, *Journal of Political Economy*, Vol. 88, pp. 473–491.

Lerner, A., 1947, Money as a creature of the state, *American Economic Review*, Vol. 37, No. 2, pp. 312–317.

Llewellyn, J., and Thompson, S., 2019, The Great Depression in Germany, *Alpha History*, https://alphahistory.com/weimarrepublic/great-depression.

Lucas, Robert, 2008, Ben Bernanke is the best stimulus right now, *Wall Street Journal*, December 23.

Lucas, Robert, and Rapping, Leonard, 1969, Real wages, employment, and inflation, *Journal of Political Economy*, Vol. 77, pp. 721–754.

Mankiw, Gregory, and Romer, David, eds., 1991, *New Keynesian Economics*, Cambridge, MA: MIT Press.

Markowitz, H., 1952, Portfolio selection, *Journal of Finance*, Vol. VII, No. 1, pp. 77–91.

McDonald, John, 2015, *Postwar Urban America*, New York: Routledge.

McDonald, John, and Stokes, Houston, 2013, Monetary policy and the housing bubble, *Journal of Real Estate Finance and Economics*, Vol. 26, pp. 437–451.

McDonald, John, and Stokes, Houston, 2015, Monetary policy, fiscal policy, and the housing bubble, *Modern Economy*, Vol. 6, pp. 165–178, published online.

Meade, J. E., 1952, *The Balance of Payments*, London: Oxford University Press.

Minsky, Hyman, 1975, *John Maynard Keynes*, New York: Columbia University Press.

Mitchell, Wesley Clair, 1941, *Business Cycles and Their Causes*, London: Cambridge University Press.

Mundell, Robert, 1961, A theory of optimum currency areas, *American Economic Review*, Vol. 51, pp. 657–665.

Mundell, Robert, 1963, Capital mobility and stabilization policy under fixed and flexible exchange rates, *Canadian Journal of Economics and Political Science*, Vol. 29, No. 4, pp. 475–485.

Murphy, Robert, 2019, The upside-down world of MMT, *Mises Daily Articles, Mises Institute*, January 23.

Myrdal, Gunnar, 1944, *An American Dilemma: The Negro Problem and Modern Democracy*, New York: Harper and Row, 1944 (original edition), Brunswick, NJ: Transaction Publishers, 1966.

Paul, Rand, and Spitznagel, Mark, 2015, If only the Fed would get out of the way, *Wall Street Journal*, Vol. CCLXVI, No. 65, Sept. 10, 2015, p. A15.

Paul, Ron, 2009, *End the Fed*, New York: Grand Central Publishing.

Phillips, A. W., 1958, The relation between unemployment and the rate of change of money wages in the United Kingdom, 1861–1957, *Economica*, Vol. 25, pp. 283–299.

Pigou, A. C., 1927, *Industrial Fluctuations*, London: Macmillan.

Pigou, A.C., 1936, Mr. J. M. Keynes' general theory of employment, interest and money, *Economica*, New Series, Vol. 3, pp. 115–132.

Quiggin, John, 2010, *Zombie Economics: How Dead Ideas Still Walk Among Us*, Princeton, NJ: Princeton University Press.

Rauchway, Eric, 2015, *The Money Makers: How Roosevelt and Keynes Ended the Depression, Defeated Fascism, and Secured a Prosperous Peace*, New York: Basic Books.

Reinhart, Carmen, and Rogoff, Kenneth, 2009, *This Time Is Different*, Princeton, NJ: Princeton University Press.

Ricardo, D. 1821. *The Principles of Political Economy and Taxation*, 3rd ed., London: J.W. Dent (Everyman Library), 1962 reprint.

Rich, B, and Janos, L. 1994, *Skunk Works*, New York: Little, Brown & Co.

Rockoff, H., 1990, The 'Wizard of Oz' as a monetary allegory, *Journal of Political Economy*, Vol. 98, No. 4, pp. 739–769.

Rodrik, Dani, 2015, *Economics Rules*, New York: Norton.

Romer, Paul, 1990, Endogenous technological change, *Journal of Political Economy*, Vol. 98, pp. S72–102.

Samuelson, Paul, 1939, Interactions between the multiplier analysis and the principle of acceleration, *Review of Economics and Statistics*, Vol. 21, pp. 75–78.

Samuelson, Paul, 1940, The theory of pump priming reexamined, *American Economic Review*, Vol. 30, pp. 492–506.

Samuelson, Paul, and Solow, Robert, 1960, Analytical aspects of anti-inflation policy, *American Economic Review*, Vol. 50, pp. 177–194, May.

Schumpeter, Joseph, 1942, *Capitalism, Socialism, and Democracy*, New York: Harper & Row.

Schwartz, Anna, 2009, Origins of the financial crisis, *Cato Journal*, Vol. 29, pp. 19–23.

Service, Robert, *The End of the Cold War*, New York: Public Affairs, 2015

Shiller, Robert, 2009, *The Subprime Solution*, Princeton, NJ: Princeton University Press.

Simons, Henry, 1936, Rules versus authorities in monetary policy, *Journal of Political Economy*, Vol. 44, pp. 1–30.

Skidelsky, R., 1983, 1992, 2000, *John Maynard Keynes*, Vols. 1, 2, and 3, London: Macmillan.

Skidelsky, R., 2009, *Keynes: The Return of the Master*, New York: Public Affairs.

Skousen, M., 2005, *Vienna & Chicago: Friends or Foes?* Washington, DC: Capital Press.

Smith, Adam, 1776, *An Inquiry into the Nature and Causes of the Wealth of Nations*, New York: The Modern Library edition of 1937.

Snowdon, Brian, and Vane, Howard, 2005, *Modern Macroeconomics*, Cheltenham, UK: Edward Elgar.

Solow, Robert, 1957, Technical change and the aggregate production function, *Review of Economics and Statistics*, Vol. 39, pp. 312–320.

Stiglitz, Joseph, 2016, *The Euro: How a Common Currency Threatens the Future of Europe*, New York: Norton.

Stiglitz, Joseph, 2020, *Rewriting the Rules for the European Economy*, New York: Norton.

Stockman, David, 1986, *The Triumph of Politics: Why the Reagan Revolution Failed*, New York: Harper & Row.

Suits, Daniel, 1962, Forecasting and analysis with an econometric model, *American Economic Review*, Vol. 52, pp. 104–132.

Sundstrom, William, 1992, Last hired, first fired? Unemployment and urban black workers during the Great Depression, *The Journal of Economic History*, Vol. 52, pp. 415–429.

Taylor, John, 1993, Discretion versus policy rules in practice, *Carnegie-Rochester Conference Series on Public Policy*, Vol. 39, pp. 195–214.

Taylor, John, 2009, *Getting off Track*, Stanford, CA: Hoover Institution Press.

Temin, Peter, and Vines, David, 2014, *Keynes: Useful Economics for the World Economy*, Cambridge, Mass.: MIT Press.

Thornton, M., 2009, The economics of housing bubbles, in R. Holcombe and B. Powell, eds., *Housing America: Building Out of a Crisis*, New Brunswick, NJ: Transactions, pp. 237–262.

Tobin, James, 1958, Liquidity preference as behavior towards risk, *Review of Economic Studies*, Vol. 25, pp. 65–86.

Tobin, James, 1965, The monetary interpretation of history, *American Economic Review*, Vol. 55, pp. 464–485.

Tobin, James, 1969, A general equilibrium approach to monetary theory, *Journal of Money, Credit, and Banking*, Vol. 1, No. 1, pp. 15–29.

Tobin, James, 1970, Money and income: Post hoc ergo propter hoc, *Quarterly Journal of Economics*, Vol. 84, pp. 301–317.

Van Overtveldt, Johan, 2007, *The Chicago School*, Chicago: Agate.

Wallison, Peter, 2015, *Hidden in Plain Sight*, New York: Encounter Books.

Wicksell, Knut, 1906, *Lectures on Political Economy*, Vol. 2, Translated by E. Classen, London: Routledge and Kegan Paul, 1935.

Woods, T., 2009, *Meltdown*, Washington, DC: Regnery Publishing, Inc.

Woodward, Bob, 2000, *Maestro: Greenspan's Fed and the American Boom*, New York: Simon & Schuster.

Wray, L. R., 2015, *Modern Money Theory*, 2nd ed., New York: Palgrave Macmillan.

Wray, L. R., 2016, *Why Minsky Matters*, Princeton, NJ: Princeton University Press.

Yellen, Janet, 1984, Efficiency wage models of unemployment, *American Economic Review*, Vol. 74, No. 2, pp. 200–205.

Yellen, Janet, 2015, Inflation dynamics and monetary policy, *Board of Governors of the Federal System*, September 24, 2015.

Zandi, Mark, 2009, *Financial Shock (updated edition)*, Upper Saddle River, NJ: FT Press.

Zandi, Mark, and Hoyt, Scott, 2015, U.S. macro model methodology, *Moody's Analytics Report*, West Chester, PA, April.

Index

Note: Page numbers in *italics* indicate a figure and page numbers in **bold** indicate a table on the corresponding page.